THE **BIG** HANDOUT

THE **BIG** HANDOUT

HOW GOVERNMENT SUBSIDIES

AND CORPORATE WELFARE

CORRUPT THE WORLD WE LIVE IN

AND WREAK HAVOC ON OUR FOOD BILLS

THOMAS M. KOSTIGEN

Rodale books may be purchased for business or promotional use or for special sales. For information, please write to:
Special Markets Department, Rodale, Inc., 733 Third Avenue, New York, NY 10017
Printed in the United States of America

Rodale Inc. makes every effort to use acid-free ♾, recycled paper ♻.

Book design by Sara Stemen

Illustration credits: page 25, Physicians Committee for Responsible Medicine; page 44, Alyssa Bieler

Library of Congress Cataloging-in-Publication Data

Kostigen, Thomas M.
    The big handout: how government subsidies and corporate welfare corrupt the world we live in and wreak havoc on our food bills / Thomas M. Kostigen.
        p.   cm.
    ISBN 978-1-60961-113-2 (hbk.)
    1. Subsidies—United States.   2. Agricultural subsidies—United States.
    3. Industrial policy—United States.   4. United States—Commercial policy.
    5. United States—Economic policy.   I. Title.
HC110.S9K67   2011
    338.1'873—dc22   2011014674

Distributed to the trade by Macmillan

2   4   6   8   10   9   7   5   3   1   hardcover

We inspire and enable people to improve their lives and the world around them.
www.rodalebooks.com

For Jeannie

CONTENTS

INTRODUCTION ix

I. **THE GROCERY STORE** I

2. **THE ADVENT OF SUBSIDIES** II

3. **THE MEAT COUNTER** 2I

4. **POULTRY** 3I

5. **PORK** 4I

6. **DAIRY** 53

7. **SUGAR AND BEVERAGES** 65

8. **BREADS AND CEREALS** 77

9. **RICE** 89

IO. **COTTON** IOI

II. **FRUITS AND VEGETABLES** III

I2. **FISH** II9

I3. **OIL AND GAS** I3I

I4. **STEEL** I43

15. **THE GROWTH OF SUBSIDIES**   155

16. **WHY THEY MAKE US POOR**   165

17. **WHY THEY MAKE US FAT**   177

18. **WHY THEY MAKE US HATED**   189

19. **WRECKING THE ENVIRONMENT**   201

20. **WHO BENEFITS**   213

21. **POWER PLAYERS**   223

22. **WHAT CAN WE DO TO CHANGE?**   237

23. **WHAT WOULD THE WORLD LOOK LIKE WITHOUT
    SUBSIDIES?**   247

    CONCLUSION   257

    SOURCE NOTES   267

    ACKNOWLEDGMENTS   273

    INDEX   275

INTRODUCTION

We spend more than $200 billion annually, or more than $1,500 per US household, in subsidies. For that we get higher prices at the checkout, a greater likelihood of obesity, increased environmental damage, and terrorism from abroad.

Every year, we spend $3.65 billion on oil and gas subsidies and, on average, $5 billion in direct farm payments alone.

I was shocked to learn just how much each of us pays in taxes to support big businesses, the biggest and most profitable businesses in the world, businesses whose only interest is self-interest: increasing the bottom line. I am not speaking about businesses that we subsidize with tax dollars to provide a public service. I am speaking of cold, hard cash outlays to corporations for the sake of those corporations. Companies such as Exxon Mobil, BP, and Royal Dutch Shell. And, indirectly, Monsanto, Cargill, and ConAgra. Wealthy individuals and celebrities who own lifestyle farms and ranches, too, often get the big handout.

Subsidies are the squirrelly, government-sanctioned means by which this occurs. And that is what this book is about: what we pay for and what we get for it. You will, I believe, be as surprised as I was to learn what goes on behind the scenes and between powerful interest groups that prosper at our expense.

A subsidy is a grant made by the government to a private business that is deemed advantageous to the public. The theory is that we need to assist producers of things such as cotton, wheat, corn, soy, and petroleum—the most subsidized commodities in the United States—to make American industry more competitive by lowering how much it costs to produce them. That way, the materials can be offered for sale more cheaply at home and abroad.

At one point in history this might have been a fine idea, but today subsidies do farming more harm than good. Rather than increasing competitiveness, they crimp business efficiencies and fly in the face of globalization. Moreover, they've pushed out the small farmers who are in need and created a racket for big, powerful interest groups to profit by.

In short, subsidies are a sham, and we taxpayers are getting bamboozled.

The Big Handout doesn't pull any punches in explaining how the money for subsidies goes from our bank accounts, to the government's bank account, to the bank accounts of Big Business, and then to the bank accounts of the politicians who set the subsidies and appropriate the funds. Despite the fact that we pay for subsidies out of our tax dollars, we are by design and deliberate law kept in the dark about who our money goes to and what it's spent on. These brokered pacts are what keep the subsidy system in place.

In these pages you'll find out exactly how much subsidies cost you—down to the price you pay for your chicken, fish, milk, eggs, and pretty much every other product that is supported directly or indirectly by the massive subsidy system that's in place today.

Few realize how out of control the system has gotten and how many of our tax dollars go to some of the wealthiest people on earth.

The Big Handout explains how the subsidy system works in very simple terms by breaking down the process and showing you the bottom line: how subsidies affect the prices we pay, the quality of our food, the health and welfare of the planet, and already vastly complicated international relations.

I didn't write this book as an academic treatise on the subsidy system. My eyes glaze over as much as the next guy's at just the mention of the word "subsidy." I wrote this as an accessible guide to get the everyday person through the maze of confusing and overcomplicated policies and practices put in place to direct our attention away from the heist that is going on before our eyes—literally before our eyes. Every time you buy a can of soda, a gallon of milk, a carton of eggs, or a pair of blue jeans, you are being fooled.

It wasn't always this way. For almost 150 years the United States went along just fine largely without subsidies. Total annual government spending until the early 1900s averaged $125 per citizen. Today, the the federal government spends more than $10,000 per head. Yet, the average federal tax bill in America is $17,000. Where does all of our money go?

The Big Handout explores how subsidies make us unhealthy. Most of the food produced in the United States comes from factory farms. Factory farms are subsidized more heavily than small, organic farms. These factory farms artificially plump up chickens, fatten hogs and cattle, and use pesticides and fertilizers that make our food grow bigger and faster—but not better. A lot has been written about this, and many people are aware of the food problem in America today. But what goes unmentioned in many stories is the fact that the majority of food subsidies go to these factory farms (71 percent). In other words, we subsidize corporations with our tax dollars so they can churn out volumes of food at the lowest prices possible—but not in the healthiest possible ways.

Besides health problems, subsidies lead to other problems, too—terrorism for one. Farm subsidies in rich countries like ours depress world market prices, so much so that they induce the governments of poor countries in Africa and elsewhere to import food that their local farmers could otherwise produce more efficiently. These farmers in poor countries are then left without incomes and, in the worst cases, without food for themselves; they can't afford to grow it. Hostility festers.

This is how violent problems arise. Out-of-work, poor farmers in developing countries who bear malice toward America are being recruited by terrorist organizations, especially in places such as Uganda and Somalia. Indeed, piracy off the coast of Africa is the product of similar circumstances.

I wish I could say that these ugly manifestations of government policy are exaggerated or academic, but they are playing out on the world stage today. And whether we know it or not, we are all complicit.

When we buy a $1 hamburger or a new pair of socks we are, very likely, initiating a chain of events that curses our own future and the fortunes of others.

Take the environment. The heavy use of pesticides and fertilizers by subsidized factory farms does more than facilitate plant growth; it degrades land, water, and even the air that we breathe. Concentrated factory farming relies on artificial practices that ruin the soil, foul water supplies with toxic run-off, and magnify air pollution.

However, unlike many of the world's ills that require breakthroughs in medicine or technology to solve, subsidies and their nasty ramifications can be done away with through the swipe of a pen.

Subsidy programs are regularly put before politicians for action. Farm bills come up every five years for congressional vote. Corporations lobby. Industries campaign.

Change can be accomplished by you and me, average Americans, if we step forward and stand up for ourselves. We can effect change. There are many ways to do it. The most effective ways don't even cost anything.

Change begins with knowledge and awareness. *The Big Handout* brings a bit of both by shining the spotlight on subsidy programs, the people behind them and affected by them, and the places where they do harm. It also reveals what the world might look like without subsidies, a world where there would be more money in our pockets. And a world where everyone is given an equal chance to prosper, not just the chosen few.

THE **BIG** HANDOUT

CHAPTER ONE

THE GROCERY STORE

Forty-five thousand square feet. It's the average size of a grocery store in America and it's about the size of the one I am standing in front of on a sunny California day as I watch shoppers come and go. For context, 45,000 square feet is about 20 times the size of the average home in the United States.

An older, white-haired man in a red checkered shirt, jeans, and bright white sneakers pulls up in his beige Honda Accord and rushes inside. A pregnant woman in a black Range Rover shuts her door and a "chirp" from the SUV confirms she's locked it with her remote key. A Mexican man in a Chevy truck gets in and starts the engine, wolfing down a handful of chips (part of his lunch?) before taking off. A student—identifiable by her knapsack—parks her bike. A family of four. Several older women. A mixed bag of men—young, old, with kids and without. All park their mostly American-made cars and SUVs and walk inside. The 175-space lot is in constant flow, a stream of people just like you and me, coming and going.

This, my friends, is the most common meeting place in America for citizens like us. And it's a fake. It's a racket. You and I are its victims. We're getting conned out of the money we exchange for food at the cash register.

All that, like the rhythm of a popular song, continues without much thought to what's behind it—not the words, not the meaning.

Inside the grocery store this scenario I've sketched comes alive: In the produce section, Deep Blue Something's "Breakfast at Tiffany's" plays over the intercom system. The track is broken by the sound of fake thunder over the speakers. And then there is a spray of mist as the sprinklers keep the produce on the shelves wet.

A young woman in a workout outfit, basket in hand, takes a large package of Supreme sweet corn from the shelf. Its crooked black-and-white tag advertises "Special. $5.99." It's a four-cob pack.

The corn is wrapped in plastic. And the package is wet. Needless waste, of course. It's an apt metaphor for agricultural subsidies. Showering packaged vegetables is like the government subsidizing farmers to produce the vast amount of corn that is already grown in California. More incentives aren't needed.

I get approached by a store worker. I think he's going to hassle me for standing around taking notes and—admittedly—gawking at customers. But he only tries to push some peaches on me. "Forty-nine cents a pound," he says. "Today, last day of sale."

Over in the meat section there are things marked "Reduced for Quick Sale." Things like bologna and sausages and hot dogs and packaged pork in gravy find themselves relegated to this shelf.

"Save Big. Lunch Meat." It's another teaser.

A heavyset woman wearing a T-shirt and sweatpants walks by and grabs two packs of boneless chicken thigh fillets from the bin. They are priced at $1.99 a pound. It catches the attention of an older Asian woman. She reads the sign and takes two packs.

Chicken. Beef. Turkey. Pork. All for sale, on sale.

At the checkout counter the coupons are passed, the scanner beeps, club cards are handed over, and tiny paper receipts are handed back to customers as they leave, their carts—sometimes two each—now full of plastic bags, filled with all the fixings for meals yet to be served: breakfasts, lunches, dinners.

A man argues with a cashier about the price of something. If he only knew. If he only knew how that item was really priced and the factors that determine those digits displayed on shelves. He probably doesn't. Few dare go down that path of inquiry.

The average person in America spends about $120 per week on food. It's a number that has been climbing steadily and is expected to rise at an even faster rate as food costs soar.

From 1990 to 2008, the period for which the most recent government data are available, food expenditures rose close to 50 percent. You might think that's a lot. And it is, especially in the down economy the world is experiencing as this book goes to press. But the increase in the amount we spend on food in America is a crumb compared to the rise in global food prices.

Over a period of just two years—between 2006 and 2008—average world prices for the commodities that compose most of our diets more than doubled. Prices for rice rose by 217 percent, wheat by 136 percent, corn by 125 percent, and soybeans by 107 percent. You may recall the food riots that occurred around the world during this time. Indeed, some 40 riots broke out in Mexico, Haiti, Egypt, and other countries short of basic food items.

Subsidies aren't even doing their job of keeping prices down in America. Instead, they create perverse ways for food companies such as Archer Daniels Midland, Cargill, ConAgra, and Monsanto to profit wildly; savings aren't being passed along.

Think about that lady at the grocery store who reached for that package of Supreme sweet corn. Imagine her having to fight for it, the package ripping open, the four ears of corn tumbling to the ground. A scuffle forming and hands desperately pecking at one another trying to catch the scattering kernels. Or that woman in the sweatpants who took two packages of chicken thigh fillets for $1.99 each. No way she'd get away with it. Imagine fierce battles over the basics we need for survival. Food. Water. The staples of our existence. Low down on the food supply chain, in poor, developing countries, things are getting ugly.

Corn, rice, wheat, and soy are the grains that feed us. They are the feed for the animals we consume. They are the makings of our breads and cereals. And dairy products, of course, come from animals that eat grain. When the prices of these grains rise, the increases ripple through the rest of the food chain.

Moreover, myriad circumstances are challenging our food supply. Droughts and other severe weather events in grain-producing nations have crimped supplies. These droughts are expected to only worsen as the world's climate changes. In addition, rising oil prices have affected the costs of fertilizers, food transportation, and storage.

The floor for food prices keeps rising, and for some it's a step they can no longer afford to make. Roughly 1 billion people throughout the world live in a state of hunger. And these aren't just people in developing countries. One person in eight in America gets food from one of the more than 200 food banks of the country's largest hunger-relief charity alone.

You read that correctly. In the most affluent country in the world, people can't afford to eat. In many cases they go hungry. It doesn't make the headlines, but it should.

Much of the starvation around the world is, ironically, caused by subsidies. Food subsidies, designed to lower prices so people wouldn't starve, are now having the opposite effect.

Here's how: The US government subsidizes the production of certain foods (corn, soy, rice, etc.). We export that food at below-market costs to other countries. Poor countries' governments buy the cheap food subsidized by America to feed their hungry. The farmers in these countries cannot compete with these prices, so they go out of business and join the millions who can't afford to eat. Back at home, meanwhile, local farmers—real farmers, not the big agricultural corporations that get the bulk of government subsidy money and produce most of the agricultural output today—can't compete with these artificially low prices either, and many of them join the ranks of the unemployed and undernourished.

It gets worse, and even more complicated. Because we "dump" cheap food on the world market, some countries impose trade barriers and other policies that jack up the prices of their foods that we import. That, plus the currently low value of the US dollar around the world as compared to other currencies, makes the food we import more expensive. Bananas and coffee, which are virtually 100 percent imported, are especially prone to this type of price rise.

Across the economic spectrum, subsidies and protectionist trade policies put certain food items out of the reach of certain people. This makes the choices among basic necessities hard, very hard.

According to the 2010 *Hunger in America* report by the charitable organization Feeding America, of all hungry households in the United States almost half had to choose between paying for utilities or heating fuel and food, 39 percent said they had to choose between paying for rent or a mortgage and food, 34 percent reported having to choose between paying for medical bills and food, and 35 percent were forced to choose between transportation and food.

That's here in the United States, where food programs like Feeding America are available. Now think about a farmer in Uganda, a country where even with the cheap imports from the United States' food programs, they can't feed their poor. These unfair trade practices cause feelings toward the United States to become negative, sometimes even violent. It's why Secretary of Agriculture Tom Vilsack's role sometimes overlaps with that of Secretary of State Hillary Clinton's on matters of US foreign policy. But we'll get into that backlash later.

What's important to know is that higher food prices are being felt all over the world. So let's get back to the United States, where in 2007 the average household spent $777 on meats, poultry, fish, and eggs; $387 on dairy products; $600 on fruits and vegetables; and more than $1,241 on junk food and other items.

The grocery store, while a painful reminder of our increasingly stretched household budgets, is also the source of pains much bigger in scope: It's the gateway for so many of the world's problems. Indeed, behind the sign that hangs in front of your grocery store is one end of the many pathways that connect us to the world—the routes bananas trek from Panama, coffee takes from Columbia, tea travels from China, and fish voyage from the middle of the vast oceans.

Subsidies interrupt and corrupt what seems like a very basic system: growing goods and bringing them someplace to sell. The "market" that throughout time decided prices—(*"Hey, Lucius, my fellow Roman farmer. You are charging what for your grapes? I'll charge the same, too, per bunch."*)—has become infected with price distortions. (*"Lucius, guess what? The government just said they will pay us to grow our grapes. Let's lower our prices and get some more business."*)

The first supermarket didn't open in America until 1930. Rather than being just a local hub of commerce, it has grown to become a political and scientific outpost. It connects us to Washington, DC, where food policies are set, and to laboratories on university campuses the world over where researchers craft food "alternatives" and additives for our diets.

It's also the place that is most directly tied to our health and well-being. It's mostly responsible for where and how we get fat.

To take a page out of the book *Eat This, Not That! 2010*:

In the early 1970s, food manufacturers, looking for a cheaper ingredient to replace sugar, came up with a substance called high-fructose corn syrup (HFCS). Today, HFCS is in an unbelievable array of foods—everything from breakfast cereals to bread, from ketchup to pasta sauce, from juice drinks to iced teas. (Indeed, just try going to your local convenience store and buying a drink that doesn't contain HFCS!) According to the FDA, the average American consumes 82 grams of added sugars every day, which contribute 317 empty calories to our daily diet. HFCS might not be any worse for our bodies than normal table sugar, but its dirt-cheap cost and prevalence in processed foods has only served to intensify America's collective sweet tooth in recent years.

In short, it works like this: Government subsidizes corn. It becomes so cheap that HFCS can be made super-inexpensively. It gets added to all sorts of items to make them "sweeter" . . . and we gain weight.

Obesity is a big issue. But as I said, it's only one problem that subsidies promulgate and our grocery store connects us to. Another big issue that subsidies connect us to is debt. They make us poorer.

In America, we spend about $200 billion per year—more than $1,500 per household—on corporate welfare and farm subsidies. We actually pay farmers some $2 billion a year *not* to farm.

As it stands the federal government was projected in 2010 to spend $30,543 per household and collect taxes of $17,879 per household, resulting in a budget deficit of $12,664 per household, or $1.5 trillion. It means that for the first time in US history we'll be a 100 percent debtor nation, making less money than we owe with our deficit exceeding our gross domestic product. Subsidies add to that bill.

These are statistics that should be laid at the feet of Senator Debbie Stabenow, the Democrat from Michigan who chairs the Senate Committee on Agriculture, Nutrition, and Forestry, and Congressman Frank Lucas, a Republican from Oklahoma who chairs the House Committee on Agriculture.

But most people are too busy worrying about paying for their food and don't have the time to call and raise a stink with their elected representatives.

So back to the grocery store and your own weekly or monthly food bill: Add to that tally all the taxes we are paying to subsidize farmers and you'll find that we as individuals and families have even bigger food tabs to pay. It equates to thousands of dollars more per year.

Yet, what if I told you that over the long term, ending subsidies would actually lower food prices? After the immediate spike in prices we might experience after doing away with subsidies, costs would gradually fall as more international markets were opened to us. Many jobs, too, would arguably be more secure and even increase in number because they wouldn't be based on false premises and government underwriting.

We historically have paid more than double the world price for sugar because of protectionist trade policies that keep import tariffs high to keep cheaper products from being imported. We also pay higher prices for milk, butter, and cheese because of federal policy on the domestic and international fronts.

Sure, we might initially pay a lot more for a hamburger without subsidies—if we relied solely on domestic feed and cattle. But remove trade restrictions and on the world market the price of that hamburger would fall below what we pay now—and our cattle ranchers would have a bigger market to serve, too. Protectionist trade policies also drive up prices for peanuts, orange juice, canned tuna, and other products.

As three Cato Institute directors put it in an article addressing this issue titled "Six Reasons to Kill Farm Subsidies and Trade Barriers" in the libertarian magazine *Reason,* "If American farm subsidies and trade barriers were significantly reduced, millions of American households would enjoy higher real incomes." Less tax equals more income, if the savings are passed along to us.

Isn't it about time for *that* type of America? Instead, we get a grocery store littered with lawmakers, lobbyists, and all sorts of corporate and special interest groups. Walk down the aisles and you can practically see them hanging off the shelves, filling up bins, posing behind glass counters. And there, waiting for you at the checkout counter, is good old Uncle Sam, hand out, waiting to take his share.

It is at the grocery store that we get hit hard by subsidies. Sure, energy gets its piece and so too do the textile makers. But it all comes together at the supermarket. After all, we likely drive our cars there using fuel that is subsidized. And, unless you're a curious sort, you are wearing clothes, the materials of which are likely subsidized, too. (Cotton is a heavily subsidized crop.)

There we are: sad creatures pushing along our four-wheeled shopping carts that shake and rattle as we somnolently walk through a fluorescent-lit (also subsidized) store listening to Muzak that somehow always seems to be about something tragic.

There we stand, American consumers, among the 47,000 items that the typical supermarket stocks, in a place we typically travel to twice per week.

How'd we end up here?

CHAPTER TWO

THE ADVENT OF SUBSIDIES

Blame Herbert Hoover. It was under his presidency that the subsidy system we know today began. And it all began with the Federal Farm Board. It was created in 1929, a year most of us associate with Black Tuesday, October 29—the great stock market crash, the beginning of the Great Depression. It's all connected. Subsidies were born in dark times.

The federal Farm Board was created as a promise of hope. Yet that promise has been abused, almost right from the start.

"I invest you with responsibility, authority, and resources such as have never before been conferred by our Government in assistance to any industry," President Hoover said in addressing the Farm Board's first meeting July 15. And he wasn't kidding. The Farm Board received more money— $500 million—than almost any other government agency had in history.

What, pray tell, was the Farm Board to do with all this cash? The board, which was directed to promote a series of farm marketing cooperatives throughout the country, was to figure out ways to farm better and give America a leg up in the agricultural trade wars that had begun after World War I. It was, in essence, the first government bailout of its time and it was massive. Not only was the money designed to assist farmers' livelihoods, it was designed to give government a hand in the business of agriculture—not an altruistic hand, mind you, but one that got something in return.

The Farm Board, which over time guaranteed farmers' incomes by purchasing surplus supplies of some crops and setting prices, also poured money into research to help farmers become more productive by using better irrigation techniques and pesticides.

The offices of the Farm Board, as part of the US Department of Agriculture, which absorbed its functions (as did various other agencies throughout its history), today can be found sitting in the shadow of the Washington Monument at the very beginning of the National Mall that leads to the Capitol building in DC. It doesn't get as many visitors as the Smithsonian next door or the White House or the halls of Congress. (The pathetic 1,000-square-foot garden out front isn't much of a draw, nor is the farmers' market it hosts June through October.) Still, its importance is shown through the sheer size of the buildings in which it is housed: more than 2 million square feet of space where more than 6,000 employees work.

The USDA is, I would say, the most powerful and influential governmental agency because it oversees one thing we can't live without: food. That's a lethal weapon. And it didn't take the government long to figure out how to aim it.

Soon after the Farm Board was created, it was realized that controlling how much agricultural product was available on the world market affected supply and demand. The result of controlling this ratio was the ability to control prices. On a global scale, this meant hegemony. And it's a testament to the Farm Board's role in international affairs that the US State Department

provides the most comprehensive synopsis of its evolution as
well as the rationale, from the federal government's standpoint
anyway, for agricultural subsidies:

> The good years of the early 20th century ended with falling
> prices following World War I. Farmers again called for help
> from the federal government. Their pleas fell on deaf ears,
> though, as the rest of the nation—particularly urban areas—
> enjoyed the prosperity of the 1920s. The period was even more
> disastrous for farmers than earlier tough times because
> farmers were no longer self-sufficient. They had to pay in cash
> for machinery, seed, and fertilizer as well as for consumer
> goods, yet their incomes had fallen sharply.
>
> The whole nation soon shared the farmers' pain, however,
> as the country plunged into depression following the stock
> market crash of 1929. For farmers, the economic crisis com-
> pounded difficulties arising from overproduction. Then, the
> farm sector was hit by unfavorable weather conditions that
> highlighted shortsighted farming practices. Persistent winds
> during an extended drought blew away topsoil from vast tracts
> of once-productive farmland. The term "dustbowl" was coined
> to describe the ugly conditions.
>
> Widespread government intervention in the farm
> economy began in 1929, when President Herbert Hoover
> (1929–1933) created the federal Farm Board. Although the
> board could not meet the growing challenges posed by the
> Depression, its establishment represented the first national
> commitment to provide greater economic stability for
> farmers and set a precedent for government regulation of
> farm markets.

There are two main things to take away from the synopsis above. One, the USDA forged the steroid-based, fatten 'em up, and unnaturally increase the production of agriculture culture we live with today. And two, the Farm Board set a precedent for government regulation.

The politics of all this are, of course, interesting. And it's worth getting into that heady space for a bit before we discuss why the USDA decided it needed to mess with the lives of the fruits, vegetables, and animals that we eat.

The economic climate after World War I wasn't good. Businesses were afraid cheap products from Europe would flood America. Europe had big war debts and lots of unemployed people. They could well afford to undercut US prices. American businessmen were in favor of jacking up tariffs, which are basically import or export taxes. But President Woodrow Wilson refused to raise the flag of protectionism. He said, "If ever there was a time when Americans had anything to fear from foreign competition, that time has passed. If we wish to have Europe settle her debts, governmental or commercial, we must be prepared to buy from her."

That was a nice thing to say, an eloquent and high-minded principle, the type of thing I could see Barack Obama saying today. Unfortunately for President Wilson and the country, his successor, Warren Harding, didn't much agree. During Harding's presidency Congress enacted the Emergency Tariff Act of May 1921 and the Fordney-McCumber Tariff Act of 1922 to help out the struggling agricultural industry. The laws established the highest tariff rates in history, with tariffs on some products reaching 400 percent. Everything from leather to lace was affected. Almost anything of foreign origin saw its price rise dramatically. That, dear reader, is protectionism to the highest degree.

Politically, therefore, things got testy between the parties, with Republicans calling Harding "mad." The international community seemed to agree, and a huge trade war erupted. Some say this at least added to, if not precipitated, the Great Depression and the stock market crash of 1929. In any case, prices for agricultural products were depressed due to world-wide surpluses, leaving farmers in deep financial trouble. Because European countries had recovered more quickly than expected after World War I, exports of US farmers' products were no longer required in large quantities to feed them.

Financial journalist Brian Trumbore observes that "when it came time for the presidential election of 1928, Republicans looked at the overall economic climate across the country and reached the conclusion that high tariffs worked."

The Smoot-Hawley Tariff Act of 1930 was passed and foreign countries went nuts. It seemed as though the United States had made "a virtual declaration of economic war on the rest of the world," as Trumbore reported historian Richard Hofstadter stating. Within two years of Hoover's election in 1928, 25 countries had retaliated against the US tariff scheme and foreign trade took a huge hit. America had exported $5.24 billion in goods in 1929 and by 1932, the total was just $1.6 billion—largely due to tariffs designed to help the agricultural industry.

Trumbore related that David M. Kennedy wrote in his book *Freedom from Fear: The American People in Depression and War, 1929–1945,* that "Hoover went along with his party's plan for tariff revision because he wanted two things: higher duties on certain agricultural imports as part of his program to aid farmers, and a strengthened Tariff Commission, with power to adjust import duties by 50 percent." The famous and influential journalist Walter Lippmann said that Hoover's tariffs had "surrendered everything for nothing." He said Hoover "gave up the leadership of his party. He let his personal authority be flouted. He accepted a wretched and mischievous product of stupidity and greed." Hoover, it should be noted, was reportedly personally opposed to tariffs, protectionism, and even subsidies. Lippman obviously took great issue with Hoover's abandonment of values.

Stupidity and greed are two adjectives that keep coming up when subsidies are discussed.

Trumbore, who is the editor of StocksandNews.com, discovered this fact when researching the history of subsidies: "1,028 economists had earlier petitioned President Hoover to veto the [Smoot-Hawley] bill, but with enactment, tariffs hit all-time levels on some 70 agricultural products and 900 manufactured items. The economists had warned that [the bill] would raise prices to consumers, damage export trade, hurt farmers, promote inefficiency and promote foreign reprisals." And as he notes, that's exactly what happened.

Conservative author and blogger James Bovard writes that "the federal government wrecked the agricultural sector after World War I and . . . the Agriculture Department became a permanent lobby for 'socialism in one industry.' "

> In a harebrained effort to enrich farmers, the Farm Board
> destabilized the grain trade, substantially reduced U.S.
> exports, and created a massive price-depressing surplus,
> greatly weakening American agriculture. Argentinean,

Canadian, and Australian farmers weathered the Great Depression far better than American farmers did largely because their governments did not abandon export markets. Canadian and Australian exports actually increased in the 1930s. The prices of American wheat and cotton declined far more than those of other domestic crops between 1929 and 1932. . . .

Geza Feketekuty, a former economist at the U.S. trade representative's office in the White House, observed in 1988, "The world protectionist binge of the 1930s started as a result of efforts to protect American farmers from low world market prices." After the federal government had driven U.S. crop prices far above world prices, politicians had no choice but to close U.S. borders or abandon their price-boosting scheme. The Farm Board debacle convinced many farmers that foreign trade was the only thing standing between them and far higher prices. The farm bloc put its weight behind an extreme protectionist measure, the Smoot-Hawley Tariff Act [of 1930], that boosted tariffs on agricultural products far more than it boosted tariffs on industrial products.

Numerous history observers point to the tariffs imposed by the Smoot-Hawley Act as exacerbating the worldwide depression.

Tariffs, it needs to be remembered, are subsidies' twin. They play defense whereas subsidies play offense in the policy game book.

The health issues associated with the advent of subsidies haven't received as much attention as the financial aspects in the history books, but they deserve mention as well.

The roots of artificial approaches to raising livestock and growing produce can be traced to the Hatch Act of 1887.

Basically, the Hatch Act created funding for "agricultural experiment stations" where farmers and scientists could work on ways to fight crop and livestock disease and therefore increase productivity. These stations, which still exist in every state and are affiliated with universities, put, as I like to say, the lambs in the lab, the cattle in the classroom.

With the growing population needing more and more food, the government needed new ways to make agriculture flourish. Parasites are a big deal to the farming community, especially livestock producers. In the 1870s and 1880s, "Texas cattle fever" was crimping Northern herds, some to the point of eradication. The state of Kansas closed its borders to cattle crossings by herds driven north from Texas to Illinois for slaughter. This was also the beginning of "food migration" diseases (think Mad Cow today), and they perplexed ranchers and farmers. The government funded research for solutions. It had no way of knowing that eventually the research would result in not only increasing yields by fending off disease, but also devising new ways to increase the sizes of pigs and potatoes.

By this time scientists such as Robert Koch of Germany and Louis Pasteur of France had already found ways to stave disease through vaccinations. US government scientists went looking for similar success with cattle fever—and they found it. Artificial injections started to become more common.

As the agricultural community developed into more and more of a business rather than a way of life, the scientific aspect of food (research and development) also grew. Today, scientists study ways to vary crops and increase yield, as well as produce livestock more efficiently through technology advancements. Fruits, vegetables, and animals have come to be thought of as agricultural "products" rather than living things. And just like any other product, the more that can be produced at the cheapest possible cost, the more profitable the product.

That's how we ended up with supermarkets that stock on their shelves thousands of products that don't go bad for months or years . . . or decades.

Giant supermarkets have even become symbols of America. Ask a foreigner what his or her biggest impression from a visit to America is and it will often be our supermarkets. They marvel at the quantities of food we have at our disposal.

In Washington, DC, I went looking for the grocery store nearest to the USDA building. It's a Safeway, and it's located to the south of the building, past the fish market and across from the popular waterfront area that houses hip restaurants. I'm not sure if anyone has ever mapped this—the location of the capital of food policy, the USDA, to its nearest outpost, the grocery store—but here it is, located in a modern, new building advertising "stylish living" on its upper floors. Residents say they welcome the supermarket because there isn't another to be found in the area. Odd, considering I'm staring at the National Institute of Food and Agriculture, which is around the corner. You'd think this would be foodie central. In any event, I head into the closest outpost of our nation's food policy. And I go straight to the meat counter.

CHAPTER THREE

THE MEAT COUNTER

At the grocery store meat counter, there are stacks of beef. Plenty of packages of beef. And if I don't want the ones in plastic, the butcher behind the counter is all too happy to grind me some.

The lady next to me orders two pounds of ground chuck. I ask her what she is going to do with it. "Hamburgers," she says. Just one word. She looks at me skeptically. "Why?" An alternative translation might have been: "What's it to ya?" I tell her about my assignment—investigating food prices. Then I ask her how much more she would be willing to pay for any type of beef. She gives a good answer: "I already pay too much."

That's the mentality of most consumers. We shoppers want everything for free, or at a discount. And that is the advantage that subsidized industries have over us. Their prices fit our desire for deals and discounts.

"Would you pay $200 for a burger?" I ask. Now she really thinks I'm nuts. "No," she says declaratively, and she is off. Halfway down the aisle I notice that she glances back to make sure I am not following her.

The reason I am quizzing her is this: the hamburger. It's distinctively American. It can be had for a dollar at fast-food restaurants. At a grocery store like Safeway, hamburger meat will set you back just a few bucks per pound. There are many types, too: ground chuck, ground sirloin, different grades of leanness. No matter, they all seem, well, inexpensive; prices are within cents of each other.

Yet this hamburger of the Fourth of July block party, staple of the political candidate and everyman dinner along with fries and a Coke, is the ultimate symbol of Fake America. It's a total fraud.

Subsidies pervert the price of beef in the market. The USDA even admits this. It says its policies create "distortions" in the marketplace. Distortions mean beef prices aren't what they should be. The USDA reports that we provide millions of dollars in price supports—read "assistance"—for beef exports, which amount to $3 billion per year. Indeed, price supports are so out of hand that the government is now trying to reel them in. Other countries have squawked too much and rebelled against our meat. Foreign citizens have even staged protests about our beef exports (their imports).

What's all the mooing about?

American cattle ranchers have an unfair advantage in the world marketplace. The rest of the world's cattle are largely grass fed, but American beef producers get grain for feed, water, land, and even energy to raise their herds on the cheap thanks to US taxpayer subsidies.

The director of beef quality assurance for the Montana Beef Network explains it this way:

> The U.S.—along with our neighbors in Canada—has a highly differentiated beef production system compared to most other beef producing nations. This difference can be summed up in one word—*corn*. The colossal farming resources granted by

the U.S. Corn Belt have shaped domestic beef genetics and production systems for decades. Beef producers put this unique advantage to work in creating "high-quality" grain fed beef products that virtually no one else in the world enjoys. . . .

The bottom line is that few countries have the economic luxury of being able to turn corn into beef protein on a scale large enough to define an industry.

Corn, of course, is the most-subsidized agricultural product in the United States. Add that to the other subsidies ranchers can get (for such things as water and land), and you can see how it becomes "Advantage: America" in the international contest to dominate the beef industry.

And it's a big industry. There are approximately 1.5 billion cattle on earth. Considering that a beef cow is worth about $700, we are talking about a trillion-dollar industry. And it's going nowhere but up as developing countries such as India and China get wealthier and more of their people can afford to eat beef. When incomes rise, so does beef consumption. America, of course, already has its seat at the beef table.

According to the National Cattlemen's Beef Association, the total annual retail value of US beef alone is more than $80 billion. That's a lot of money spent on beef—almost twice as much as was spent in 1980. Also, what's really interesting about the data is that the amount of meat gotten from one American cow has risen by 41 percent during that time period, from 449 to 632 pounds per cow.

Okay, so I can see how with population growth and rising incomes worldwide more meat is consumed. And I can see how more cattle have to be raised to meet that demand. But how's it that cows themselves are growing? Are cows exercising less and getting fat? Is there some strange genetic phenomenon among the cow population that the news media missed? Or could it be that these cows are getting artificially plump on cheap corn and hormones?

Graze where you will on grass, my beautiful Brazilian bovines, to keep your lovely figures, but you ain't got nothin' on US fatties at the slaughterhouse!

To be sure, without subsidized assistance, and taking into account the cost of clearing land for cattle raising, a burger and fries might, in fact, run you $200. It's an exaggerated figure, and one that is tossed about on the Internet. But, depending on how one calculates the value of subsidized land, disaster relief programs, water allotments, grain, fuel, and a slew of other determinants, it's feasible to come up with that amount—though it's a stretch. Anyway, who wants a burger that costs anywhere near that much? Not me. And if subsidies are nixed, prices don't have to go to that level. To be sure, beef prices would go up because the corn and other grain producers that provide the cattle feed that is the largest expense in putting that there fine steak on your plate also get subsidized. And take that subsidy away and prices rise. But create a more open market and competition from other countries would keep prices reasonable.

It wouldn't help to go looking outside the US border for beef either. Beef in other countries is expensive. In London, for example, a pound of ground beef is already about two and a half times more expensive than in the United States, and in Paris, a little more than three times as much.

On the world market, subsidies help make good ol' "Made in the USA" ground chuck pretty cheap: It costs less than $3 per pound, according to national store averages. Besides, the

United States imposes a 26 percent tariff on beef imports. That means if you want to buy Kobe beef from Japan, on top of the market factors and premiums charged, you're going to pay an extra 26 percent.

If, however, tariffs were eliminated, the price of beef without subsidies wouldn't skyrocket into the stratosphere. It would likely double and level off. And that may not be such a bad thing, anyway.

The illustration below comes from the nonprofit health advocacy group the Physicians Committee for Responsible Medicine. It's meant to show—and does, nicely, I believe—the contrast between what foods are subsidized and what the USDA recommends we eat to be healthier.

In case the point is lost on you: Subsidies contribute to unhealthy foods being far less expensive than their healthy counterparts. Price parity just might help make America healthier.

Why Does a Salad Cost More Than a Big Mac?

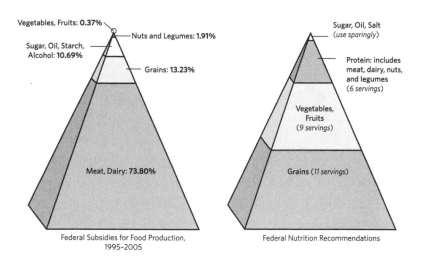

Vegetables, Fruits: **0.37%**
Nuts and Legumes: **1.91%**
Sugar, Oil, Starch, Alcohol: **10.69%**
Grains: **13.23%**
Meat, Dairy: **73.80%**

Federal Subsidies for Food Production, 1995–2005

Sugar, Oil, Salt (*use sparingly*)
Protein: includes meat, dairy, nuts, and legumes (*6 servings*)
Vegetables, Fruits (*9 servings*)
Grains (*11 servings*)

Federal Nutrition Recommendations

Perhaps a hamburger that reflects the real value of what it takes to produce is the answer. Cattlemen wouldn't have to resort to artificially fattening cows with corn feed. The environment wouldn't suffer as much as a result, either. For example, subsidizing water use by cattle ranchers results in overuse and waste. Texas, the second-largest agricultural state in the country, is now America's driest region. And raising cattle causes more environmental damage and pollution than transportation. You need lots of land to raise cows, too; 25 percent of all the land on earth, as a matter of fact, is being used for raising cattle.

Let's be blunt: When food is cheaper, people eat more.

Obesity rates in America are rising. A majority of Americans are by definition overweight. The heaviest are black people and the poor. The poor and non-Hispanic blacks also eat the most beef. If you really care to, map where most fast-food restaurants are located: They're in poor neighborhoods. Fast-food restaurants are the biggest consumers of beef. It doesn't take a political scientist to see that subsidies may be resulting in a new form of oppression in America.

A cheap hamburger can have all sorts of health consequences. As John Robbins points out in his book *The Food Revolution,* one Double Whopper with cheese has 130 percent of the maximum saturated fat daily value for adults according to the US Department of Health and Human Services. The same sandwich has 200 percent of the saturated fat daily value for an eight-year-old. Eating excess saturated fat contributes to myriad health problems. It is the main dietary cause of high blood cholesterol, which in turn leads to heart disease, among other problems.

We adults would benefit from healthier and more expensive meat in another way as well: Our tax dollars wouldn't be going toward a system that results in added health care costs and strains. (Too many "extra value" meals and chances are that that overweight kid is going to experience some type of health issue.)

The Centers for Disease Control and Prevention estimates the medical costs directly tied to saturated fat and which can be directly linked to cheap hamburgers and other such foods high in saturated fat run close to $100 billion per year. Now, of course, the US taxpayer is footing the bill for those costs through subsidized health care. Emergency room visits for heart attack victims, diabetes treatments, and other hospital care can all be linked back to food subsidies.

The madness has to end, and the buck should stop with the dollar burger.

Okay, you ask, exactly how much more expensive would a burger be without subsidies? My estimate is anywhere from a dollar more a pound to more than double the price.

The previously cited $200 hamburger figure comes from a study conducted in India and includes the costs of clearing rain forest to raise the cattle and of subsidizing the feed, water, transportation, and seemingly everything the researchers could think of. They even cite cattle raised on government land that is leased for 1 cent per acre.

The vast majority of US cattlemen work hard to pay expensive land leases. (Only 3 percent of beef industry cattle are grazed for $1.35 a month per animal on publicly owned lands.) Still, all that said, livestock ranchers receive millions of dollars per year in direct payment subsidies, plus they get indirect subsidies that discount the price of the feed and water they need to raise their stock. So the increased price of nonsubsidized beef, therefore, would be somewhere between the extremes of $1 and $200.

The easiest—and, admittedly, very inexact—way to estimate a likely increase is to search for the price of beef from small producers' grass-fed cattle. This eliminates the feed subsidy and likely any land subsidy. It likely puts tier water rates in line with market prices to give a fair assessment of what beef would cost without subsidies, although certainly the economies of scale enjoyed by bigger producers as well as the price-lowering effects of a much larger field of competition are left out of the equation.

As I write this, the Bureau of Labor Statistics puts the US city average price for a pound of 100 percent ground chuck beef at $2.96 and that for uncooked beefsteaks at $5.96. A flash through some Web sites showed the cheapest grass-fed ground chuck to be $7 per pound and the cheapest 12-ounce steak, $12.

Is $7 for ground beef too much? Is $12 for a good steak?

A study conducted by two researchers at the University of Nebraska at Lincoln found that people actually *would* pay more for beef they liked, up to $1.61 per pound more. Given that, it's reasonable to assume that people might pay even more for better-quality meat. And therein lies the problem with raising prices.

As discussed, low-income people in the United States eat more beef than do those with higher incomes. And overall, non-Hispanic black people eat the most beef—77 pounds each per year compared to 64 pounds each year for non-Hispanic white people.

This income statistic may seem to fly in the face of the worldwide data showing that as people become more affluent, they consume more beef. But that is way down on the income pyramid where people are climbing out of poverty and into the middle class.

Still, would the higher unsubsidized beef prices take food out of the mouths of poor people who could no longer afford that source of protein? It's a good question that warrants more analysis than I'm giving it here. But it's worth revisiting the fact that the biggest beef purchasers in America are fast-food restaurants that churn out products that are widely considered to be less healthy. The real question is, what would America look like without cheap beef? We'll see that portrait later.

Direct beef subsidies amount to $2.4 billion per year in feed grain and another $1 billion in land subsidies. Indirectly, as the USDA reports, the beef industry gets billions in assistance. Pretty much every dime of that comes from US taxpayers.

The Congressional Budget Office, which is just up the road from where I am doing my research in Washington, DC, highlights in a report, "Export subsidies reduce the net cost to foreign buyers of U.S. agricultural products, in effect subsidizing foreign consumption at the expense of U.S. taxpayers."

The exact same connection is true domestically: Subsidies reduce the cost of products—at our own expense. The expense goes beyond the price at the checkout counter or at the drive-through window. It's an expense that increases health care costs, taxes, and environmental damage around the world. It, of course, isn't the price of only hamburgers that wreaks these ills. There are other meats at the grocery store that are culprits, too.

Let's take a gander at the subsidy costs of some of them.

CHAPTER FOUR

POULTRY

Instead of wringing the necks of chickens, perhaps thought should instead be given to the throats of others. Here's why: The chicken industry has been a major winner thanks to changes in US agriculture policy over the past 15 years, while family farmers and taxpayers have lost out.

The above isn't my statement (okay, the wringing of necks part is); it's a paraphrasing of the conclusion of a 2006 Tufts University study. The study, the researchers reported in *Feeding the Factory Farm: Implicit Subsidies to the Broiler Chicken Industry*, revealed that the 1996 Farm Bill lowered the market prices of soybeans and corn so much that they could be purchased for far less than it cost to produce them. The meal of those grains is used to feed our fine, feathered friends that we turn into sandwiches, salads, and potpies, and the savings from the low-cost feed translated into $1.25 billion per year for corporate chicken ranches.

Notice the "corporate" in front of "chicken ranches." It's important, because while these chicken factories are churning out poultry and profits, small ranchers are struggling. Indeed, the net incomes of all small, family farmers are stagnant, at best, and in many cases falling.

As I made my way in a taxi across the Potomac from DC to Virginia, I thought about how that could be. When feed constitutes 65 percent of the production cost of chickens and you smack the price of it down by about 25 percent, as the 1996 Farm Bill did, profits should—artificially, at least—fly. Sort of like chickens themselves do when they're tossed in the air. But it isn't how a chicken is raised that has become a big fake in America; it's how chickens are sold.

The consolidation of the chicken industry has created a subsidy monster called an "integrator." And this integrator controls how chickens are sold. As the Tufts study explains:

> Through the early part of the 20th century, most chickens were raised on small farms or in backyard flocks, and their meat was largely a by-product of egg production. Independent feed mills, breeders, hatcheries, producers, and processors traded with each other in a system of often unstable spot markets. Beginning in the 1940s, however, feed stores began selling chicks, feed, medicine and equipment to growers, and then buying the grown chickens back for processing and sale. This system, pioneered by Georgia feed store owner Jesse Jewell, marked the beginning of a process of consolidation and control of the production chain by one central party.

The one central party—the integrator—is one of the big agricultural corporations of today.

Because these businesses are "vertical," meaning that they have ownership stakes in the entire life cycle of the chicken product—the feed, medicine, equipment, straight through to the sales process—the lower costs of production thanks to subsidies on one end translate into profits in each and every business stage.

It works like this: Farmers of soybeans and corn, the two grains that are the primary bases for most chicken feeds, receive direct payments from the US government to produce those grains at artificially low prices. The farmers then sell their grain to grain processors. This is where the integrators pick up the ball. These giant corporations purchase the low-cost feed and pass these initial savings on to their feedlots and processing plants and sales outlets.

A small, family farm doesn't have this advantage. In fact, it likely buys the feed, equipment, and medicine to raise its livestock from the same giant agribusiness to which it ultimately sells its product. This, of course, puts agribusinesses in the catbird's seat. Family farmers and ranchers don't stand much of a chance to profit. In fact, most family farmers ultimately sell out and become independent contractors for what I'll call Big Chicken (it sounds better than "agribusiness," which makes me yawn).

Anyway, Big Chicken monopolizes the industry. In the 1930s, the hatching of broiler chicks was spread among some 11,000 independent facilities with an average capacity of 24,000 eggs, according to the Tufts study. By 2001, the number of hatcheries had declined by 97 percent—to only 323—but with an average incubator capacity of 2.7 million eggs. In other words, the chicken industry has shrunk by thousands of ranches to just a few hundred, but—and this is big—it's pumping out millions more chickens per year: About 173 million broiler chicks are now "placed for meat production" each week in the United States. Not only has the number of chicks grown, but also the average live weight of a broiler: It rose from more than three pounds in 1945 to more than five pounds today.

Yipes!

This is something to be scared of. When controlled prices enrich the few and subject the masses to selective products, it flies in the face of a free market. Yet America is heading down this dangerous path with the guidance of the subsidy system.

Of course, no one within the Big Chicken subsidy system would dare to admit that they get any type of government assistance, as I learn when I pick up the telephone and call the National Chicken Council (NCC), which represents the producers and processors of 95 percent of the chickens produced in America. I ask whether the industry receives subsidies, and "no" is the curt answer I get from its spokesman. "What about indirect subsidies from feed, water, transportation, land?" I ask. Dick Lobb, the NCC's spokesman and director of communications, says the industry receives "no indirect subsidies. We're not part of the Farm Bill. Nothing like that."

Okeydokey, then let's ignore the fact that the chicken industry, according to the USDA, is the largest consumer of grain feed—poultry eat more grain than cattle, hogs, dairy cows, or any other type of livestock. And that grain feed is subsidized.

Make no mistake, Big Chicken is responsible for the largest share of protein in the American diet, which—ipso facto—means subsidized corporations control our diets.

The average American eats 83.6 pounds of chicken per year. As I write this, the average US city price for a whole chicken is $1.28 per pound—16 cents less than a dozen eggs. For comparison's sake, in Germany the price per pound for whole chicken is $6.

How in the world can a live animal that needs to be fed and watered as it is raised and then slaughtered be sold so inexpensively in the United States? You got it: subsidies.

A chicken will naturally live for 6 to 10 years. But those bred to be eaten are slaughtered within six weeks of being hatched, pumped up like those weird birds on the Foster Farms chicken commercials.

There are 18.5 billion chickens alive in the world at any one time, more than any other species of bird. There are about 2 billion chickens in the United States and almost 9 billion in China. These are the two largest chicken populations on the planet. And there is a chicken war underway. Wanna take a stab at what it's over?

China imposed tariffs on US chicken products "on the result of an investigation that found that subsidies had created an unfair advantage for U.S. chicken producers," the *Wall Street Journal* reported on April 29, 2010. (Kinda sheds some light on why the chicken industry doesn't want to admit that it gets any subsidies, direct or indirect.) The World Trade Organization backed China's finding.

China's Ministry of Commerce's Fair Trade Office said US corn and soybean subsidies give American chickens an unfair price advantage in international markets.

Yes, even with its nearly 9 billion chickens, China still imports about $700 million worth of US chicken products per year (they especially like our chicken feet).

I'm not looking for chicken feet at the Virginia grocery store I visit, I'm looking to see how much people spend on whole chickens and chicken parts.

The fresh chicken products that are spread out neatly in rows in front of me include breasts, thighs, legs, wings, and whole roasters. There are chicken parts to be had as well as whole frozen chickens to take home and keep for a week or more before eating.

The chicken section of the supermarket organizes its cuts well. In fact, two butchers in long white coats splattered with blood stand on either side and rearrange the packages, and rearrange the packages, and rearrange the packages. I figure out soon enough that they are biding their time to investigate what I am doing there with my pen and notebook in hand. I am taking notes on the contents of the shelves: They start with breasts and work their way over to whole chickens and Cornish game hens. In between are drumsticks, half breasts, bone-in, boneless, skinless, party wings, and leg quarters. Some parts are "Organic." Some parts are "All Natural." Some parts are "Fresh." In another aisle there are even "Frozen Fresh" whole chickens and chicken parts.

For some reason, on the day when I was in the market, every person who selected chicken was a man. And every answer to the question of what factored into their selection was the same: price.

"Price-wise."

"Just price."

"Doesn't matter [what type of chicken]. Price matters."

Et cetera.

American chickens are so cheap that we do lots of weird things with them. We famously make nuggets. We make buffalo wings. We chop them up with celery and mayonnaise and call it chicken salad.

We also waste a lot of chicken. In America, we scrap 25 percent of the food we prepare each year. Considering that poultry is the biggest protein source in our diets, we could be tossing billions of pounds of bird in the trash. Moreover, it costs more than $1 billion a year to dispose of food waste in the United States.

Because indirect chicken subsidies amount to more than $1 billion, too, as a taxpayer you might as well take a $20 bill out of your wallet, crumple it up, and throw it away. That's about the subsidized cost of wasted chicken per household per year in the United States.

Without the indirect grain subsidies, chicken would cost almost 30 cents more per pound. Put another way, taxpayers are supporting some 30 cents of every pound of chicken consumed.

I asked all the dude chicken shoppers at the supermarket, "Would you pay more for chicken?" Their answers were surprising: If they had to.

Okay, so what would we get with more expensive chicken? This is where it gets interesting and where Big Chicken gets its feathers all in a ruffle.

The 2008 documentary *Food, Inc.* and the 2006 book *The Omnivore's Dilemma* by Michael Pollan explain the benefits and virtues of eating the meat of sustainably raised, cage-free chicken pastured on grassland instead of being confined in cages. These birds aren't jacked up on antibiotics and hormones, and in their idyllic surroundings, they naturally fertilize the land. Of course, raising a chicken this way—the "free range" way—makes for more expensive chicken products for consumers.

These chickens likely contain more nutritional value, are better for the environment (because they fertilize the land and avoid the arsenic and concentrated waste problems associated with large-volume production facilities), and, according to many people, taste better.

Free-range operations produce 10,000 broiler chickens a year on 100 acres of land. Big Chicken pops out, in 20,000-square-foot warehouses, 10,000 broiler chickens every three weeks, on average.

There's no need to go into the details of Big Chicken's operations. *Food, Inc.* did that well. It's nasty and includes growth hormones, beak cutting, and generally inhumane treatment of the animals. (Check out the Humane Society of the United States' Web site, www.humanesociety.org, for more information on this.)

Big Chicken takes issue with the way it's portrayed, of course. The NCC lashed out at Michael Pollan for *Food, Inc.*, for example, in a press release directed at consumers: "Would you like to pay a lot more for your food? Would you like to have fewer choices in the supermarket?" the release asked. Clearly, it had done the same type of research I had at the grocery store, hitting the two points shoppers seem to care about most.

"*Food, Inc.* is a one-sided, negative, and misleading film about the way food is produced and sold in the United States. It is a documentary about the American food system the way *Raiders of the Lost Ark* was a documentary about archaeology," the release sniped. Despite the whining, it did make a good point: "The model favored by the makers of *Food, Inc.*—essentially local, small-scale production—is a viable niche in the overall food system, but a very small one. Small-scale farms and ranches simply could not provide sufficient food for 300 million Americans and millions of other people around the world. There is simply not enough land or labor available to make the model work." It goes on to point out what an America of small-scale chicken production would look like. "If the mainstream commercial chicken industry tried to raise its annual production of nine billion birds in a similar fashion, it would need 45 million acres! That's more than all the farmland in Georgia, Alabama, Mississippi, and Arkansas—combined."

But isn't there a happy medium? Something between cheap, mass-produced chicken and the boutique version, between Wal-Mart and Louis Vuitton? Mall chicken?

As it stands, subsidized chicken can be harmful to our health as well as our financial well-being. Check this out: Russia found US chicken so repugnant (because we wash chickens with chlorine) that it banned imports in 2009—an $800 million hit to Big Chicken as well as to hundreds of thousands of poultry workers.

When cheap chicken is deemed harmful to health and welfare, as Russia and the European Union claim US chicken is, it hurts the economy far more than it helps it.

Tim Wise, director of the Research and Policy Program at Tufts University's Global Development and Environment Institute and one of the authors of the study on the broiler chicken industry, told me that an America without subsidized chicken would look not very different from the America we live in today. Except, perhaps we'd have more money in our pockets (because we wouldn't be spending our tax dollars on it) and likely better-quality chicken to eat (because subsidies wouldn't be encouraging factory farming).

Wise is quick to point out that because the chicken industry relies heavily on implicit feed subsidies and because those feed prices change, it's easy for the industry to duck (no pun intended) claims of chicken subsidies and say they don't matter to them. (When market prices for a feed grain such as corn rise, subsidies to corn producers diminish. Indeed, the prices and subsidy data given throughout this book likely fluctuated while you were reading it.) But in the long run, subsidies are built into price cycles, and this cushion of support bears itself out in both positive and negative ways.

Wise says that it wouldn't be smart to eliminate the subsidy system altogether. "A more rational approach is needed," he says.

Subsidy elimination would crush rural land values, he says, which would affect mortgages that in turn would affect the banking system, and that would weigh too heavily on the general economy and the prices of goods and services, he says. Rural and poor communities would suffer most. That's where most farms are located.

To be sure, agricultural reform is needed, Wise says. Scaling back subsidies to the richest farmers and developing forms of assistance to small, family farmers is the way to go, he says, with the health and welfare of family farmers the focus.

Wise says plans for reform should start with a simple question: "How can farm policy support the things we value?"

For example, he says, "industry would tell you that bigger is better. But look at hogs."

Okay, let's do that . . .

CHAPTER FIVE

PORK

Pigs live up to their name. Despite there only being a little more than 100 million hogs in America, they consume almost as much feed grain as 2 billion chickens, ranking second to poultry in terms of the total amount consumed, according to the US Department of Agriculture.

Because the feed grain industry is so heavily subsidized, you'd think this would give a little piggy a leg up when it goes to market and make it cheap. Feed represents as much as 85 percent of the cost of hog production. Margins for pig farming are thin, however, and the consumer's price per pound of pig ain't cheap. Pork is two to three times more expensive than chicken, depending on cut, and almost 50 percent more than ground beef. Hence, there are more cheap burgers and chicken nuggets at fast-food restaurants than ham sandwiches. Even bologna is twice as expensive as chicken. Sliced bacon, at the time of this writing, was $4.20 per pound.

Still, this doesn't mean that pigs aren't plentiful around the world. In fact, pork, the most widely eaten meat globally, is experiencing a consumption boom.

The number of pigs on the planet has been on the rise. There are about 1 billion pigs in the world today, up from less than 750 million three decades ago, according to the Food and

Agriculture Organization of the United Nations. According to the *Wall Street Journal,* agricultural economists believe the number of hogs and other livestock will keep rocketing higher in the long term, as developing-world incomes rise and meat demand booms. The newspaper explains "pigs provide a relatively cheap source of protein."

The H1N1 virus, or swine flu, dampened demand for pork around the world at the pandemic's height in 2009. But a renaissance is occurring outside America. While the size of the American hog population has been stagnant for years, developing countries are raising more pigs to meet their people's higher demand. Take Vietnam. It has among the largest pig populations in the world (27 million), according to the *Journal.* The pigs generally are owned by local farmers or companies rather than large, international meat producers and there "isn't enough farmland for all the animals in densely populated Vietnam," the paper said. "As a result, pig farmers increasingly locate operations near urban areas."

I am yammering on about pig farming here and abroad because it brings up issues that are directly related to subsidies in America. The US government purchases surplus pork from producers, effectively guaranteeing them income in a form of federal subsidy—on top of the indirect feed and environmental subsidies—yes, environmental subsidies. Because pigs are messy, their effluent causes myriad environmental concerns, and we taxpayers pick up the tab for keeping things clean.

The federal government buys surplus pork from producers because although our pork is cheap, it isn't *as* cheap as pork imported from Asia, so the imported stock sells better. Uncle Sam lends a helping hand to keep American producers in business. In a normal market scenario, lower demand for US pork results in less US production. And to some extent, that's what has been occurring in the pork industry—just not 100 percent. Pork producers should be thanking their lobbyists. Us, not so much.

According to the most current data I could find, the hog industry receives more than half a billion dollars in implicit subsidies. Here's how that works: Industrial hog operations (defined by the USDA as those housing more than 5,000 pigs) feed their stock a mixture that averages 80 percent corn and 17 percent soybean meal. Assuming that feed accounts for 60 percent of production costs (as noted earlier, it can account for as much as 85 percent) for industrial hog operations, preliminary calculations by researchers at Tufts University suggest that a scenario in which industrial hog producers had to pay full cost of production for the corn and soybean meal used in hog feed would have increased industrial hog operators' total production costs by an average of 13 percent from 1997 to 2005. With subsidies, the opposite happened and the operators saved that much.

It is very important to note that the EPA classifies livestock operations that keep and raise animals in "confined situations" according to size. This is done to permit the EPA to adequately regulate and monitor these large concentrations of animals for their impacts on the environment and public health. These concentrated animal feeding operations (CAFOs) are designated as "large" CAFOs if they house 2,500 or more hogs weighing more than 55 pounds or at least 10,000 weighing less than 55 pounds. "Small" CAFOs have less than 750 hogs of 55 pounds or more or fewer than 3,000 weighing less than that. Meanwhile, diversified farms grow the crops to feed the livestock they raise in free-range environments.

Diversified farms have been losing market share and are struggling to compete with the larger farm operations. Hog industry observers report that the industry is headed in the direction the poultry industry has taken, with large integrators taking over.

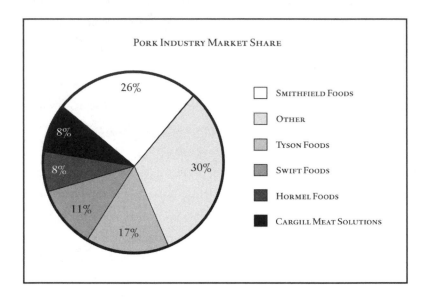

Indeed, in contrast to smaller operators, large operators can afford to do business in a market where volatile feed prices and disease outbreaks can crimp profits. Larger operators can spread losses among different aspects of their business (feed, medicine, processing, retail), and at the same time, they get the bulk of US subsidy dollars because they buy more grain feed. In addition to that, as noted, on top of the feed subsidies, the federal government spends hundreds of millions of dollars each year buying pork directly from the industry. Let me rephrase that: directly from the big hog operators. These Boss Hogs get priority on

environmental subsidies, too, by virtue of the threat their massive operations pose to the environment and public health.

In a 2001 article, the *Washington Post* colorfully described
the Boss Hog business in North Carolina:

> Embraced by politicians and business leaders as an alternative
> to tobacco and all its uncertainties, large factory-style hog
> farms—some housing 10,000 or more animals—have brought
> jobs and wealth to depressed rural communities and generated
> fat profits for the handful of big companies that dominate the
> industry.
>
> But prosperity has an unpleasant byproduct. Besides the
> stench that sometimes wafts into neighboring subdivisions,
> the untreated waste that hog farmers store in open lagoons and
> spray onto their fields has sparked broad concern about
> potential threats to streams and drinking water.

That stink isn't specific to North Carolina. Pretty much
every hog farm produces such wafts. I've come down to Alabama to get closer to the hog industry and the hog farms that
populate the area. Here, too, there is that stink in the air.

I drive through residential subdivisions, past strip malls,
by golf courses, to larger and larger tracts of open land. Tree
cover thickens. The environs get more rural.

Sand Mountain, Alabama, is one such rural area, an
approximately 120-square-mile plateau in the lower Appala-
chian Mountains that is populated mostly by the rural poor. It
was singled out by the poultry producer Gold Kist Corporation
of Atlanta, already entrenched in the region, as a fine place in
which to establish its new hog operations.

Gold Kist built three CAFOs on Sand Mountain, and as one local observer, Wayne Cummins, put it, "Those families unfortunate enough to be bordered by a hog CAFO soon lived in the misery caused by the incredible stench of football field–sized raw manure ponds."

Raw manure is flushed from the buildings housing the pigs directly into the holding ponds. This is standard procedure. Hogs produce two to four times more waste than humans, and let's just say that no pig has ever claimed that what comes out doesn't stink. Then consider this: A relatively small hog CAFO of 4,000 hogs—classified as medium sized by the EPA—produces the same volume of manure as a town of 16,000 people.

But the stench was only half the problem at Sand Mountain. According to local news reports, holding ponds can be built near property lines, literally up to the edge of a neighbor's front yard.

How lovely.

Anyway, concerns like this resulted in new and costly regulations being issued by the EPA. But have no fear; lobbyists were there to ensure that taxpayer dollars paid livestock producers to implement preventive measures and remedies to the environmental damage caused by their operations.

In its 2001 article, the *Washington Post* described the position of one farmer:

> To L.D. Black, the support seems only fair. A burly, third-generation farmer who wears Reeboks and a look of perpetual amusement, Black, 40, switched from tobacco to hogs in 1993 and raises nearly 6,000 of them under contract with Prestage

Farms Inc., one of [North Carolina's] largest producers of pork and poultry. "In my view, we're feeding the country," he said. "If they want to eat cheap, someone's got to pay the costs."

And we do. All livestock producers—including the largest and most profitable ones—are eligible for up to $50,000 in assistance per year, or a total of $200,000 over 10 years, to defray the costs of environmental projects.

According to the *Post,* "Environmental groups and advocates for small-farm owners call [the environmental assistance] a clear case of corporate welfare and one that highlights the clout of agribusiness on Capitol Hill. Because the . . . program gives priority to livestock operators facing the biggest environmental challenges, lifting the size cap diverts resources from small operations to large ones, which hastens the demise of the family farm."

But that position falls on deaf ears, especially in Washington, where the full-on Helen Keller effect is abundant. Take, for example, the position of Representative Frank Lucas, the Oklahoma Republican who chairs the House agriculture committee. "Farm bills have been very successful since 1933," he told the *Post.* "We eat cheaper than anyone else in the world."

Cheap food, of course, comes at a cost. And that is known as a different kind of "pork" in DC.

No matter how cheap its cost, some countries have banned US pork imports due to concerns about swine flu—a point I'll get to in a minute. Rather than scaling back production in response, however, Boss Hog turned to the US government for more support and assistance.

"The National Pork Producers Council has asked the US Department of Agriculture to spend almost $300 million buying American pork," according to a 2009 news story from the Australian Broadcasting Corporation. The story bore the headline "US Pork Industry Seeking Subsidies." It explained that "the US pork industry is hoping to be the next sector to benefit from increased government assistance."

I called the NPPC, which states its mission is to "protect the livelihoods of America's 67,000 pork producers," and was told that the industry actually didn't get the $300 million in assistance that it had sought; it got $150 million. That, to be clear, is money on top of its usual take.

The taxpayer assistance that Boss Hogs suckle from the government puts farmers' jobs at risk.

As Tufts University research shows: Industrial operations are getting a 13 percent discount on their operating costs due to US agricultural policies, so they are enjoying a cost advantage over hog farmers who grow crops and raise livestock in free-range environments.

That cost advantage could be what is allowing CAFO-based hog production to out-compete the small, diversified farmers who grow their own feed at a higher cost. Eliminating grain subsidies could lessen the advantage that industrial operations currently have over those diversified, independent producers.

Now about those health concerns that I said I would address.

A paper published in the January 2008 issue of the *Canadian Journal of Veterinary Research* reported that hog herds on large, high-density farms were more likely to have been exposed to the H1N1 (swine) flu virus and to harbor it continuously. This finding—more pigs in more confined quarters slopping around and sharing fluids and whatnot passing a virus around—shouldn't be shocking. H1N1 flu is quite common among pig populations. What isn't common is a virus jumping from pigs to humans.

Now here's where it gets interesting. A 2009 paper in *Environmental Health Perspectives,* published by the National Institute of Environmental Health Sciences, says that the "CAFO environment may be more likely than smaller farms to facilitate the evolution of novel strains."

A novel strain of the swine flu is what caused pandemic concerns among humans in 2009. It had RNA from two different pig and human flu viruses, meaning that the viruses combined in either a pig or a human infected with both at the same time.

Although no one will ever know exactly how or where the novel H1N1 virus came about, it seems like it might be a good idea to avoid putting animals and humans together in crowded conditions that might "facilitate the evolution of novel strains" of viruses.

I really shouldn't have to connect the dots from our tax dollars to government subsidies that enrich Boss Hog at the expense of piglet (smaller, diversified) hog farms and pose serious global health concerns.

The NPPC is correct when it says that "pork production in the United States is a vital part of the economy." Its most recent figures show the industry is responsible for about 35,000 full-time jobs and an additional 515,200 indirect jobs. "The industry," the NPPC says, "produced nearly $21.8 billion in personal income from total sales of more than $97 billion and added $34.5 billion to the country's gross national product."

The NPPC also says that "today there are more than 67,000 pork operations compared with nearly 3 million in the 1950s. Farms have grown in size; 53 percent of them now produce 5,000 or more pigs per year."

That is the growth of Boss Hog in a nutshell. Yet, what it doesn't show is the growth of subsidies paralleling Boss Hog's maturation. Implicit subsidies to the hog industry were about $81 million in 1997. As stated earlier in this chapter, they have grown to exceed $500 million.

And what do we get in return? Is it really the "cheap food" that politicians claim? Over the past decade alone, pork prices have increased by 40 percent. That trickles down to the shelves at the grocery store and to the prices of hot dogs at the ballpark.

If your bologna has a first name, it's likely not O-S-C-A-R anymore. It's T-Y-S-O-N or S-M-I-T-H-F-I-E-L-D. Tyson, Smithfield, Swift, Cargill, and Hormel own 70 percent of the $50 billion pork industry.

I pull into the parking lot of a Piggly Wiggly supermarket just outside of Huntsville, Alabama. Inside, the meat department displays the usual suspects, all neatly vacuum-packed and organized by cut: pork loin, pork chops, pork tenderloin, pork cube steak, pork shoulder, pork neck bones, and giant packs of spare ribs half the size of my arm.

The fluorescent lighting reflects off the plastic wrap and gives each pack a dull glow. It makes some seem more appetizing. Others suffer from the lighting and packaging, which just add to the unappealing look of the brown mix of muck that's inside.

The short ribs, for instance, have a nice, bright highlight on the strangely attractive streaks of white fat revealed by the clear package they're in, while bologna suffers under what looks like the queasy anaerobic conditions of its cardboard-backed box.

Bacon jumps out at you, displayed like long keys from an accordion. There is bacon coated in brown sugar, classic smoked bacon, and Canadian bacon, which actually comes from Wisconsin.

Hormel seems to own this display at this store. Its packages litter the shelf. They even offer a fully cooked ham weighing 25 pounds and costing $70. That's a lot of dough. Granted, you could feed a large family with it, but I see now why pork is "the other white meat." It's too expensive to be the mainstay. Even with grain subsidies, prices are high. That means demand will likely stay low—lower than the other, cheaper meats, anyway.

I am the only one in the pork section.

The dairy industry once found itself faced with a similar circumstance of declining demand. Let's find out what happened there, and what issues subsidies have brought along with our milk consumption.

"Got milk?" Yep, lots of it in the next chapter. We'll go to where the happy cows live: California.

CHAPTER SIX

DAIRY

The word "dairy" comes from the Middle English word for dairymaid, *"deye."* In even older times, "deye" meant a "kneader of dough."

In any case, the word describes an action, kneading—whether dough or teat. The dairy business has come to rely so heavily on subsidies at our expense that one researcher calls this use of subsidies "milking the customer."

But I don't want to get ahead of myself. I'll start at the beginning. Okay, not so far back as days of yore, when dairymaids frolicked in fields. I'll start in 1937. That's when it was found that injecting dairy cows with bovine growth hormone (BGH), a hormone produced naturally by a cow's pituitary gland, increased the cow's yield of milk.

To put 1937 into context, it was when the New Deal farm programs were in full swing and the government was pushing millions of dollars onto farmers and ranchers as well as agricultural scientists to find innovative ways to increase yields so America could dominate the world food market, as we saw in chapter 2.

In the beginning, BGH was used rather sparingly because it had to be removed from the dead cow. To avoid the science and engineering lesson, I'll give you the summary: BGH—

which is also called bovine somatotropin (BST)—basically stemmed the rate of mammary cell deaths. More mammary cells equals more milk. Weaker cows produce fewer mammary cells and therefore produce less milk.

The idea was simple enough: Isolate the hormone from the pituitaries of dead cows, purify it, and inject it into healthy cows to fend off cell death. This increased yields. But there were problems with getting and purifying BGH, so it was little used.

The great minds at the agricultural seed and pesticide behemoth Monsanto decided to take matters into their own hands. In 1979, the company started developing a synthetic form of BGH, which is called recombinant bovine growth hormone (rBGH) or recombinant bovine somatotropin (rbST). Almost 60 years after its first tests in dairy cows, in 1994 Monsanto introduced rBGH to dairy farmers, after having secured FDA approval for its commercial use in November 1993.

Guess what happened next? The synthetic version went into wide use. Yields increased by 10 to 20 percent. The milk business could boom by getting more milk from fewer cows.

All the while, of course, dairy farmers were getting their usual batch of government assistance through various programs that dole out everything from marketing fees to "loss contract" payments. Increasing yields meant dairy farmers could still get the same amount of government subsidy—or more.

In the past 40 years, dairy farms have been swallowed up by corporations just like the rest of the agricultural business. Since 1970, the number of farms with dairy cows has fallen sharply, from about 650,000 to about 75,000. Unlike the rest of the livestock industry, the number of dairy cows has fallen, too—by millions of cows. Still, total milk production has increased.

Fewer farms. Fewer cows. More milk. Big Ag. And, some say, big problems.

The federal government subsidizes milk by the gallon (to the tune of up to $2.5 billion a year) so corporations win by doing more with less. (If the subsidies were to be calculated by cow, it would be about $277 a head.)

The problems lie with the fewer-producing-more philosophy. The rBGH that allows this amazing fake to continue is reportedly harmful to the health of cows … and possibly to us.

The Center for Food Safety (CFS), a nonprofit environmental and public health advocacy organization based in Washington, DC, says:

> After approving the use of rBGH in 1993, the Food and Drug Administration has turned a deaf ear to the pleas of consumers, food safety organizations and scientists to reverse its approval of the hormone, or to simply require labeling of foods containing rBGH. Even a legal challenge by CFS could not force FDA to reexamine the health threats of rBGH. The FDA's decision stood despite regulatory bodies in both Canada and Europe rejecting the hormone due to numerous animal and human health concerns.
>
> In cows treated with rBGH, significant health problems often develop, including a 50 percent increase in the risk of lameness (leg and hoof problems), over a 25 percent increase in the frequency of udder infections (mastitis), and serious animal reproductive problems, i.e., infertility, cystic ovaries, fetal loss and birth defects.

There are other effects, too. To combat the increase in mastitis, farmers use more antibiotics, antibiotics that can find their way into milk and other dairy products. These residues contribute to bacteria becoming resistant to antibiotics, which is a serious public health problem for humans. When antibiotics don't work, they can't help the immune system combat infections, and sometimes that proves fatal. In addition, some people develop allergic reactions to the antibiotic traces.

Another problem with rBGH is that, according to CFS, the milk from cows treated with it has a higher level of another hormone, insulin-like growth factor 1, or IGF-1. IGF-1 can survive digestion and enter the human bloodstream. As CFS reports, "Numerous studies now demonstrate that IGF-1 is an important factor in the growth of cancers of the breast, prostate and colon." (In some test cases, IGF-1 increased the risk of cancer fourfold.)

It would be one thing if the government required a label for rBGH products. Just like on packs of cigarettes, there could be warnings plastered on milk cartons advising consumers that artificial growth hormones had been used. But there aren't.

Monsanto defends this practice. "Milk marketing claims differentiating milk based on Posilac use are meaningless," it said. (Posilac is the trade name of Monsanto's rBGH product.)

Monsanto has litigated to ban dairy producers who don't use the hormone from using an "rBGH-free" label on their products . . . and won. This battle is playing out at the state level right now before our eyes, or not, depending on where you live.

It should be noted, asterisked, and highlighted that rBGH is used mostly by large factory dairy farms. It was injected into 43 percent of cows in herds of 500 or more, says a USDA report.

Meanwhile, fewer than 10 percent of small dairy farms (those with fewer than 100 cows) used it.

That's the health bit about the dairy industry (partially, anyway). Now for the money part.

Who gets most of the dairy subsidies? Everybody say, "Large factory dairy farms."

For simple animals that eat massive amounts of feed per day and do little more than offer up their udders for us to milk, dairy cows sure are complicated from a monetary standpoint.

Let's start with their feed. Each day, a cow eats about 100 pounds of hay, grain, and silage in a variety of combinations, depending on the farmer. They drink up to 50 gallons of water a day.

This costs about $5 per day per cow, of which at least some—less than 5 percent—is likely indirectly subsidized via corn, wheat, water, or other government subsidies.

Considering how many dairy cows there are in the country—9 million—that still adds up to $2.25 million in indirect or implicit subsidies per day to dairy farmers. Chop the estimate in half to be really conservative and we are still talking hundreds of millions of dollars in subsidies per year—just on feed.

Now let's get to the direct subsidies that the federal government doles out to the dairy industry. (It should be noted that states have their own programs, too.)

Federal marketing orders for milk began being used in 1937. Dairy price-support programs started in 1949, and an income-support program was added in 2002. Today, as mentioned, dairy subsidies cost taxpayers up to $2.5 billion annually. (The government pays dairy farmers based on how much milk they produce, so the amount farmers get varies from year to year.)

The libertarian think tank the Cato Institute says, "Dairy programs stifle dairy industry innovation and raise milk prices for consumers."

Huh? Yep, the billions of dollars we spend per year on the dairy industry to subsidize and support it actually *raise* prices at the checkout counter. I was shocked to discover that this is a well-known and accepted practice.

Moreover, two other programs were added in 2008 that insure milk producers against revenue losses.

The Cato Institute has done a lot of research in this area, and it identified five ways that the government influences the dairy market:

> **MARKETING ORDERS.** The Federal Milk Marketing Order system sets minimum prices for milk products. About two-thirds of milk is produced under federal marketing orders in 10 regions of the country. Most of the rest is produced under California's separate system of regulations. . . .
>
> Marketing orders essentially create cartels that limit competition. Entrepreneurs are not allowed to supply milk at less than the government prices. The system also limits the ability of milk producers from lower-cost regions, such as the Midwest, from gaining market share in higher-cost regions, such as the Southeast.
>
> **PRICE SUPPORT PROGRAM.** The Milk Price Support Program keeps market prices artificially high by guaranteeing that the government will purchase any amount of cheese, butter, and nonfat dry milk from processors at a set minimum price. . . . Note that the price support program props up dairy prices at the same time that the income support program

encourages overproduction, which puts downward pressure on prices.

INCOME SUPPORT PROGRAM. The Milk Income Loss Contract program . . . provides cash subsidies to milk producers when market prices fall below target levels. . . .

IMPORT BARRIERS. U.S. imports of milk, butter, cheese, and other dairy products are limited by "tariff rate quotas," which are tariffs that vary by import volume. Import barriers are a complement to dairy price supports because they help keep domestic prices artificially high. Without import barriers, U.S. consumers could simply purchase lower-priced foreign dairy products. . . .

EXPORT SUBSIDIES. The Dairy Export Incentive Program . . . provide[s] cash subsidies to U.S. dairy producers who sell in foreign markets. Because U.S. dairy policies keep domestic prices above world prices, producers would otherwise have little interest in selling abroad. Thus, dairy export subsidies create an incentive to export and help remove surpluses caused by overproduction from the domestic market.

Net, net the federal government and the large corporations that pretty much control the dairy business have conspired to keep prices high for the American public in the name of ensuring farmers an adequate income. This is not a secret conspiracy, mind you. It's occurring out in the open, documented in public records and news accounts.

If that hasn't soured you on milk, the following story will. I read about in many different publications.

In 2003, an Arizona dairy farmer named Hein Hettinga started bottling his own milk. He sold it for less than the competition by staying outside the traditional milk production system. The effect was enormous: Retail prices across the state had to follow suit.

Of course, this didn't sit well with the establishment. A coalition of major milk companies and dairies spent millions of dollars over three years, lobbying Congress to force Hettinga to join the traditional milk production pools. Most dairy farmers participate in regional pools run by the federal or state government that give them a guaranteed market for their milk at the price that is dictated by the current marketing order. Hettinga opted not to do this by bottling his own milk. He fought the coalition, but was eventually crushed. In 2006, Congress passed a law banning this practice. As the *Washington Post* reported on December 10, 2006, " 'I had an awakening,' the 64-year-old Dutch-born dairyman said. 'It's not totally free enterprise in the United States.' "

It's understandable why the dairy industry wants to keep prices high (what producer doesn't?), especially in light of falling milk consumption. Americans now drink 23 gallons of milk each year, about half of what they did in 1941, milk's banner year at 45 gallons per person.

The National Dairy Council, established in 1915 to represent America's dairy farmers, has gone to great lengths to get more people to drink milk and eat dairy products. It funds research and puts forth volumes of data about the "health benefits of consuming milk and milk products throughout a person's lifespan."

Competition from other beverages and milk alternatives such as almond milk, soy milk, and the like are cutting into dairy farmers' business. But, I ask you, after reading about rBGH, is there any such thing as "real milk" anymore?

A block from the beach in Santa Monica, California—California, where, it's widely advertised, "happy cows come from"—I walk by a corner grocery store. On the sidewalk is a standalone sign that I think odd. It says in large black, block letters: "MILK $3.80 A GALLON."

It's meant as an enticement. Way before I even began to write this book, I was wondering who drinks milk these days. I was forced to drink it growing up. My mother would push a glass on me at dinnertime. Then college came, and there went that.

On average, Americans drink about eight ounces of milk daily.

Still, the grocery store clerk at the corner store in Santa Monica tells me that they can't stock milk fast enough. "As soon as it's delivered, two days later it's gone," he says.

I examine the crowd of milk drinkers in these parts. Surfers. Cyclists. Young people, mostly. They come and go in packs. They hop on their beach cruisers (some equipped with side mounts for their surfboards) and they're off.

The grocery store clerk tells me that management insists that they advertise their milk prices. But when I ask those passing by and those who stop in whether the price of milk matters, they say cost is relegated to second place. It's convenience that counts. It's *there.*

The clerk confirms this. "We just want them to know that we sell it here," he says.

The nearest grocery store is only about a half mile away. But just like in New York or, I suppose, any place with a lot of corner stores, it's easier to grab something at the closest one than to schlep even a few blocks for staple goods.

The milk industry counts on this. It's like sugar or eggs or coffee or bread. The very simplest things, the things we give little consideration to, are designed to be available, to be abundant, to be priced at just the right amount to not give people pause—even if the prices are far more than what the average world market commands.

The milk at this corner store is shelved inside a glass refrigerator. Gallons, half gallons, quarts. All for the taking. No label mentioning anything about whether it contains artificial hormones or antibiotic residue. A quick survey of people tells me that no one even knows what rBGH is. Most buy whole milk.

Growing up, we had milk delivered in glass bottles to our door. The milkman would come a few times a week to drop them off. He'd also collect the bottles we'd used. It was systematic.

The absence of the milkman as part of everyday society might be making some of the difference in the milk consumption rate; milk isn't part of the American fabric of life anymore. Sure, people still buy it, but it isn't automatic. When was the last time you saw a milkman? Milk is no longer even a must-have in the fridge. There are alternatives.

My milk-drinking days were before the advent of rBGH, too. When I look at that sign in front of the corner grocery store, many different associations come to mind, chief among them the politics that went into setting that price per gallon.

Politics and the milk industry have always been tightly bound. And a typical test of a politician's "Americanness" is to be able to quote the price of a gallon of milk.

In 2008, presidential candidate Rudy Giuliani famously failed this test. And President George H.W. Bush similarly was taken to task for being out of touch with the American people for his purported amazement over a grocery store price scanner. But my favorite story involving a politician and the milk industry features President Richard Nixon. It exemplifies the symbiotic relationship between the aw-shucks happy-cow industry that is really Corporate America and the underbelly of Washington, DC.

In an archive of the Watergate tape recordings, I found one, from March 1971, that shows Nixon and his staff discussing the milk industry's power. Here's an excerpt:

JOHN CONNALLY: These dairymen are organized; they're adamant; they're militant. This particular group, AMPI, which is the American Milk Producers Institute or something, uh, represents about forty thousand people. The one that parallels them on the East, uh, Mid-Con, or something—

CLIFFORD HARDIN: Mid-American.

CONNALLY: Mid-American group represents about forty thousand. The Southeastern group, uh, Dairymen Incorporated, whatever their name is, represents a lesser number, but probably in the range of twenty thousand members. They, uh, very frankly, they tap these fellows I believe it's one-third of one percent of their total sales or ninety-nine dollars a year whichever is—

NIXON: Like a union.

CONNALLY: Oh, it's a check-off. No question about it. . . .

They're asking for, for an increase in the cost, uh, in the price of a hundredweight up to four—$4.92 ...

[After some more John le Carré–like dialogue back and forth like this, Nixon gives the takeaway quote.]

NIXON: ... like they told us this morning, we won't raise the price; we'll cut back on production. ...

Now that's more than spilt milk to cry over; it's the reality of the relationship between politics and agriculture: If prices can't be raised outright on one end, then production can be scaled back on the other end—netting the same result.

Let's look at a modern-day cover-up, one that is responsible for myriad health issues, not the least of which is obesity, including childhood obesity.

It's time to take a look at America's sweet tooth.

CHAPTER SEVEN

SUGAR AND BEVERAGES

Curiously and in a very odd case of kismet, as I was beginning to write this chapter on sugar and beverages I read in my daily dose of the *Financial Times* that the Corn Refiners Association was asking the FDA for permission to change the official name of high fructose corn syrup (HFCS) to the duller, easier to say and spell, but much more misleading "corn sugar."

This would be a mighty important change.

The reporter wrote, "The request comes amid growing alarm in the US about rising obesity levels and the growing public perception that high fructose corn syrup is worse for the daily diet than table sugar.

"That has in turn led some food companies to highlight the fact that some of their products do not contain the sweetener."

HFCS is a derivative of corn made by using enzymes to alter the sugar composition of cornstarch. It was developed and made on the back of corn subsidies. When subsidies drove the price of corn very low in the 1970s, it gave some mad agricultural scientists incentive to see what else they could do with corn besides develop ways to grow more of it to feed to pigs and cattle. They went into their labs and came out with ways to feed it to us as a cane sugar replacement.

Companies such as Coca-Cola (which serves a billion of its beverages a day—yes, *1 billion a day*) liked this mad-scientist-devised cheap sugar replacement because, as you can guess, it's cheap. (HFCS is half the price of cane sugar.) Coke made the switch over to HFCS in 1985. Pepsi and other beverage makers followed suit. So did other food makers, and before you knew it, HFCS was the go-to sweetener in our food chain. (When Coke and Pepsi alone switched, it wiped 8 percent of the demand for cane sugar from the market. It saved them both $90 million the first year.)

This switch to HFCS had begun in the 1970s and bled into the 1980s, which is also when America began to get really fat. Numerous studies have pointed out the parallel tracks of increased HFCS consumption and the rising obesity rate. More than 60 percent of Americans are overweight or obese, which is defined as having a body mass index (BMI) of 25 or higher. BMI is a calculation of body fat based on height and weight. Using this system, a six-foot-tall man weighing 200 pounds would be overweight, as would a five-foot-five woman weighing 150 pounds.

I'll get into the details of increasing body weight and HFCS use in other chapters. The science, some say, is out on whether HFCS makes us any fatter than cane sugar does. But what isn't arguable is that the birth of HFCS was the result of corn subsidies. Call it corn sugar or HFCS or crap, the fact is that we ingest too much of it (about 40 pounds per year, the average weight of a five-year-old.)

Still, the popularity of HFCS did little damage to the sugar industry; instead, it helped its cause. The US sugar industry doesn't rely on the market for its pricing and profits, silly reader, it relies on the federal government. Eighty percent of the sugar consumed in America comes from US sugar growers because high tariffs block foreign growers from selling their cheaper sugar products here.

Rather than taking another walk down the aisle of yet another supermarket or grocery store or even visiting the small corner store, I decide to head to the largest retailer of food in America: Wal-Mart.

Sugar is a big part of this place. It greets me when I arrive at the front door in the form of soda (two-liter bottles for $1.25 each). It escorts me down the aisle in the forms of doughnuts, cookies, and chips. It sits there stacked up in one-pound bags with familiar names, household names, coaxing me to choose among them: Twizzlers, Hershey's, Snickers, Reese's, M&M's, 3 Musketeers, Kit Kats.

Their jingles play in my head as I scan the shelves. Child-hood memories came back: Oreos. Chips Ahoy. I don't just see these items. I feel these items. They are embedded parts of our culture. Goldfish. Milky Ways. I don't eat any of these things anymore. But I can almost taste them. The packaging alone brings my taste buds to life. Fritos. Ruffles.

Mounds of sugar. Mounds of packaging. Baked, twisted, and coated into forms that scream "Happy." "Good." "Sweet." Frosted sugar cookies. Two dollars and 98 cents for 12. I am tempted by them. I want to rip open the package and bite into them.

I move on and look for something I would eat these days. It's sad. The only thing I can come up with are some nuts. Otherwise, none of the snack foods on the shelves at Wal-Mart meet my low-sugar-diet restrictions.

Other shoppers, however, are clearly finding things they want. Many of these people are dressed in sweatpants. Most have their shirts untucked. The majority of the shoppers are over-weight. The most disturbing part of this portrait isn't the shoppers themselves, however. It is those who have a seat: the children sitting either in shopping carts or in baby seats on shopping carts. They play, coo, and point as their mothers push them down the aisles. I noticed that the candy packaging was much more colorful than that for the other foods.

America has a sweet tooth, and despite the fact that the global price of sugar is way below what we pay for it (meaning that worldwide it is a fine way to make profits based on the free market alone), sugar prices remain high. According to the USDA, raw cane sugar outside the United States is 10 cents per pound whereas US raw sugar prices are 22 cents per pound. The agency unapologetically explains, "U.S. sugar prices have been well above world prices since 1982 because the U.S. Government supports domestic sugar prices through loans to sugar processors and a marketing allotment program."

Big Sugar (and this time I haven't dubbed it that, many people already have) reaps about $1 billion per year from government programs that support it by keeping prices at or above a certain amount; direct payments to farmers aren't made. And you can add that on top of the industry's profits—artificially high profits, of course, because Big Sugar isn't playing fair: It gets to charge us inflated prices. Of course, the American Sugar Alliance, which represents American sugarcane and sugar beet farmers, doesn't see the world this way. It says that it "works to assure that farmers and workers in the U.S. sugar industry survive in a world of heavily subsidized sugar."

HFCS, remember, reaps subsidies by virtue of being made with corn and therefore can keep its prices low.

Table sugar is a whole different world.

"Some people win the lottery; other people grow sugar," author James Bovard quipped. "Congress protects consumers from the roller-coaster by pegging American sugar prices on a level with the Goodyear blimp floating far above the amusement park."

It's true. "Sugar sold for 21 cents a pound in the United States when the world sugar price was less than 3 cents a pound. Each 1-cent increase in the price of sugar adds between $250 million and $300 million to consumers' food bills," according to Bovard.

"A Commerce Department study estimated that the sugar program was costing American consumers more than $3 billion a year," he continued. That's a mighty costly program that is being funded by . . . us. (Sugar allotments vary greatly by year and it should be noted that the tariffs imposed, which increase the price of the sugar on the shelves for us, are far more damaging to our wallets than sugar subsidy programs, which come and go.)

A friendly reminder here of the segment of the population that consumes the most sugar: the poorest. Thanks, Big Sugar, you are doing the country a solid.

Don't get me wrong. HFCS is just as bad if not worse than cane sugar for the American consumer. McDonald's, Taco Bell, Subway, KFC, Jack in the Box, Burger King, Arby's, and Blimpie, among other fast-food restaurants, use HFCS prodigiously in menu items beyond the obvious sodas. How else do you think they can afford to offer "dollar value meals" and such?

At stores like the Wal-Mart I walked through, HFCS goods fill up many a shopping basket.

Consumers, however, are getting wiser. And in direct response to consumer backlash, Hunt's stopped using HFCS in its ketchup.

"In direct response to consumer demand, Hunt's is pleased to offer ketchup sweetened with sugar and containing only five simple ingredients," said Ryan Toreson, Hunt's Ketchup brand manager. "Parents are looking for wholesome meals and ingredients they recognize."

That quote is from a press release Hunt's sent out at the time of the swap (May 2010), and it came with a footnote: "The 2009 HealthFocus Trend Report indicated consumer concern over high fructose corn syrup has risen from 27% of shoppers being extremely or very concerned in 2004 to 45% of shoppers in 2008."

Hunt's was wise to switch. When almost half of your consumer base says it doesn't like what you are selling, change isn't a choice, it's a business necessity—no matter what cost savings could be had otherwise. (Hunt's said its ketchup's retail price would stay the same.)

Still, by choosing to use sugar instead of HFCS, Hunt's is shaking its head at one industry and giving a nod to another.

You might make the assumption that the corn industry and the sugar industry are pitted against one another (HFCS versus cane sugar)—until you explore the meaning of a word I've come to deplore: ethanol.

Just so the poor sugar farmers didn't feel left out by the ridiculous—and I mean ridiculous—amount of money corn farmers are getting from ethanol subsidies, the government gave Big Sugar a piece of the action in the 2008 Farm Bill.

Ethanol subsidies were designed to entice farmers to grow more products, such as corn and sugar, that could be turned into "clean energy." Ethanol was once thought to be a source of clean fuel. As numerous studies have shown, however, it's anything but clean.

According to a report by the food and agricultural consulting firm ProMar International, ethanol subsidies essentially create "a very expensive and uneconomic program to divert surplus sugar into production of fuel ethanol without regard to taxpayer costs." It cited in particular the more restrictive import quota and allotment provisions that "raise the cost of sugar to consumers and to food and beverage manufacturers by an average of 2 cents per pound, equal to $400 million a year or $2 billion over the life of the farm bill."

And then there are the job costs. ProMar predicted that the increased costs for sugar in the US market relative to sugar in other markets would accelerate US job losses because foreign manufacturers would have an increased competitive advantage. "Since 1997, 75,000 such jobs have been lost." The report continued:

> The higher market prices will stimulate sugar production in both the United States and Mexico, leading to surplus supplies that must be removed from the market at taxpayer expense.
>
> Federal budget costs will be considerably greater than the $1.3 billion projected by the Congressional Budget Office. We estimate that the cost over the ten-year budgeting horizon will be $5.4 billion.

Both the corn and sugar industries have already gotten away with robber baron–like profiteering at consumers' expense.

Ethanol subsidies only serve to promulgate the sick system that is hailed by many as bad for everyone—except Big Business and Big Government.

Big Sugar defends itself vigorously, by the way. The American Sugar Alliance says two-thirds of Americans believe sugar is inexpensive. Moreover it says that it isn't to blame for any type of food price increases even though sugar is used in 70 percent of manufactured food. Instead, it says, "Food manufacturers pocket lower sugar prices to boost profits instead of sharing the savings with shoppers." Also, it claims that sugar farmers don't receive government subsidy checks. Rather, "America's sugar producers support 146,000 U.S. jobs" and "Sugar producers generate nearly $10 billion a year for the U.S. economy."

And all of the above is true, if you don't take into account what's really going on with Big Sugar. It isn't direct subsidies that cause the Big Fake, it's sugar tariffs.

Tariffs, or covert subsidies, fuel sugar growers' propaganda—and even covert affairs. To skirt sugar tariffs, entrepreneurs in the past resorted to importing high-sugar products, such as iced tea mixes, and sifting out the sugar to sell it at the higher domestic price.

What's bizarre about the US sugar industry is that it shouldn't really exist to begin with. America doesn't exactly have the same climate as Cuba or the Dominican Republic or any of the more apropos environs for growing sugar. Parts of Florida, for sure, have the right temperature for sugar growing, and that's why so much domestic sugar comes from that state. But even an objective observer should admit that sugar protectionism—keeping a majority percent of the US market for ourselves—strains Florida growers and/or gives them a virtual monopoly.

Bring in sugar from other warm climates, such as Mexico, and fair competition would begin. The US sugar industry cries foul at this notion (which took effect in 2008 as part of the North American Free Trade Agreement) and has and is lobbying for even more support because of the "competition."

"Fourteen years after NAFTA came into effect, the last remaining barriers to agricultural trade in North America were dismantled [in January 2008]. Mexican corn farmers and American Big Sugar hate this unreservedly," said the author of an opinion piece published in the *New York Times* in February 2008. "American sugar barons are right to be afraid. Free trade in sugar within North America will allow cheaper Mexican sugar to flood in, undercutting the government system of sugar supports, which guarantees farmers high prices and costs consumers about $1.5 billion a year."

Don't worry. Big Sugar, by lobbying for provisions in the latest Farm Bill, included added compensation for itself if business was lost to producers from Mexico or any other exporting country that interferes with its stranglehold.

Even if foreign sugar does start to creep in, that food companies are beginning to use cane sugar in their products again will likely increase demand for it. Besides food companies such as Hunt's reverting back to cane sugar as an ingredient, soft drink makers, too, are responding to consumers' calls for "old school" soda. As it stands, every Pepsi and Coke (except for what they dub "Kosher for Passover" colas, which can be purchased around that holiday), and a few other specialty drinks they make in America, is made with HFCS. Outside the

United States, not so. That's why a cold bottle of Mexican Coke tastes so damn good.

To be sure, Mexican Coke is more expensive, which is likely why I can't find a bottle on any of Wal-Mart's shelves. All the soda here is made with the cheaper HFCS.

We consume about 10 percent of our daily calories in the sweetener in soft drinks. A switch to cane sugar would surely be a boon to Big Sugar. Health-wise, the jury is still out on whether it would make much of a difference.

Perhaps if food companies actually served us real ingredients and the growers of those ingredients got real with their prices, we'd be able to better cast our votes based on taste, price, and health at the checkout counter.

Cane sugar, as we've seen, is rife with tariff-related issues, making it artificially expensive in the US relative to the world market. And the much cheaper alternative, HFCS, is raft with issues that allegedly exacerbate health issues. No matter which one we choose, our choice of sweetener comes with a bitter ending. Subsidy policies need to change for HFCS and tariff policies need to change for cane table sugar, in order to put them both on equal footing and give us a fair choice between them.

At the Wal-Mart checkout, every single customer—I repeat, every single customer—has at least one junk-food item on the black belt waiting to be scanned. Why not? They're cheap. They're within arm's reach.

Whatever practices Americans choose to partake in, whether it's becoming so fat that they need to pay for extra seats on airplanes or eating so much sugar in whatever form that health insurance gets even more expensive, one thing is for sure: Sugar isn't going away; it's here to stay.

Since Indians learned how to crystallize it in the sixth century AD, making its transport easier, and since HFCS made a sweet liquid of corn, we have liked our sugar fix.

I know I need mine. I'm still drawn to the vending machine outside my office, where I pay 65 cents for a can of Coke several times a day. I know that it's HFCS in there from all the research I've done. But if I were a regular consumer I wouldn't know it. I'd only know that it tastes sweet. There would be no way for me to know that for every half cent I spent I'd be supporting the corn industry or for every penny I spent I'd be supporting the sugar industry. For that I'd need a cane-sugar Coke and a whole lotta time to do some research. I might also want a sandwich and a bag of chips to go with it. Which brings us to the subject of bread subsidies.

CHAPTER EIGHT

BREADS AND CEREALS

Cut off the crust of a slice of bread. What's left is what the slice really should look like, because that's how much we are really paying for—without subsidies.

Subsidies finance about 20 percent of the cost of bread in America. Same amount for cereal. Might as well scoop out and toss a bowl of those Wheaties. What's left in the box is the honest Breakfast of Champions.

We spend $2.2 billion a year to subsidize wheat farmers in the United States. They produce about $10 billion or more in sales depending on market prices, and export half that bounty.

Wheat grain is used for flour, pasta, bread, cereal, cakes, and cookies. It's hugely important. A 2009 Senate committee report flat-out stated, "It is no exaggeration to declare that 'grain is the only resource in the world that is even more central to modern civilization than oil,'" quoting author Dan Morgan from his best-selling book *Merchants of Grain.*

The report also looked back a few centuries and found that the importance of wheat hadn't changed: "No man qualifies as a statesman who is entirely ignorant of the problems of wheat," it quoted the fifth-century-BC philosopher Socrates as saying.

No sense worrying about driving our cars or heating or cooling our homes if we can't eat. And wheat is a staple food. To butcher another line from the past: We can't eat cake if we can't make bread.

So I get why the government would think it wise to keep bread cheap—in order to help us live. Then why does it cost so damn much?

I looked up the national average price of bread in March 2011, and it was running at about $2.30 a loaf. Having just been to the market and kvetched about spending four bucks on a loaf, I thought the discrepancy odd. I rationalized by thinking that I live in a nice area and had bought a multigrain variety that probably cost a hell of a lot more than a loaf of Wonder bread in Detroit.

Which got me thinking about whether the rich really are different—even when it comes to food. So I went to find out. I sought bread elsewhere. I chose Beverly Hills.

Paris Hilton, I'm told, shops at the grocery store I chose. So does Nicole Richie. And I have it on good authority that George Clooney has strolled the aisles of this store, a Bristol Farms smack in the middle of celebrity territory. The famous "press junket" Four Seasons, where stars are interviewed about their new films, is just a couple of blocks away.

Bread here is, in fact, different. It isn't in the aisles. It's put below the glass cases of sliced meats as if to pair the offerings. The choices are magnificent: Cracked wheat, pumpernickel, Irish soda, English toasting, and 100 percent whole wheat. There's original oat nut, country potato, country white, seven grain, healthy multigrain, raisin, and sourdough, among other varieties. The prices go from a high of $4.99 (Irish soda) to $2.99 (oat nut). All in all, nothing was more than five bucks. I figured that for what may be the ritziest place in the country, that wasn't so bad. Perhaps bread isn't all that expensive in America.

Then I took a look at the prices of breads in other countries around the world. Despite our double-digit subsidy, we pay one of the highest, if not the highest, price for bread. In Morocco, the government subsidizes 50 percent of the cost of bread. A loaf there is 20 cents. Cut that subsidy to match ours and double the price and it's still just 40 cents. In France, where bread is famously subsidized by the European Union, a loaf is a bit more than a buck, and sometimes you can get a fresh baguette for less. Even in the ridiculously expensive United Kingdom, bread costs less than it does here.

Each year, each American taxpayer pays the equivalent of six loaves of bread to the wheat industry. And what do we get in return? Bread that costs more than it does pretty much anywhere else on the planet.

Here's why: There is a built-in disincentive for wheat farmers to produce more wheat, which would increase supply and lower prices.

The largest recipients of a government program called ACRE (Average Crop Revenue Election) are wheat farmers. This pays farmers when wheat prices and/or yields drop. (I wish someone would pay me when I produce less and lose money.) Because of advanced technologies available today, farmers have a pretty good idea about how their growing season might fare and they are typically very knowledgeable about the world's crop supply. As such they can opt to plant other crops on their lands to accommodate these conditions. (I get into some of the factors that interfere with these decisions later on.) Some of these crops will even pay them more money as they wait for supplies to get lapped up—and then they can go back to planting wheat again.

"Decision Time Looms for Wheat Farmers," the *Wall Street Journal* headlined a story on August 8, 2010. "Wheat farmers in the U.S. and elsewhere are gearing up to make a crucial bet on the health of the world's grain supplies," its authors wrote. "Many farmers must decide within the next few weeks whether to plant more wheat to take advantage of rising prices."

It's a difficult choice to decide whether to plant wheat to try to make money or to not plant wheat to try to make money.

The National Association of Wheat Growers says it has four priorities—all of which center on the proposition of to grow or not to grow. These priorities are:

- Encouraging investment and innovation in U.S. wheat with the goal of increasing yields for U.S. wheat growers by 20 percent by 2018
- Increasing the focus on capturing the benefits of energy policy
- Improving risk management programs to support U.S. wheat growers, including federal farm policy, crop insurance and transportation policies
- Creating a unified voice supporting U.S. wheat, by working with U.S. Wheat Associates and other industry groups

What's driving farmers away from wheat are those dreaded ethanol subsidy programs that pay farmers more for their crops than they could usually get on the open market. Already large swaths of land previously farmed for food are being planted for fuel (up to one-third of wheat farmland, some reports say).

And then there's Wall Street. Don't blink, you read that right. Driving up the price of that sandwich in your hand that has already been subsidized by the US government are commodities traders.

This isn't Corporate America disguising itself as poor farmers and reaping Big Government subsidies while running multinational businesses. This is high finance driving up the cost of food for profit without owning or producing anything. Think of it as hedge funds in your food.

Indeed, Michael W. Masters, a hedge fund manager, testified before the Senate that "institutional investors are one of, if not the primary, factors affecting commodities prices today." Masters noted that in 2007 Americans consumed 2.22 bushels of wheat per capita. Meanwhile, he said, the 1.3 billion bushels represented by the 2008 wheat futures contracts stockpiled by index speculators was "enough to supply every American citizen with all the bread, pasta and baked goods they could eat for the next two years!"

In other words, the amount of wheat being traded was exponentially disproportionate to the amount of wheat being consumed in the country. This created a totally false market and a totally false sense of supply and demand. In turn, prices were manipulated—and soared.

The large-scale food riots that occurred around the world in 2008 highlighted the issue of food prices so well that Congress held more than 40 hearings on the issue of financial market trading in commodities markets. *Nothing* much came out of those hearings. Then the USDA got in on the act. It said of Wall Street's involvement in food prices:

> The funds held an increasingly large percentage of open interest in the futures market for agricultural commodities, as well as of nonagricultural commodities such as metals and energy. These investors only had a financial interest in the markets and did not intend to take delivery of the agricultural commodities. Indeed, it is likely that in general, neither the investors nor the financial managers that directed the funds' investments knew much about the fundamentals of agricultural commodity markets. *It is unclear to what extent the effect of these new investor interests had on prices and the underlying supply and demand relationships for agricultural products.*

The italics are mine and I ask: On what planet do lawmakers and the USDA live? If farmers use price indicators to decide how much or how little to plant the next season, and some Big Swinging Dick on Wall Street is trading around for a profit and messing with those prices, of course it's going to affect how much or how little food will be grown.

Financial speculators don't usually intend to "take delivery" of the contracts they buy. This means they are just in the commodities business for the money.

It's worth investigating how that happened—and continues to—because I don't know about you, but I don't want some grubby hedge fund manager's fingers in my pie. (And that saying takes on a whole new meaning now, don't it?)

Commodities futures contracts are agreements "to buy or sell a set amount of a commodity at a predetermined price and

date. Buyers use these to avoid the risks associated with the price
fluctuations of the product or raw material, while sellers try to
lock in a price for their products. Like in all financial markets,
others use such contracts to gamble on price movements,"
according to Investopedia.

Gambling on price movements is akin to gambling with
the price of our food, because that is exactly what many commodities traders do.

To be sure, recent financial reform legislation coming out
of the economic crisis limits some of the financial speculation
that has infected food trading in the past. But there are still a
lot of measures to be taken to get Wall Street out of the business
of speculating on food prices. It's a business they were never
supposed to be in.

US commodity futures markets were developed in the
mid-nineteenth century as a way to help farmers. Improved
transportation and technology were allowing them to sell their
products around the world, and forward contracts allowed
them to better manage price risks and sell grain over longer dis-
tances and periods of time.

Here's the business strategy behind it: Grain elevators collect grain from farmers; either purchase it from or hold it in storage for the farmer, who pays a storage fee; and either sell it or
coordinate its transportation to the final buyers. They do this
either by straight cash payments or through forward contracts
that specify a date in the future for the delivery of a commodity,
say, wheat. The contracts specify the amount, grade, date, and
price for the contract payment, and are usually done in advance
of harvest time, which allows farmers to guarantee a crop price
and eliminate the risk of falling crop prices.

That is logical. I give something to you, which you either buy outright or act as a middleman for. I either get my money up front in cash or collect it at some point in the future when you sell the item on my behalf.

But then grain elevators got more sophisticated with their forward contract payments, and hedged their own risk. As the Senate report on financial speculation in the commodities market explains:

> In order to protect themselves from the risk of falling crop prices, elevators usually hedge their cash or forward purchases by entering into futures contracts on the futures exchanges to sell the grain at a price they expect will cover their expenses. . . . Once the purchase of a cash crop is hedged with a futures contract, any decline in the value of the crop in the cash market should be offset with a gain in the futures market.

All fine and dandy if everyone buying and selling can take physical delivery of the commodity. Buy 1,000 bushels of wheat, for instance, and you'd better have room to put it somewhere. And for the most part, people with vested interests participated in the commodities market (albeit with a certain amount of speculation) until 2006.

Then, a massive amount of speculation entered the market. Investors who were pure speculators began trading food—commodities—like stocks. So much of this was going on that the American Bakers Association, among many others, alerted the Commodities Futures Trading Commission of their concerns. The bakers' association warned that as a result of the increasing commodity index trading, "the commodity exchanges have moved away from their original intent—to allow producers to sell their product in a transparent, regulated manner to physical users of the commodity."

In short, hedge funds and the like started trading in the commodities market, jacking up prices. This didn't translate into profits for farmers—most had already sold their grain contracts to grain elevators, remember. And it didn't help grain elevators. They had already set their price in the futures market. When it's time to settle up and actually deliver the product to the final purchaser, grain elevators, to simplify, have to buy back their futures contracts at a higher price. Meanwhile, the jacked-up market price was what set prices at the supermarket, increasing food costs for you and me. Everyone gets screwed in this scenario—except for the speculators, Wall Street.

Some very smart guys on Wall Street had figured out that they could make a killing on food because there was no limit on how much they could buy, and that someone else would have to—have to!—come in and buy their contracts from them at the last minute to actually buy the stuff. The trick was to create enough trading to increase prices. This they did—in a very big way.

Since 2008, limits and other technical barriers to keep Wall Street out of our food cabinets have been set. But Stopgambling onhunger.com, a Web site devoted to trying to get financial institutions out of the commodities business, says that while there has been regulatory and financial reform, Wall Street is *still* gambling on hunger. One of the examples the site gives is that farmers, granaries, and mills pay a higher tax rate than financial institutions, adding that pension funds and endowments pay no taxes on money made in the commodity markets.

The group is lobbying to have all participants in the commodities markets pay the same tax rate, which, it claims, would basically end the problem of commodity indexes and investment funds messing with our food business.

As you can see, it's no longer just Big Business and Big Government exploiting the world's need to eat at any cost. The ultimate financial whore has gotten in on the act: Wall Street, where greed is good.

Perversely, we fund all of this. It's our tax dollars that drive the engine that subsidizes farmers so they can stay in business, allowing grain elevators to hedge so Wall Street can profit (and pay less taxes on those profits). Lobbyists make sure Washington is taken care of. And we consumers find ourselves scratching our heads at the checkout over the cost of a bologna sandwich these days. Or worse.

As the author of a piece posted on rense.com wrote about the 2008 food crisis:

> Consumers in rich countries feel it in supermarkets but in the world's poorest ones people are starving. The reason—soaring food prices, and it's triggered riots around the world. . . .
>
> Wheat shortages in Peru are acute enough to have the military make bread with potato flour (a native crop). In Pakistan, thousands of troops guard trucks carrying wheat and flour. In Thailand, rice farmers take shifts staying awake nights guarding their fields from thieves. The crop's price has about doubled in recent months, it's the staple for half or more of the world's population, but rising prices and fearing scarcity have prompted some of the world's largest producers to export less—Thailand (the world's largest exporter), Vietnam, India, Egypt, Cambodia with others likely to follow as world output lags demand. Producers of other grains are doing the same like

Argentina, Kazakhstan and China. The less they export, the higher prices go.

The author of an August 2010 *Financial Times* opinion piece asked,

> So what lessons were taught by the 2008 crisis? It was in part the consequence of long-term neglect of investment in agriculture in developing countries and poorly thought-out agriculture subsidising policies in industrialised countries. It was then set off by adverse weather and exacerbated by inappropriate policies, such as export bans, hoarding by importing nations and lack of appropriate regulation of trade in commodities.

Sure we can feel bad for some farmers, but many still get their subsidies, more, even, if their revenue falls and they lose money. Sure we can feel bad for the owners of grain elevators, many of which are . . . dunt da na na! . . . big agricultural companies such as Cargill and Archer Daniels Midland. And we can feel bad for ourselves. None of us is dying, however, from food price speculation. Overseas and south of our border, people really are dying because of US subsidies and commodities speculation.

As I wrote in my Dow Jones *Ethics Monitor* column on April 9, 2010: "US subsidies lead to poverty and death."

It doesn't get any plainer than that. That's the real America we live in. And that's the real America people outside the country live with.

The lines between food and finance are merging more and more around the world. So let's take a hard look at our foreign policies, which matter a lot—right down to a grain of rice.

CHAPTER NINE

RICE

Being of Irish descent, I was never much of a rice man; potatoes have always been my starch of choice.

In America, rice isn't a huge slice of our diets; we are responsible for 12 percent of the world's production and we keep only half of that for ourselves. This is unlike most of the world's population. Rice is the most important grain for the human species as a whole. In Asia, especially, rice is a big deal. More corn may be grown throughout the world, but it has other uses besides human consumption (ethanol, animal feed). Rice, on the other hand, provides one-fifth of the calories consumed by humans. Other than eating rice as a grain, rice is a component of processed foods, beer, and pet food—in that order, from biggest to smallest usage.

Rice isn't indigenous to America. It came here with immigrants, first arriving in America in 1672. Africans who had learned to plant and cultivate it before being enslaved adapted their methods to cultivating the crop in South Carolina.

Plantation owners saw profits in the making and rice growing eventually spread to Georgia and throughout the South. Now more than 100 varieties are produced primarily in six states—Arkansas, Texas, Louisiana, Mississippi, Missouri, and California.

Rice cultivation in California came along with the estimated 40,000 Chinese laborers who immigrated to the state during the Gold Rush. They grew rice for their own consumption. Growing went commercial in California in 1912.

So rice is probably the thing we grow in America that is most like most of us Americans: We didn't originate here; we came from other countries, but we've grown and flourished and now dominate the same places from which we came.

Our subsidy system, you see, ensures that we are a dominant world player even if rice isn't a huge part of our diets or agriculture. Rice production in the United States amounts to $1.8 billion a year. Subsidies lower the retail price at the checkout counter by about 12 percent.

Of all the crops that I have researched and written about, I understand best why we need to subsidize rice growers: The stuff isn't supposed to be here. We don't have the right climate for it to grow properly and so we've had to create an artificial process to allow it to thrive.

Rice is best grown where rainfall is abundant and labor costs are low because it takes so much work to tend and harvest. Does that sound like America to you?

In this country, where we are experiencing water crises and our labor costs are famously high, rice isn't the first crop that comes to mind as a smart thing to grow. Thirty-six US states are in danger of drought on a regular basis, including Texas, which is now the driest region in the country, and—as I mentioned a few paragraphs back—where we grow a good amount of rice.

Rice requires ample water to flourish, so farmers typically flood their fields before planting. I am sure you can picture rice paddies. They are like swamps festooned with green shoots, inside of which are little seeds that after harvesting are milled into brown rice (by removing the husks) and white rice (by removing the bran).

I spent some time in a rice paddy in Malaysia and I can attest to the fact that growing rice isn't easy. You have to wade through the field, pick each plant, and then get into milling it. Not easy work.

I always thought shucking corn was a pain in the ass, but rice is in a different league. In the 17th century, separating the rice from the husks, or hulls, was done by putting whole rice kernels in a pan and throwing them in the air as the wind blew. The husks were blown away, but the rice fell back into the pan. Apparently, this worked because the hull isn't nearly as dense as the rice.

In any case, the basics of producing rice are the same the world over, even here in America: plant, harvest, dry, mill, store, and package. (Winnowing, which is what removing those husks is called, is mechanized now, of course.)

I visited a rice farm located almost dead center in the geographic middle of California near the San Joaquin Valley, in the most productive agricultural region in the country. Intricate canals and irrigation systems are used to flood the fields. Which is a controversial thing these days. Water subsidies, you see, are being examined more closely, much to the ire of the population that lives off this land. All over Kings County and Kern County and Merced County—famous California farming regions—are yellow signs that read: "Congress Created Dust Bowl." Others name names: "Stop Cardoza, Pelosi, Boxer. Water Crisis." They put Xs over the congresspeople's names.

Crimp the water and you crimp the crop. Costs rise.

Here's why that's a big deal: The Web site of Koda Farms, the rice farm I visited, explains that Koda has a seed development program in which it individually selects each panicle of rice (the cluster of grains on a stalk) to be grown. Those grains from the selected panicle are then planted in their own row on a small plot. A half-acre seed plot can contain more than 1,000 rows, and all of these need to be watered uniformly. As the rice grows, it is monitored for undesirable traits, and when these are found, all of the plants from that panicle of grains are cut from the seed plot. The rice is harvested at the end of the season and the process is repeated the next year, the Koda farm says. In the third year, the seeds harvested from the seed plot plants the year before are planted in a 10- to 20-acre field. More water. In the fourth year, the seeds from those plants are dropped by airplane onto a larger seed field. Even more water. In the fifth year, the seeds those plants produced are used to produce the rice that Koda sells. (Note that this intensive program is one that Koda undertakes to meet its high standards for "purity and quality control." Most rice is grown in a much simpler process that sees a crop planted and harvested each season, without the four-year seed development phase.)

According to Koda, which is a well-respected family farm (although you'd never think it was a family farm; the operation is enormous, with fields quite literally stretching as far as the eye can see), once the rice is harvested, it is dried and then milled. The grains, which have been removed from the plants by the threshing machine, first go into a dryer. Picture conveyor belts, drying stands, and storage tanks. Then the rice is milled, with the husk, bran layer, and germ being removed from each grain. The rice is then packaged, labeled, and shipped.

As you can see, water is a critical element in the growth process, from start to finish. And that's why water subsidies are coveted by rice farmers, who band together to lobby politicians as the USA Rice Federation. It's comprised of producers, millers, and merchants from across the country.

In Southeast Asia there is no need to lobby for water: The natural rainfall does the trick of watering rice crops. In Cali, it's a man-made phenomenon.

Mist rose from the fields on the day I visited the Koda rice farm. It made everything seem spooky. Or perhaps the dogs that surrounded me, baring their teeth, when I arrived added to my emotional stir. I stood still and then pretended to toss something to the other side of the car. The dogs got distracted. I jumped back in the driver's seat. They soon figured out my deceit and in unison the three of them stretched their necks and began to howl.

I sat there and looked at the six massive storage silos that look like spaceships, the little campus of beige office buildings, and, sticking out of seemingly nowhere, 29 palm trees. Flat land splayed out to the horizon in every direction. Patches of brown and green. And there: Trees that no more belong on this land than the rice that is grown all around them does. Palm trees, like rice, aren't indigenous to this area.

The Koda family, which hails from Japanese samurais, has worked the farm—10,000 acres—since the 1920s. They admit that growing rice isn't cheap in America. "Most of the 'advancement' in the new strains has come in the form of higher yields and lower production costs, while taste and quality have been sacrificed," the company's Web site says. But when production costs rise, as they do when water subsidies are lowered, the whole local farming economy is threatened. Farmers howl.

In countries where the price of labor is low and rain plentiful, such as those parts of Asia I mentioned, rice production
makes more economic sense. Unfair labor practices are issues
to be discussed, but the reality is that wages are far lower in that
part of the world than they are here, in the world's richest
nation. It costs, for example, twice as much to grow and mill
rice here in the United States as it does in Vietnam. However—
and here is where it gets interesting—America exports as much
rice as Vietnam does.

Hmm. How can we compete? "Massive handouts to US
farmers to support uneconomic rice production" is how an article in London's *Times* summarized the conclusions of a report
by the charity Oxfam. The report found that US subsidies
effectively created their own type of export industry, putting
farmers in the Third World out of business.

According to Oxfam, American rice, sold at prices lower
than the cost to produce it, prevents local rice farmers in countries such as Haiti, Ghana, and Honduras from selling their
crops because they can't compete with the subsidized American exporters.

Oxfam used Riceland Foods, an Arkansas farmers' cooperative, to exemplify the tragedy of US rice price supports.
According to the report, the cooperative received almost half a
billion dollars in subsidies over eight years; at the same time it
saw its profit rise exponentially. Oxfam said the profit spike
was due mainly to increased exports to Cuba and Haiti. "Companies such as Riceland can compete because the US taxpayer
pays two thirds of the cost of production," the *Times* report said.

Oh yeah, by the way, the Koda farm I visited? It has
received millions of dollars in subsidies over the years. The

"extra effort and expense" they lament in growing their specialty rice was offset by approximately $4 million in subsidies between 1995 and 2004 alone, according to Environmental Working Group (EWG) data. In 2002, Koda received more than $1.1 million in federal crop subsidies and some $500,000 in water subsidies, EWG reported.

Phil Bloomer, at that time the head of Oxfam's campaign for fair trade, was quoted in the *Times* report as saying of rice subsidies, "This is an example of rigged rules and double standards at their baldest.... It is scandalous that poor countries are forced to compete with the US. Worse still, they are denied the opportunity to defend themselves from dumping."

It's bad enough that US subsidies force farmers in some of the poorest countries in the world out of business, but there is more. The United States also uses its clout with the World Bank and the International Monetary Fund (IMF) to influence what countries get loans and for how much. This is an abuse of power that doesn't get as much attention as it should.

In his book *Confessions of an Economic Hitman,* John Perkins, an economist who for years advised the World Bank, IMF, United Nations, and a number of developing countries (to those countries' detriment), explains how the United States uses its economic power in the Third World to push exploitative debt and financial instruments on poor nations, supposedly as tools for developing infrastructure. The same practices are used in agricultural policy.

"Many poor countries have been forced to lower tariff barriers that protected their rice farmers, as a result of pressure from the World Bank, the IMF and bilateral trade agreements with the US," the *Times* of London wrote in its report on

Oxfam's findings. "Haiti, the poorest country in the western hemisphere, where half of all children are malnourished, was encouraged by the IMF in 1995 to cut its rice import tariff from 35 per cent to 3 per cent."

Wow. Seriously? Talk about a sick abuse of power. It's like a professional fighter picking on a grade school kid.

The *Times* said the cut in Haiti's tariff dropped the price of imported rice so much that imports tripled—and 95 percent of that rice is coming from the United States. Meanwhile, the 50,000 rice farmers in Haiti saw their market share plummet. Now, three-quarters of the rice consumed in Haiti comes from US farms.

Monica Mills, the director of government relations at the nonprofit group Bread for the World, tells me that one of her biggest peeves with US subsidy policy is its treatment of and effect on Haitian farmers. "They just cannot compete," she says of them. "And that happens in a lot of markets."

Let's take a step back and take a look at Haiti's suitability for growing rice: It obviously has a cheap labor force. And its rainfall averages 54 inches per year. In California, average yearly rainfall amounts to 17 inches. Get what I am saying?

Dan Griswold, the director of the Cato Institute's Center for Trade Policy Studies, was more blunt than I am in explaining rice subsidies in a 2006 trade briefing paper.

> Americans pay for the rice program three times over—as taxpayers, as consumers, and as workers. Direct taxpayer subsidies to the rice sector have averaged $1 billion a year since 1998 and are projected to average $700 million a year through 2015. Tariffs on imported rice drive up prices for consumers,

> and the rice program imposes a drag on the U.S. economy
> generally through a misallocation of resources. . . . Globally,
> U.S. policy drives down prices for rice by 4 to 6 percent.

That's a global average Griswold is citing. When it comes to shoving US exporters' goods down developing countries' throats at lower prices than they cost to produce, the price effect can be many times that. This is what is meant by "dumping" goods on a nation's or the world market. It happens with a variety of products, from rice to steel to sugar.

Imported rice selling at lower prices than local producers can match perpetuates poverty and hardship for millions of rice farmers in developing countries, undermining our broader interests and our standing in the world, Griswold points out. He says this also leaves the US open to costly world trade challenges.

Dumping can result in the importing country imposing "countervailing duties" on the dumped goods, which are fines or penalties. (Technically, "countervailing duties" seek to help a country's own producers be competitive with foreign companies whose goods have been subsidized, while "antidumping duties" are applied to raise the prices of imported goods that have been dumped in a country. A product doesn't have to be subsidized to be dumped on a nation; excess supply can be dumped, too.)

The United States has been whacked with millions of dollars in fines for violating WTO dumping provisions, and the backlash ends up costing US consumers and taxpayers because we pay the fines levied by the nations that we dumped goods in with our tax dollars or have to pay more for foreign goods whose prices have been raised in retaliation.

Cumulatively, we have paid billions of dollars in fines and penalties because we are trying to protect the American farmer. Or should we substitute "American business interests" for "American farmer"?

A revamping of the WTO system is needed to create a fair international marketplace. And it's not such a pie-in-the-sky prospect.

Fixing what he judges to be a fundamentally sound and effective WTO would require just four things, according to a news release about a Council on Foreign Relations report by Robert Z. Lawrence, a Harvard University professor and a member of the President's Council of Economic Advisers from 1998 to 2000:

- Allow greater participation by multinational corporations and nongovernmental organizations that have a stake in the proceedings
- Open hearings before the dispute settlement panels to the public
- Allow countries to appeal decisions in which the panel has authorized the plaintiff to retaliate
- Increase the resources of the dispute settlement mechanism so as to accelerate decision-making

Food can be used as a weapon. And bad policy can be particularly devastating to the people who are most vulnerable to food issues: the impoverished. To ensure that those people's rights aren't abused, the establishment of an international commission on fair trade is of great and urgent importance. It should be put together, like, now.

US rice exports are a perfect example of why such a commission, or a WTO with some real teeth, is needed. I don't think you can choose a more striking example to illustrate this than the differences in quality of life between the United States and Haiti.

In Haiti today, people are increasingly resorting to eating biscuits made of mud rather than rice or other foods they could grow. Food prices have soared because of the natural disaster, crop damage, and other factors. So people eat discs made from dried yellow clay mixed with water, salt, and vegetable shortening. The biscuits are known to locals as *"terre,"* which means "earth." They have traditionally been eaten by pregnant Haitians and children as an antacid because the clay is a source of calcium. Now, however, they have become a staple diet.

The Food and Agriculture Organization of the United Nations has expressed concern over food prices in the Caribbean, and especially targets the rising cost of rice as cause for concern. Haiti is the poorest country in the Western hemisphere, with most of its people living on less than $2 a day.

Meanwhile, the Haitian market is flooded with US rice imports (called "Miami rice" because it's shipped from Miami). The decline of rice production in Haiti has put even more people out of work. It also means they are even more reliant on imported rice. Haiti's rural population is desperately poor, so poor that some have resorted to eating mud. Mud!

We in the United States are so immune to such a possibility that we often don't appreciate the abundance we have. For example, a quick stop at the market can stock our cabinets with enough food for us to live on for weeks on end. Our food choices are almost unlimited.

At the entranceway to a farmers' cooperative store in California, I grab a plastic basket to test this theory. The co-op is a store designed to give farmers a permanent place to sell their goods and consumers the opportunity to buy local agricultural products without having to track down when and where the next outdoor market is.

This market attracts a hippie mix of people and displays organic foods as well as alternative medicines. It's set up just like any other grocery store, but it's about the size of two food aisles at one of the big chains.

Unlike in Haiti, where the local food supply is sporadic, here there are literally tons of local foods and products, including rice from Koda Farms.

I step past the fresh flowers and hit the rice section. At the aisle's end is a display that showcases nine different varieties of rice, all from the same California farm. Its slogan is "from our family farm to your family table."

For $2.99 a pound I can get whole grain, brown, white, and combinations of black and mahogany rice. Quite a number of choices. No mud cakes anywhere. And this is just the rice section.

Fair trade can only truly exist in a world of free trade. The government subsidizing local farmers doesn't make trade among nations fair. Indeed, it creates the opposite: an unfair and unbalanced market. It isn't just in Haiti that the imbalance is felt. That is just one of the many developing countries that are impacted by our farm policies.

And rice isn't the only product in which free and fair trade is an issue. US cotton growers also ruin lives and livelihoods overseas because of the subsidies they receive.

CHAPTER TEN

COTTON

It is literally the price of a shirt off your back; that's how much each of us—every man, woman, and child in America—pays to the cotton industry every year through various subsidy programs. It amounts to $5 billion, or, on average, more than $15—about the price of a shirt—per capita in the United States. It's an awesome number, the same as the National Cancer Institute's budget for cancer research. And it's unnecessary, wasteful, and a leading reason, many say, that the United States is so hated around the world.

For all that money, here's what we get: A bigger tax bill and the pleasure of seeing American cotton growers receive up to 73 percent more for their cotton than they would on the world market.

Subsidies should result in cheaper prices for us Americans—but they don't. You see, we pay farmers export subsidies that make things cheaper overseas, not here in America.

This cheap trade doesn't help foreigners much either, as we've seen in the case of rice. We don't do it to be charitable. We do it to stomp out the competition.

Pesky cotton farmers in developing countries can grow on the cheap and charge less. Blah. Not while rich Uncle Sam is here to throw inexpensive cotton around like confetti to foreign buyers. Why buy local in Bangladesh when you can buy Made in the USA for a whole lot less?

Of course if you happen to be a cotton farmer in Bangladesh, the US government dumping cheap cotton in your market doesn't help business. In fact, the cheap-dumping practice likely pisses you off. Might even put you out of business. Might even make you so angry that crazy Osama who lives down the block might not sound so crazy after all when he tries to recruit you to join his little gang and fight back against the West.

This scenario isn't conjecture; the Cato Institute reports that US agricultural policies are having this effect in certain developing countries.

All this goes down right before our eyes, but few are paying attention. After all, how can we know? We don't live in Bangladesh. Many Americans can't even pinpoint Kansas on a map, never mind a foreign country. Generating enough sympathy for a Bangladeshi or any other Third World cotton farmer to make a difference ain't gonna happen in our lifetime.

The price for a bale of cotton is about $1,000. Without US subsidies, the world price would rise by about 10 percent, directly impacting the lives of millions of Third World farmers—for the better. Nixing cotton subsidies would also benefit small US farmers by leveling the playing field for all cotton growers.

According to the Environmental Working Group, the top 10 percent of cotton farms—all of them large commercial operations—receive the majority of all subsidies.

Cotton subsidies provide very little value relative to their costs. According to the *Iowa Ag Review,* which is published by Iowa State University's Center for Agricultural and Rural

Development, the cotton industry receives 13 percent of all subsidies and returns just a 2 percent share of value to America.

The National Cotton Council of America, the central organization for the cotton industry and the "unifying force in working with the government," apparently has convinced members of Congress that that trade-off is a good one.

Cotton subsidies are not only ridiculously unfair here at home, but also breach world trade rules. The United States was forced to pay a whopping $830 million to Brazil in 2010 because we subsidized our cotton so much that it altered world trade balances.

Add that to the US taxpayers' tab.

Moreover, we US taxpayers now must further compensate Brazil by subsidizing *its* cotton farmers. It isn't enough that we have been supporting our own cotton industry. We have also been supporting the *illegal* practices of our own cotton industry. And we got busted, bad, by the World Trade Organization (WTO).

The "cotton problem" began in 2002, when Brazil and four other countries big into cotton argued before the WTO that US cotton subsidies had caused world cotton prices to decline and reduced the five countries' export revenues.

The United States was allowed to support the domestic cotton industry with subsidies to the tune of $1.7 billion per year. Yet Brazil and the other four countries, Benin, Burkina Faso, Chad, and Mali, discovered that we had actually paid as much as $4 billion to our cotton farmers via subsidies. Whoops. That imbalance caused a huge shift in world prices. Considering that the worldwide value of cotton production at the time was about $30 billion a year, the price swing that subsidies provided added up.

When the WTO's decision was handed down, the *New York Times* wrote:

> Without the subsidies, Brazil estimated that United States
> cotton production would have fallen 29 percent and that
> American cotton exports would have dropped 41 percent. That
> would have led to a rise in international cotton prices of
> 12.6 percent, which would have helped Brazil's cotton farmers.

The millions of dollars the United States agreed to pay will go into the Brazilian Cotton Farmers Fund, managed by the Brazilian government.

We in America also vigorously guard the cotton inside our borders by applying quotas and tariffs on imports as we export the stuff like mad all around the world.

The United States is the third-largest cotton producer in the world. China produces the most and India is second. Together, the top five, which also includes Brazil and Pakistan, account for almost 80 percent of world production.

But production is not consumption. We consume far less cotton than we produce. (We consume only about 4 percent of the world's supply.) Yet, we are by far the world's largest *exporter* of cotton. We export about three times as much cotton as any other country in the world. And we allow as little as possible into our country (free trade agreements be damned). Our high import tariffs—imposed when a quota limit is reached—are meant to keep Made in the USA on our shelves and in our closets.

Which, I must say, is odd—though not from a policy point of view. I get that. From a practical, man-on-the-street point of view. When was the last time you saw Made in the USA on store shelves?

I'm in a Macy's department store. On the shelves are shirts, ties, pants, underwear, and T-shirts from different designers in different patterns and colors and textures and sizes and shapes—all the variations and options that fashion gives consumers so we will buy, buy, buy.

There is one option missing, however. There is not one— not one!—thing I can find that has "Made in the USA" on the label. Therefore, there is not one item that I can point to and say, "Oh, yes, my tax dollars went to offset the price of this garment, and that is why it's cheaper than the rest." Nope, not here, not anywhere that I can see amongst the piles or on the racks.

The scent of men's cologne changes subtly as I go from section to section—from musky to fruity to downright pungent, the odors pervade.

There is a Ralph Lauren dress shirt for $39.99, made in China; a Calvin Klein one for $52.50, made in Indonesia; a Tasso Elba for $34.99, made in Nicaragua. A Van Heusen for $40, made in Honduras, and a Tommy Hilfiger for $59.50, made in Thailand.

It's like the United Nations here, but the United States isn't represented. Bangladesh, Egypt, Malaysia, Vietnam, El Salvador, and the Philippines are, though. Socks, shirts, underwear. DKNY, Alara, Hugo Boss, and Kenneth Cole. Designers from here, cotton from there—labels everywhere, it seems, but from America, where we spend billions to support our cotton farmers so that they can compete on the world market, have a leg up, and dominate the cotton industry. In other countries, perhaps we are the cotton victor, but not here. Here, on its home turf, the USA cotton industry isn't even represented.

I am not the first to notice this. After his own trip to a department store, Mike Barnett, the publications director for the Texas Farm Bureau, wrote on his blog,

> One bale, approximately 480 pounds, is enough cotton to make 765 business casual shirts, 4,321 socks and 1,217 T-shirts. Those items would sell as follows:

> • 765 business casual shirts at $90 a pop would sell for $68,850. At half price they would sell for $34,425 and at 30 percent off half price would sell at $24,097.50. One shirt contains a little more than a half pound of cotton. The farmer gets about 68 cents per pound for higher quality cotton. No matter what the price—$90, $45, or $31.50, the farmer received about 41 cents per shirt.

> • Those 4,321 socks translate into 2,160 pair with one left over. Retail at six pair for $18 comes out to $6,480. The farmer received about 91 cents for the six pair or a little over 15 cents a pair.

> • And the Nike T-shirts? 1,217 T-shirts would retail at $34,076 for full price; $17,038 half price. The cotton farmer gets about 17 cents per shirt no matter what the price.

So here's where we're at. While our domestic textile mills and manufacturers have almost completely disappeared, foreign workers are making $90 shirts, $18 socks and $25 T-shirts out of bargain-priced cotton and shipping them to the United States. No Made in USA labels here. Meanwhile, our economy is in the pits, unemployment is over 10 percent and farmers struggle to make ends meet.

The price of shirts needs to come down. The price of cotton needs to go up.

There is, I've learned while writing and researching this book, a large disconnect between the various factions in the supply chain. And this is important to recognize. Lots of farmers, or growers as they are sometimes called, get screwed the most in the business scheme of cotton (you could insert any commodity here; in fact, let's insert the word "life"). They have become suppliers to the owner of the supply chain, who outfits them with equipment, chemicals, seeds, storage, distribution, and everything and anything else they need to keep them alive—just barely.

Cotton farmers end up selling a product that likely gets shipped overseas to be manufactured and then shipped right back to the mall down the street in the form of a blouse or a button-down shirt.

It's the corporate product line mentality and philosophy that are destroying things for all of us, small farmers included; it's plain but not so simple Corporate American greed.

In other chapters, I've written about the health effects of food: how large, subsidized agricultural farms have turned into multinational corporations that control the food supply chain. To keep food cheap, they skimp on the foods' healthfulness.

This brings the effect of Corporate America's monopoly home far more vividly than the extra dime we spend at the checkout counter. Health effects get people to sit up and take notice—fast.

"I'm not eating that; it can kill me" is a stronger statement than "I'm not gonna wear that, it costs an extra dime."

But get this: We actually eat more cotton than we wear or sleep on.

According to the Organic Consumers Association:

> About 80% of all the cottonseed and almost all the gin trash go
> right into our milk. The other 20% of the cottonseed is made
> into oil, meal and cake and winds up in many different junk
> foods. An average of eight pounds of cottonseed is fed out to
> most dairy cows in the US every day. Large amounts of gin trash
> are fed out or used for bedding for dairy cows and beef cows.

Who knew? And while it's stunning to imagine that "gin trash"—the stem and other plant parts that remain after a cotton gin separates them from the cotton—could be anything other than healthy feed for us or cows, one also has to realize that most cotton being grown in the United States is genetically modified—"most" as in about 75 percent or so.

The type of genetically modified cotton that is used in about one-third of all cotton crops is called *Bacillus thuringiensis,* or "Bt" for short. It has had genes from a common soil bacterium that kills insects inserted into the cotton DNA, so the plant produces the insecticidal substance as it grows—killing the bugs. But it is also suspected as being the cause of deaths in animals and other crops. It can wreck the soil. Now put that in your food and eat it (or drink it).

We also export vast amounts of Bt cottonseeds.

In India, some policy analysts have linked Bt cotton (and its failures) to farmer suicides. The seeds haven't performed as hoped in many Indian farm districts. Some farmers in these areas who planted Bt cotton subsequently went into debt because of their poor yields. When the crop dies, so does hope—and some committed suicide.

Genetically modified cotton, while developed to ward off pests, itself uses a lot of pesticides and fertilizer to grow. The

Organic Consumers Association reports that the California Environmental Protection Agency found that pesticides used on cotton in that state were known to be some of the most toxic chemicals in the world. Seven were probable cancer-causing pesticides, eight caused tumors, and five caused mutations, Cal EPA and the US EPA reportedly found. Many were toxic or very toxic to fish or birds or both, according to the analysis. How 'bout to us?

Some studies conclude that GMO cotton, specifically Bt cotton, can cause allergies and other immune system reactions in people. Yet, the USDA applauds Bt's use— "Biotechnology can help farmers reduce their reliance on insecticides and herbicides. For example, Bt cotton, a widely grown biotech crop, kills several important cotton pests"— and a couple of widely cited studies say that Bt-modified crops appear to be safe to eat. After all, one study says, the formula has been in use for more than 50 years with "few if any negative effects."

You can certainly take the chance and eat GM foods that contain Bt. It's your bed. Sleep on it. Or eat it in the trace amounts that find their way from cow feed into milk.

Yet I'd be cautious about buying the spin coming from the USDA. After all, Monsanto and the USDA share the same public relations agency. Yep. True.

At the end of the day, the whole GM and Bt madness boils down to subsidies and our agricultural policies that coax the cotton factory farmers to produce as much as possible on as little as possible. So much so that we now even eat it.

Subsidies create our inverse relationship with a healthy food supply: We support the bad stuff at the expense of the good. In the next chapter, we see how that has come about and why.

CHAPTER ELEVEN

FRUITS AND VEGETABLES

It would be one thing if government subsidies went to food products that are good for us—healthier foods. But the vast majority—and by that I mean 99 percent or so—of subsidies go toward food products that are more caloric.

Fruits and vegetables, which are universally healthier foods because they contain more nutrients and fewer calories, and therefore have more positive nutritional value for our diets, get the least government support—for human consumption, that is.

Corn is the most subsidized vegetable, reaping more than $5 billion a year in government subsidies. But corn is mostly used for animal feed and ethanol production. The corn we actually eat makes up just 1 percent of all the corn that is grown.

If we also exclude the kernels that get made into high fructose corn syrup and the like or become "lab rats" for scientific altering, the subsidy for corn in our diet is less than $50 million a year.

After corn, the most subsidized vegetable is soy. While it is increasingly used for derivative products such as soy milk, tofu turkey, and the like, most soy is used for feed and ethanol. Total subsidy for soy: $1.7 billion.

In terms of healthy foods, the pickings are slim. Peanuts and apples make the list of healthy foods receiving subsidies over the past decade. Apples got about a quarter of a billion dollars in federal assistance from 2001 to 2004, under a specific loss-assistance program, but have gotten none since, according to Environmental Working Group data. And peanuts? Well, peanuts have received between $100 million and more than a billion dollars per year under federal assistance programs over the past decade. We Americans eat a lot of peanuts. We make it into butter, oil, flour. It's even used to make dynamite. (Weird, I know, and fascinating.)

But if you stick with the fruits and vegetables we eat, all of them tallied together add up to 2.5 percent of farm subsidies. Compared with the rest of the food chain, the amount spent on fruits and vegetables looks a lot like a child's dinner plate: mostly meat, some starch, and a scant amount of vegetables.

When we opt to purchase nutritious foods, we pay more for them; subsidies aren't there to help.

The *Journal of Nutrition* finds that Americans are consuming more refined carbohydrates, more added sugars, and more added fats. Our total daily energy intake has increased by 300 calories per person since 1985. The average daily calorie intake for an American man is close to 3,000 calories, while for a woman it's about 2,000 calories, according to the Centers for Disease Control. A 300-calorie bump, therefore, is roughly a 10 percent gain. That can be the difference between being healthy and becoming fat.

Added fats account for 24 percent of that increase, and added sugars for another 23 percent. In all, added sugars and added fats account for almost half of the increase of our daily calories.

The Journal of Nutrition reports, "In contrast, the consumption of more expensive fruit increased by only 0.3 servings since the 1970s. In 2000 the food supply provided a daily average of 1.4 servings of fruit and fruit juices per person per day and 3.8 servings of fresh and processed vegetables. Not surprisingly, the lowest-cost items continue to be consumed the most. . . . The consumption of more nutrient-rich (but also more costly) leafy green vegetables was only 0.17 servings per day, whereas deep yellow vegetables added another 0.2 servings."

The comparison between healthy choices and unhealthy ones is startling. As you can see, there has been almost no increase in the amount of healthy foods we eat over the past several decades, while the amount of cheap, subsidized junk food we eat has skyrocketed.

Put another way, over the past 25 years the average calorie content of the food we buy has increased by 25 percent, and practically none of that comes from healthier foods such as fruits and veggies.

To be sure, fruits and vegetables get money on the state level and are subsidized indirectly through water, insurance, and land conservation programs.

Take alfalfa, for example. More than 10 percent of its price is subsidized via water subsidy programs. Alfalfa being a water-thirsty crop, when you subsidize that water, you are effectively subsidizing the crop.

You could insert any number of fruits or vegetables here for alfalfa—tomatoes, carrots, broccoli, etc. The point is that, directly or indirectly, all the food that we consume is subsidized. It's by how much and for what purpose that matters.

The higher up the food chain you go, the more subsidies. Indirect subsidies are a bigger factor the closer you get to the top of the food chain. Looking again at subsidized water, it takes just 10 gallons to grow a pound of lettuce. A pound of beef takes 1,500 gallons. Add to that feed subsidies (which meat needs and vegetables obviously don't), land subsidies (because livestock take more space than plants), and import tariffs (which we impose on meats more than veggies) and you don't have to be Einstein to calculate how much more one food group gets subsidized than the other.

It would be one thing if the food group being subsidized most—meats—were good for the American public. But it isn't. Nor are the ugly stepchildren of the subsidized meat industry: fast foods, and their brothers and sisters, junk foods.

This is where Big Government and Big Ag act like drug dealers, lowering prices and making cheap alternatives to stuff that is already really bad for you. From cocaine to crack, in the drug world the price comes down to suit the market. Ditto with our food supply: from a steak to a burger to a dollar meal.

I use a drug dealer example because this is how low you have to go to really get at the heart of the matter with our food supply.

At the lowest rung of the economic ladder, the price of food shifting a nickel, a dime, a quarter, or 50 cents matters—a lot. Elitist America, of which I am admittedly a part, doesn't get to see this world. A quarter here or there is of no concern for us. For 43 million Americans, it is. That's how many poor people in this country rely on food stamps.

We write them off and give them very few choices in life, even about what they eat. Start in the slums and work your way up through society. At every stage, people care about what they eat.

Caring about what you eat and being able to afford it are two different things, however. A UCLA study found that a typical grocery bill consumes three times as much of a low-income family's income than a middle-income family's income.

Money matters. Then there is education.

Researchers have found that the poorest and least educated communities tend to have the greatest percentages of obese people. That correlation is especially strong in Mississippi, Alabama, and South Carolina, an analysis by Media General, a communications company in the Southeast, found. It noted that "flashy ads send powerful messages to eat fast food instead of healthy food. Unhealthy food often tastes better and satisfies hunger faster than nutrient-rich fruits and vegetables. Low-income neighborhoods face additional challenges. They tend to have more fast-food restaurants and fewer places to buy fresh fruits and vegetables. Many poor people lack transportation or time to get to well-stocked stores in wealthier neighborhoods. And, eating healthy costs more than eating unhealthy food."

Adam Drewnowski, director of the nutritional sciences program at the University of Washington, found through studies that foods made from subsidized crops—like cookies and soda—cost five times less per calorie than unsubsidized foods like carrots and orange juice.

Hence, increasing subsidies for fruits and vegetables isn't the answer. We'd end up in a big, fat race to see who wins more of our tax dollars. Instead, a "fat tax" combined with education may be the solution to increasing the consumption of more nutrient-rich foods such as fruits and vegetables and seeing America become healthier.

Here's why:

Psychology professor Leonard Epstein and a group of researchers at the University of Buffalo put together a study on shopping habits and nutrition. They studied a group of mothers who shopped at a simulated grocery store, in which food items were priced the same as at a real grocery store nearby. The study, published in the journal *Psychological Science* and cited by other academic publications, had the volunteer mothers shop with plain old prices. Then the researchers changed the game: They imposed taxes on unhealthy foods, raising the prices as much as 25 percent, and imposed subsidies discounting the prices of healthy foods.

Then they sat back and watched. Taxes, they found, were more effective in reducing calories purchased than were subsidies. "Specifically, taxing unhealthy foods reduced overall calories purchased, while cutting the proportion of fat and carbohydrates and upping the proportion of protein in a typical week's groceries," as *Science Daily* summarized the results. "By contrast, subsidizing the prices of healthy food actually increased overall calories purchased without changing the nutritional value at all. It appears that mothers took the money they saved on subsidized fruits and vegetables and treated the family to less healthy alternatives, such as chips and soda pop. Taxes had basically the opposite effect, shifting spending from less healthy to healthier choices."

The solution to eating healthier, therefore, isn't to begin subsidizing healthy foods more. People will still eat junk. The solution is to reduce and/or eliminate subsidies altogether in order to create a more level playing field—and then if we really want to make an impact on Americans' health: tax the unhealthy stuff more.

We tax cigarettes more. We tax alcohol more. We can levy more taxes on junk food if need be. And how's this for a no-brainer: Have the additional taxes pay for nutritional education in the inner cities and poor areas where it's needed most.

In Harlem, an area of New York City not exactly known for its farmers' markets or green grocers, I walk into a grocery store to check out the type of food it sells. I don't walk directly into the fruits-and-vegetable section, as a shopper would in, say, a Whole Foods out in the 'burbs. Here, the bakery section is first: doughnuts, packages of cakes and cookies. It's followed by the sale section, then the fruit-and-veggie stand— which isn't bad, actually. There are stacks of apples, bananas, and berries. The prices aren't too far off from other grocery stores, either: California oranges for $3.99 a bag, rutabagas for 69 cents, tomatoes for $1.99 a pound. What gets me, though, is when I turn the corner from the produce area to the rest of the store: There are 25 massive aisles of processed and packaged foods. The fruit-and-vegetable section is 20 by 13 feet—about half the size of one of these aisles.

This layout shocks me, even though it should be no surprise. More surprising are the food deserts I learned about in the course of research. "Food deserts" are increasingly common in urban areas. A food desert is a district with little or no access to foods needed to maintain a healthy diet but often served by plenty of fast-food restaurants. Reports show that in some urban areas, grocery stores have withdrawn entirely or relocated to the suburbs. This means that the low-income earners and senior citizens who remain find healthy foods either unavailable or inaccessible as a result of high prices and/or unreachable locations. Indeed, when news organizations descended upon

Louisiana to cover the BP oil spill, correspondents were surprised to learn that they had to drive 50 miles to reach the
nearest grocery store.

In Chicago, the food-desert situation has become so bad
that drugstores have stepped in to offer fresh food to urban
residents. The Walgreens chain expanded its typical drugstore
offerings to include fresh, healthy food options featuring fruits
and vegetables to round out the usual array of potato chips and
cookies. The expansion not only fills a gaping void in many
neighborhoods, according to the blog *JustMeans,* but also seems
to be a solid business move; the fresh food is selling well. Guess
what, food producers? People in urban areas like to eat healthy,
too. So much so that Duane Reade, another drugstore chain,
opened a giant fruit-and-vegetable section in Manhattan.

Food distribution must change, and along with it more
choices for healthier foods should be made available to lower
income neighborhoods.

Clearly there is a market for healthy foods in urban areas
and inner-city neighborhoods. If the people at the drugstore
who sell me my toothbrush and toilet paper can figure it out,
then the big food chains should be able to as well.

What say you, big grocery chains: Kroger? Casey's? Rud-
dick? The Pantry? Safeway? Supervalu? Fresh Market? Whole
Foods? Weis Markets?

In the next chapter, I will take us from the inner city out to
sea, where fish subsidies swim with abundance.

CHAPTER TWELVE

FISH

I asked Dr. Marah Hardt, an environmental scientist and marine life expert who lives on the most remote islands in the world, the Hawaiian Islands, about subsidies. Way out there, far, far away from mainland USA, do subsidies make their way? Or are fish safe from the long arm of the government? Have fish escaped the harm, politics, and protectionism to which other foods have succumbed?

When I posed this question to Marah over the telephone, she told me that she hadn't really thought about fish in that context. She had investigated fish scarcity, ocean pollution, and a whole raft of other issues related to sustaining seafood, but somehow subsidies hadn't risen to the surface in her years of research.

She said she'd look into the issue, including the seafood industry's lobbying group, the National Fisheries Institute, and get back to me.

A few things about Marah: She is an extreme scuba diver and has led scientific dives from Florida to the Caribbean to the Pacific Ocean. She was a top researcher at Carl Safina's Blue Ocean Institute and generally lives for all things blue. Moreover, she is a dogged investigator searching literally to the bottom of the ocean to find out about things.

A few weeks later, she and I spoke again. This time Marah had something to say. A lot to say, actually.

"As I began to investigate the role of subsidies in seafood, I found that our penchant for propping up food systems on land has seeped into the sea, where it now fuels a feeding frenzy poised to wipe out the last wild food on the planet," she said. It got my attention. And it should get yours.

Marah found that global fisheries subsidies currently total nearly $30 billion and account for 20 to 25 percent of the total value of all wild seafood. These numbers, she said, are mirrored here in the United States.

A report last year by the Environmental Working Group (EWG) bore this out. It determined that between 1996 and 2004, US subsidies amounted to 21 percent of the total commercial harvest. US taxpayers foot the bill for an average $713 million in direct fisheries-related subsidies each year. Add in indirect subsidies and the number jumps to $1.82 billion.

Holy mackerel, that's a lot of clams. And all this money apparently does more harm than good.

Marah said she discovered that more than half of the money ($400 million per year in the United States) is spent on "harmful" subsidies—those that go toward helping fishermen increase their capacity to catch more fish, when the focus should be on rebuilding endangered and threatened fish populations (globally, about 60 percent of all subsidies go to increasing fishing capacity).

In other words, as fisheries economists put it: The global community is paying the fishing industry billions each year to continue fishing even when it would not be profitable otherwise—effectively funding the overexploitation of marine resources.

"Subsidies make it possible to constantly add new species (often lower on the food chain and from deeper depths) as we run out of old favorites," Marah said. "This serial depletion of global fish supplies has been coined 'fishing down the food web,' and it is in large part due to subsidies for research and technology that enable fishermen to catch fish from more remote, hard-to-reach environments. Subsidies for marketing campaigns also 'help' (there are several kinds of these, and they amount to about 1 percent of all fisheries subsidies). For example, a fish known as slimehead was remade via a marketing campaign into the much more appealingly named orange roughy. The campaign worked; it's now endangered, thanks in part to these subsidies."

With such powerful tools, it's no wonder the seafood industry lures us into eating more and more seafood every year—five times as much globally today as we did a century ago.

And just what types of fish are we munching?

According to the NOAA's National Marine Fisheries Service (NMFS), there's nothing tiny about our appetite for shrimp: Last year we downed a whopping 1.2 billion pounds of those little pink guys. That's about four pounds per person. We each tossed back another 2.5 pounds of canned tuna. All told, we eat about 16 pounds of seafood per capita a year. We don't indulge in the bounty of the blue as much as Japan or the Scandinavians (who eat at least 30 to 40 pounds per person per year), but there are a lot more of us than them (about twice as many as those countries combined). That adds up to a lot of shrimp cocktails and tuna fish sandwiches when you multiply it out.

In the scheme of things, seafood is a comparatively healthier protein source than, say, factory-farmed beef. But it has its own set of risks, including mercury contamination and toxic shellfish poisoning. Nevertheless, the message that fish is good for you has stuck since the fishing industry launched a big marketing effort in the 1980s, and we've been eating more of it ever since. (Also contributing to our bigger fish diets is the rise of those 45,000-square-foot supermarkets, which have made room for individual seafood counters and expanded freezer aisles, increasing demand for more kinds and quantities of fish and shellfish to adorn their glistening cases.) The United States as a nation is third in global seafood consumption, behind only China and Japan.

There are lots of fish to choose from in the United States. We catch boatloads off our coasts, and when that supply isn't good enough, or delectable enough for some palates, we import more.

I gaze at all the seafood I have available to me at my fish market. There are sea scallops, Mexican shrimp, oysters, Clare Island salmon, barramundi, salmon patties, salmon steaks, arctic char, South African lobster, ahi tuna, cobia, hiramasa, catfish, king salmon, Pacific red snapper, blue tilapia, albacore tuna, Chilean sea bass, yellowfin tuna, Alaskan halibut, opah, mahimahi, striped bass, New Zealand snapper, rainbow trout, John Dory, skatewings, swordfish, monkfish, wahoo, dungeness crab, Canadian Bay shrimp, and other variations. Right: a boatload of fish.

Marah tells me this is all an illusion. Quoting Dr. Daniel Pauly, a fisheries researcher at the University of British Columbia, she says that despite the appearance of abundant fish supplies, global fish catch has declined by about 700,000 tons since the late 1980s. In fact, 90 percent of all the big fish on earth have vanished over the past 50 years because of factory fishing, climate change, and pollution, among other things. We've caught or killed off entire species. But don't feel a fool for thinking otherwise—for thinking, as I did, that because the seafood market is brimming with fish and the grocery store freezer case is full of everything from fish sticks to fresh cod that seafood is ample.

Fisheries scientists who are supposed to track these things were also duped into believing the global fish catch was rising. Turns out that China's fisheries agents were getting rewards for catching their quota. So for each report, they wrote down that quotas were made—even if the fish never hit the docks. Then some researchers started looking a bit more closely at China's numbers and discovered that they were completely bogus.

Because Chinese fishermen catch so many fish (we Americans import most of our fish from there), China's inflated numbers made it look as if the oceans were providing more and more every year. The UN's Food and Agricultural Organization (FAO) now reports global fish catch with and without China's numbers. We now know that in reality, fishermen have been fishing harder and catching less—for decades.

But how is it that fishermen can afford to keep doing this? You guessed it: You and I pay them to.

As explained by Reneé Sharp, a senior scientist at the EWG, "With help from the US taxpayers, fishing operations have bought many more boats, fuel, and equipment than the oceans may be able to handle . . . like other government supports, harmful fishing subsidies have contributed to the destruction of the already fragile ecosystem off our shores."

Marah explained to me that subsidies lead to what's called "overcapacity"—meaning the fishing fleet has the capability of catching more fish than is allowed or is biologically sustainable (leaving enough fish to reproduce and replace what's been taken out).

Globally, almost three-quarters of fish stocks are currently fully exploited or overexploited. According to the World Wildlife Fund, there are about 2.5 times as many boats employed in fishing as would allow for a sustainable catch worldwide. The FAO estimates it is slightly less than this, at about 30 percent overcapacity, and states, "Overcapacity is a significant, if not the primary, reason for overfishing in domestic and global fisheries. . . . World fishing capacity would need to be reduced by 25 percent for revenues to cover operating costs and by 53 percent for revenues to cover total costs." Not only are there more boats than the ocean can support; there are also more boats than the market can support.

In the United States, things are not much better. Back in 1999, a report by the US Federal Fisheries Investment Task Force (FFTF) argued that government subsidies contribute to overcapacity, which drives declines in many marine fisheries. But subsidies have continued, and today, one-third of stocks are overfished or experiencing overfishing.

Cod is probably the most famous example of a major fishery that collapsed due to overfishing, but stocks of Atlantic halibut, ocean perch, haddock, and yellowtail flounder, which once fed millions of Americans, have been depleted as well.

"At the end of the day, all these subsidies supporting all this overfishing means that our kids and grandkids will likely be looking at an entirely different kind of seafood buffet, one that may ooze with gelatinous globs of jellyfish instead of shrimp, cod, or crab cakes," Marah conjectured.

But overfishing costs us more than just future menu options. A 2008 FAO-World Bank study entitled *The Sunken Billions* estimates that overexploitation costs the world $50 billion each year in lost revenue—you can't cash in on fish that are no longer there to catch. Over the course of the past three decades, when declines have been most severe, the price tag of this mismanagement (including the egregious use of subsidies) has been $2 trillion— about the GDP of Italy. And that is a conservative estimate.

Perhaps even more significant is the loss of a valuable source of protein for millions of people. Another study estimates that *without* overfishing, about 20 million people worldwide might have averted undernourishment in 2000.

Just as subsidies to big agribusiness squeeze out the small farmer, the majority of marine fishery subsidies benefit large-scale fishers. This occurs despite the fact that small-scale fishers—generally defined as having boats smaller than 50 feet in length or no boats at all and less energy-intensive fishing gear—employ 25 times more people, have far less bycatch (accidentally caught species that are thrown overboard, dead), and use one-quarter as much fuel to catch almost the same amount of edible fish (about 30 million tons) as the large-scale industrial sector does.

The favoritism is especially evident in Africa, where governments desperate for cash repeatedly sell off the rights to fish in their nearshore waters to European nations and other developed countries. These fleets then strip local waters of fish and carry away the catch to feed the rich or, more often, feed the fish farms that feed the rich. Through subsidies, developed countries are effectively exporting the overfishing problem to other vulnerable shores. Local fishermen are left with no fish and few alternatives for feeding their families. Many try to emigrate abroad, thinking things will be better there. Others look to a more, shall we say, historically profitable enterprise: piracy.

Rolf Willmann, a senior fishery planning officer with the FAO, sums it up this way: "Right now, no one is winning. The real income levels of fishers are depressed, much of the industry is unprofitable, fish stocks are depleted and other sectors of the economy foot the bill for an ailing fishing industry."

Too many boats chasing too few fish means stiffer competition and lower prices for fishermen, and a dismal outlook for the future of fish.

The wrongful application of subsidies to fund bigger fishing fleets has gotten so bad over the past few decades that the normally very conservative World Trade Organization has been leading negotiations to ban subsidies that enhance fishing capacity under the Agreement on Subsidies and Countervailing Measures. The fact that these negotiations have gone on for years is evidence of how difficult it is to get governments to stop paying fishermen to catch the last fish.

The first paper to actually conduct a detailed analysis of direct marine capture fisheries subsidies in the United States came out in 2010, and documented a dizzying maze of programs and policies that funnel funds from the public to fishermen. Subsidies can be found buried in state and federal tax codes or even lurking beneath school lunch programs.

But before we dive into those, let's first be clear about what we are talking about. In everyday parlance, a direct subsidy is any amount of money that is *given to* or *kept by* fishermen for doing what they do.

Thus, deferring income tax payments (so that money is *kept* by fishermen) is as much of a subsidy as government payouts at above-market prices for fish.

Here in the US, we dole out subsidies in both categories. The majority are federal and state fuel subsidies, which account for 44 percent of the total (about $2.8 billion between 1996 and 2004). These subsidies are in the form of tax breaks to fishers, who do not have to pay federal or state taxes placed on gasoline and diesel. These taxes go toward supporting road construction and maintenance and *should* be applied to fishers to pay for port construction and maintenance and other shore-based facilities fishers use. But the fishers aren't taxed. And we foot the bill for those projects in other ways, providing a massive subsidy to fishers.

At the federal level, we also provide about $285 million a year in fisheries research—and this doesn't include money for recreational, monitoring, or aquaculture activity. Other federal-level subsidies include disaster aid (4 percent of all subsidies), surplus fish purchases (2 percent of the total), and fishery access payments—where the government pays other countries to let us fish in their waters for the bargain price of about $20 million a year.

Then there are subsidies that basically make it really cheap and easy for fishers to overcome the diminished odds of catching fewer fish by building bigger, more high-tech boats. The Capital Construction Fund allows fishers to defer taxable income from fishing activities if the money is put into a special account that later is used for boat construction, reconstruction, or purchase. It's essentially an interest-free loan from the government that promotes growth of the fleet. Between 1996 and 2004 it deflected $65 million from the government coffers to the pockets of fishers.

A slightly different but similar subsidy is the Fisheries Finance Program, which lends money to fishers for construction and reconstruction of fishing boats and shoreside facilities or to buy fishing permits. Fishers get lower short-term costs with these government loans than they would with private lenders, even though most fishermen in the program would qualify for private loans.

There are state subsidies. At least 19 states have sales tax breaks on their books for everything from purchasing fishing vessels to gear to maintenance, totaling 5 percent of all subsidies.

And there are quasi-subsidies that come from entities such as the Fishermen's Contingency Fund, which is paid for by a tax on oil and gas companies to compensate fishers for lost resources due to oil and gas activities off the coast. (If you are thinking BP, your thinking is right. Hence you might recall President Obama's full-court press to get the oil giant, not the US taxpayer, to pay for the costs of the Gulf disaster's cleanup.)

Even those subsidies that are meant to decrease fishing fleet size often wind up doing the opposite. Vessel buyback programs provide a combination of public and private financing to buy back vessels, permits, or both from fishers. However, the money fishers get from selling their boats and permits is often used to upgrade and buy newer, more "efficient" vessels, which can catch *more* fish, rather than less.

In addition to subsidies working against the long-term sustainability of wild fish populations, they also are ridiculously skewed in their distribution, favoring some species and regions over others. Salmon and tuna receive more than half of all subsidies, and groundfish (halibut, flounder, rockfish, cod, etc.) receive another 25 percent. For salmon, most of the subsidies are for disaster aid and surplus fish purchases. For tuna (some types of which are at times very endangered), we're dishing out $400,000 per boat per year in foreign access payments to allow 45 vessels to fish for tuna off the coasts of several South Pacific island states. These payments in particular are why the US Western Pacific Region receives the highest subsidies payments out of all regions in the United States, despite having the lowest catch volume and landed value (price of fish at the docks).

And that's the thing about subsidies: Looks can be deceiving. The money often doesn't align with greater volume or value of catch, and small subsidies can sometimes be more damaging than large ones.

In fact, subsidies often conflict with established policies that mandate that we stop overfishing. To do that, we must reduce the number of boats on the water—we have more than twice as many as needed.

Give a man a fish, he'll eat for a day. Give a man a subsidy and he'll fish for a lifetime—even if there's nothing left to catch.

And that is exactly what will happen if all these subsidies remain in place. Removing harmful subsidies, on the other hand, could help curb pressure on dwindling stocks and allow fish to recover. Fish populations have proven quite resilient in the past, with species such as striped bass and Atlantic swordfish proving that if you cut them some slack, the fish can come back. It would also help free up funds for more beneficial subsidies, such as those that help fishermen switch to more sustainable gear types.

"We might not be able to get canned tuna from the South Pacific for less than a buck without subsidies, but at least the prices we'd pay would help ensure that our kids don't get stuck with only jellyfish burgers on their menus," Marah concluded.

To turn your stomach even more, in the next chapter we examine energy subsidies.

CHAPTER THIRTEEN

OIL AND GAS

"I used to work real close, so the price of gas didn't matter. Now, because of the economy, I have to drive an hour to work," the woman at the gas pump tells me. "We were fine then. Now things just keep going up."

She's middle-aged, spectacled. A secretary. Both she and her husband work to pay the bills. Her car is an old white Toyota Corolla.

She is just one of many people who stop and fill up. America is here. No matter what station. No matter what status. A person needs fuel to drive. And most people in America drive. A cross section of the country is here: Bentleys, Beetles, what have you.

There are three gas stations. One on each corner, just off the freeway in California: Arco. Shell. BP. On the fourth corner is an office building. The managers of each station tell the same story: Not as many people fill up. Only 10 percent pay cash. There are more credit card transactions. Since the economy fell, people struggle to pay their cars' fuel bills. As the woman at the pump puts it, "What are we going to do? We have no choice."

ExxonMobil makes about $45 billion per year. Chevron makes about half that, and BP makes a third as much. Those are profits. The entire oil and gas sector makes some $2 trillion in annual revenue.

And we still subsidize it with our tax dollars.

Americans support, with $36.5 billion in subsidies, companies such as BP, responsible for the largest oil spill in history in the Gulf of Mexico, and Exxon, which, with the *Valdez* in 1989, put the oil-spill business into the big leagues. I am going to write that again: $36.5 billion in tax dollars and tax breaks. It's a federal budget item for ten years. Annually, that works out to $3.65 billion, or more than $10 for every American citizen. Considering that about 50 percent of the population pays taxes, it's closer to $25 per taxpayer that the oil and gas industry *directly* charges us in the form of subsidies. Note the italics: The oil and gas industry, as you'll see below, also receives indirect subsidies such as tax breaks that add up to billions more.

Worldwide, fossil fuel subsidies plus tax breaks and other government financial support amount to a half trillion dollars. These are annual figures. That's 25 percent of the entire industry's total revenue. That's *huge!*

What do we get at the pump for all that support? Where I live in California, as of this writing, it's more than $3 per gallon for gasoline. At the Arco station, regular unleaded is $3.29 per gallon, unleaded plus is $3.39, and premium is $3.49. At the 76 and Shell stations across the road from where I stand, the prices are more than Arco's: $3.31 for regular, $3.41 for plus, and $3.51 for premium. The cheapest state in which to buy gas—again, as of this writing—is Texas—at $2.56 per gallon.

Considering that the average American drives 12,000 miles per year and gets about 20 miles per gallon, the annual fuel cost to drive a car is $1,800. The annual subsidized portion of that cost, then, is $225.

Here's how that works out: The Energy Information Administration, which is part of the federal government, put together a list comparing all energy subsidies by type. Natural gas and petroleum liquids such as gasoline came out the lowest per energy unit besides geothermal power. The study examined energy subsidies not related to electricity production. It showed that we support the oil and gas industry to the tune of three cents per million British thermal units (BTUs). Convert that to a gallon of gasoline and the subsidies amount to 37.5 cents per gallon of gas, or $225 per year based on the average American's driving habits.

Now, I am not saying that $225 is anything to be shrugged off, but that amount of money wouldn't keep me or likely anyone else from driving if it came down to having to pay that extra $18.75 per month. The secretary I interviewed at the Arco station, for example, now pays an extra $35 per month to commute. In her words, there's "no choice." Not if you have to get to work to make money. Not if you have to drop the kids at school. Not if you live outside of a major city, without public transportation.

If you look at the oil and gas subsidy system on a purely "get what you pay for" standard, it's a great deal: Who wouldn't pay $25 in tax dollars to save $225 in annual expenses—for driving alone? Factor in the cost savings for utility bills and the deal gets even sweeter. We Americans spend on average $2,200 per year on utilities such as electricity, heating, and cooling. As a percentage of total spending, beyond oil and gas, the federal government subsidizes about 7 percent of our coal use, which is mostly used for electricity; 26.5 percent of our ethanol use; 10 percent of our biodiesel use; almost 12 percent of our wind energy use; more than 12 percent of our solar energy use; and 21 percent of our nuclear energy use. These plus other fuel sources are mixed and matched to create energy for our homes.

The American Petroleum Institute, which represents the interests of the oil and natural gas industry, gloats that "oil and natural gas produce a substantial bargain for taxpayers when so-called 'subsidies' are compared with the amount of energy produced." It cites the EIA statistics.

Indeed, Irwin Kellner, chief economist for Dow Jones MarketWatch, tells me that it isn't subsidies that make prices seem cheap here in the United States when compared with fuel prices in other countries. "Price differences stem from other countries levying big taxes on oil and gas consumption, not subsidies here in the US," he says.

But here is the disconnect: The oil and gas industry says that if we *don't* subsidize them, the price of gasoline would go through the roof—to as much as $15 per gallon. (They claim the cost of everything from research to leases to exploration would rise, rise, rise. And, moreover, they would lose operational efficiencies and wouldn't be able to take into account government support for their price planning.) And they say they would be forced to lay off employees throughout the entire oil and gas sector. Look at the numbers. If ExxonMobil had to eat the entire industry's subsidies itself, it could—and would still have $10 billion left over. So if they are making so much money, why not just forgo all that subsidy *dinero?*

Dunno. But I do know that the oil and gas industry's argument is fake.

The *New York Times* reports that an examination of the American tax code indicates that oil production is among the most heavily subsidized businesses, with tax breaks available at virtually every stage of the exploration and extraction process.

The *NYT* cited a Congressional Budget Office study done in 2005 that shows "capital investments like oil field leases and drilling equipment are taxed at an effective rate of 9 percent, significantly lower than the overall rate of 25 percent for businesses in general and lower than virtually any other industry."

The blurred reality put forth by the oil and gas industry starts to get a little clearer. "And for many small and midsize oil companies, the tax on capital investments is so low that it is more than eliminated by various credits. These companies' returns on those investments are often higher after taxes than before," the *Times* says.

To put it really clearly, the oil and gas industry exploits its tax breaks to make even more money. Providing jobs and lower-priced fuel to the planet isn't their real mission.

Senator Robert Menendez of New Jersey was quoted in the *NYT* piece as saying, "There is no reason for these corporations to shortchange the American taxpayer."

Oh, but there is, Senator Menendez: It's called excessive greed. And the oil and gas industry will fight to keep every penny it can make. The oil and natural gas industry has spent $340 million on lobbyists since 2008, according to the Center for Responsive Politics. And when it can't lobby its way out of making money, it makes threats.

"As you begin consideration of legislation to address expiring tax provisions and other revenue issues, we urge you to avoid policies that could endanger jobs in the domestic oil and natural gas industry, an industry that is critical to both our energy and economic security," American Petroleum Institute president Jack

Gerard said in a letter to members of Congress, enlisting Mark H. Ayers, the president of the AFL-CIO Building and Construction Trades Department, as a cosigner. As any astute political observer knows, unions such as the AFL-CIO hold major political clout because they represent so many potential votes. By dropping the union "card" on congressmen, the oil and gas industry was making a heavy threat. These guys play hardball.

But some government watchdog groups say the oil and gas industry's only political interest is preserving the tax breaks. According to the *NYT,* "An economist for the Treasury Department said in 2009 that a study had found that oil prices and potential profits were so high that eliminating the subsidies would decrease American output by less than half of one percent."

There is no analysis needed for that statement: Eliminating subsidies wouldn't hamstring the economy as much as the oil and gas industry would have us believe.

There's actually a statement on the American Petroleum Institute's Web site that says the elimination of subsidies has done good for them in the past—and has been good for us: "The elimination of subsidies under the government regulations after 1981 led to the closure of many smaller, less-efficient refineries throughout the 1980s and 1990s. Those refineries left standing did a better job of bringing product to market for less. The further consolidation benefited consumers."

If the oil and gas industry could get its greedy head out of its ass, it might see profits rise and negative sentiment about its business activities fall by refusing subsidies.

Rather, we are still giving tax breaks to highly profitable companies to do what they would be doing anyway. Most people would define this as a giveaway, not an incentive.

But the tax breaks given to oil and gas companies are entrenched in history. Many of the tax breaks were originally intended to encourage exploration. In fact, some oil companies still benefit from these provisions. For example, oil companies can deduct the "lost value" from tapped oil fields even if that exceeds the amount the company paid for the oil rights to begin with. Other deductions compensate oil companies for the royalties they pay to foreign governments for drilling. And then, of course, there is the old accounting trick of incorporating in foreign "tax havens," or countries where taxes are low. By utilizing this one trick alone, five oil companies—Transocean, Noble, Nabors Industries, Weatherford International, and Global Santa Fe Corp.—have saved themselves $4 billion in taxes since 1999.

ExxonMobil is actually in favor of forgoing some subsidies to save face. Seems that a subsidy provided to oil companies under the guise of an ethanol subsidy was even too much of a fake for that oil giant.

The subsidy, a $5 billion boondoggle, was an incentive to use ethanol in gasoline blends. But instead of the money going to the biofuel provider—the corn, soybean, or sugar grower, for example—it goes to the gas blenders. And for those of you a little slow on the uptake, gas blenders are . . . big oil companies such as ExxonMobil.

ExxonMobil executives say they are content to let the subsidy expire, citing its redundancy: They are already mandated by federal law and regulations to mix a certain amount of ethanol with their gasoline. The subsidy, even to them, makes no sense. If that seems out of character for an oil company—refusing money, that is—I would have to agree. The forgoing of the subsidy is likely, then, a trade-off for better public relations.

For us gas-guzzling consumers, the subsidy, formally titled the Volumetric Ethanol Excise Tax Credit, is negligible. Robert Rapier, an energy blogger and engineer who works in the renewable energy field, explains that if the tax credit were not there, it wouldn't matter.

> ExxonMobil is still mandated to blend a certain amount, and . . . they are subject to fines by the Environmental Protection Agency (EPA) if they fail to comply with the mandates. Since the EPA can wield a big hammer, companies willingly violate EPA regulations at great corporate risk. Therefore, gasoline blenders will use the amount of ethanol they have been mandated to use, regardless of whether there is a subsidy in place.
>
> So in the event that blenders did not get the tax credit, the energy equivalent price they would pay for ethanol would be about $2.50 per gallon (based on ethanol's current spot price). The subsidy amounted to about $5 billion last year, and continues to rise with increasing ethanol production. Assuming the oil companies passed on the additional costs, that $5 billion spread over 140 billion gallons of gasoline sold in the US last year would increase fuel costs by just 3.5 cents a gallon. The only difference would be that the cost would then be borne directly by drivers in proportion to the number of miles they drive.

That is some $5 billion fake that amounts to . . . nothing. So how does such a thing ever get put into place in the first place? What group of geniuses would offer a subsidy to encourage mixing more ethanol when a federal mandate already exists?

In an online discussion about the issue, Vinod Khosla, a venture capitalist and new energy guru, explained:

> What I heard, is that well past midnight when this was being debated in the [congressional] conference committee, the oil companies inserted 2 words into the language, calling this subsidy a blender's credit. So the person who is blending it with gasoline gets it. All $2 billion of it last year was collected by the oil companies. Like they needed more money. It's unfortunate, but that's the way the system works. I talked to one of the senator's aides who was in the conference room, and he said they got to 1 a.m., and were still negotiating, and oil guys were willing to stay there.

Because the subsidy is based on the amount of fuel used, its amount can vary: $5 billion or $2 billion. The point is, it's billions.

When people hear the word *ethanol,* they usually think "clean energy." Perhaps they even believe it's a good substitute for oil and gas.

When I hear the word *ethanol,* I cringe. Subsidies for the fuel, which is manufactured mostly from corn, amount to some $6 billion per year and cost taxpayers tens of billions of dollars. These subsidies have distorted the food supply, retarded gas prices, upset American foreign policy and trade, and generally wreaked havoc on the environment.

If you want to encapsulate what is wrong with government policy and what is wrong with subsidies, look no further than ethanol.

Ethanol is actually the alcohol ingredient in the beverages we like to make us drunk. It's been around for centuries making us loopy. And now that it has crept into other aspects of our consumptive lives, it has made us stupid, too.

Both President Barack Obama and former president George W. Bush have supported ethanol subsidies.

Ethanol subsidies are our chance to "get off oil," "it's a step toward energy independence," politicians say.

Wrong.

It takes more energy to manufacture energy from corn ethanol than one can get from using that corn ethanol as energy. Researchers at Cornell University and the University of California, Berkeley, say it takes 29 percent more fossil energy to turn corn into ethanol than is yielded by the amount of fuel the process produces. "There is just no energy benefit to using plant biomass for liquid fuel," says David Pimentel, professor of ecology and agriculture at Cornell. "These strategies are not sustainable." The researchers included such factors as the energy used to produce the crop. In terms of health, there is no question that oil, gas, and even ethanol produce pollution that makes us sick, creates diseases, and adds billions to our health care costs every year. Never mind your thoughts on global warming: I am talking strictly about the air pollution that the burning of these fuels produces.

According to a National Research Council report, the hidden costs of energy production are $120 billion when you add up the increased costs of health care, fewer food crops, pollution control, and other ramifications that relate to damaging carbon emissions.

Add that to your tax bill and smoke it.

So sticking with the bottom-line nature of this book, what do we pay for oil and gas subsidies? Close to $10 billion per year, when you tally up all the direct and indirect costs from oil, gas, ethanol, and so on.

And what does that buy us? A $120 billion liability and a 37.5-cents savings at the gas pump.

No one wants to hear this, but we'd be better off if we paid higher gas prices at the pump and higher utility bills for our homes. It would decrease incentives to drive and use our home heating and cooling systems with reckless abandon. And it would decrease the amount of pollution in the air, pollution that is harmful to our health and the environment.

One very simple way to make the world a better place would be for Americans to pay the real cost of oil and gas. We are already suffering too much by its artificially cheap price.

Few things seem real or solid in America anymore. So next I decided to go to the source of "solid," the modern-day equivalent of stone: America's steel industry.

CHAPTER FOURTEEN

STEEL

It should be the backbone of America. It should be a source of pride and jobs and one of the mainstay exports on which the world relies. But the United States steel industry is in shambles. It's weak, 30 percent bankrupt, and has been on the downside of the economy—well before the economy even turned down.

In Pittsburgh, the capital of steel in America, John, my taxi driver, tells me that he used to own a successful business servicing the steel industry. His whole family worked for it: two sons and a daughter. John, 70, was forced to retire. Now he drives. His kids, too: They drive. His steel business went belly-up.

Zipping past downtown, heading to the outskirts of Pittsburgh, the city belies its polluted past. It's green. The air is clear.

Pittsburgh is transforming itself from a Rust Belt city and marketing itself as an environmental case study. "For more than 100 years, Pittsburgh was 'hell with the lid taken off.' Darkness covered the city 24 hours a day, making Pittsburgh a 'two-shirts-a-day' town," according to the Web site Pittsburghgreenstory.org. Now, "Pittsburgh isn't the Smoky City anymore. The deadly air pollution that hung over Pittsburgh's steel mills for nearly 150 years is gone, and the region has undergone a dramatic environmental transformation."

The smoke and pollution went away with the steel business. But so did a lot of jobs. "It put us out of work," John recollects as we whisk past the convention center, the world's largest "green" building. Green as they might, the city still hasn't lapped up all the jobs that have fallen with the collapse of steel.

The reason for much of the steel industry's disaster is subsidies. But not so much ours—China's.

It may seem odd to insert steel into the mix of this book. I don't cover every form of subsidy—health care and student loans, for example. I am painting a portrait of what an America would be like without subsidies in the things that we can see, feel, and touch.

We can certainly see and touch steel. It's one of the most abundant materials in our lives. Our cars, homes, and offices are full of steel, and it's even used for the cans that much of our food comes in. It's used to make the furniture we sit and eat on. It's a main ingredient in our computers, printers, and mobile phones. Steel is a big part of our physical world. Yet much of it these days has been "stolen" from us by other countries.

Our cheap energy and cheap cotton and corn underwritten by federal subsidies may give us a leg up on the world market and allow us to dominate those industries. When it comes to steel, however, we are the victims.

Because we impose steel import tariffs and because we artificially prop up the US steel industry with loan guarantees (backed by the US taxpayer) and pension benefits—yes, pension benefits, also paid by the US taxpayer—China believes it has a free pass to support its steel industry with government subsidies for as much as it wants. That has added up to more than $50 billion over ten years in Chinese government subsidies to Chinese steel producers.

What does all this mean to the people of the United States?

It means that we pay more in taxes to support the faltering US steel business, and we pay more for steel and other Chinese products than we would otherwise, due to government protectionism and retaliatory tactics.

A World Bank study on the US steel industry shows that even small increases in US import tariffs translate into big retail product price increases and cause construction prices to increase as well. Any rise in steel prices at all has a wide-ranging effect on the economy.

The total hit to the US economy promulgated by steel quotas is estimated to be $7 billion per year.

We impose import duties of up to 135 percent on some Chinese steel—more than twice the price and then some—to rectify what the US government believes is China dumping cheap steel on the domestic market. When "dumping" occurs, the steel industry and the US government claim that jobs are lost and US steelmakers suffer.

Actually, that is false. Three times as many jobs are lost when the government artificially inflates the price of steel through import tariffs, according to various studies on the issue.

In a widely quoted study on the steel tariff issue, "The Unintended Consequences of U.S. Steel Import Tariffs," by researchers Dr. Joseph Francois and Laura M. Baughman, the authors found that "more American workers lost their jobs in 2002 to higher steel prices than the total number employed by the US steel industry itself." They found that 200,000 Americans lost their jobs to higher steel prices and that these lost jobs represented approximately $4 billion in lost wages. This was nine years ago, at a time when Chinese tariffs were less than one-third what they are now.

Chinese subsidies driving down prices and dumping their goods onto the US market isn't what has stopped the US steel industry from prospering and helping provide us with less expensive goods (and more jobs). The problem is with the US steel industry itself.

According to the book *High-Tech Protectionism: The Irrationality of Antidumping Laws,* by Claude Barfield, published by the American Enterprise Institute, "U.S. steel makers long enjoyed a cost advantage because of their proximity to coal and iron ore deposits, but by the early 1970s the discovery of high quality iron deposits outside the United States (in Australia and Brazil), combined with the introduction of new ocean-going bulk tankers, drastically reduced this advantage. One study has estimated that between 1958 and 1980, by sourcing low-cost ore and using huge bulk carriers, Japan turned a 28 percent cost disadvantage on steel raw materials into a 30 percent advantage." Meanwhile, the book says, US steelmakers didn't change their ways in order to compete. "European and Japanese competitors also outdistanced U.S. companies by early adoption of another major technological breakthrough in steel making: continuous casting. Continuous casting represented a big advance over the ingot casting technology that had been utilized since the days of Andrew Carnegie. In ingot casting, raw molten steel is poured into a mold, allowed to cool into an ingot, then transported to a rolling facility where the ingot is reheated and transformed into a slab, which is finally rolled into a finished product. Continuous casting eliminates all of the steps from raw steel to slab by channeling the raw steel directly from a furnace to a casting machine that molds the steel into the slab form, after which it can be shaped into a finished product. As late as 1980, only 20 percent of U.S. facilities used continuous casting."

Still, while US steel producers toiled away with a method that can be likened to using carrier pigeons in the days of e-mail, the US government stayed by its side to lend a helping hand.

"Foreign government subsidies have been repeatedly cited by the U.S. steel industry as a rationale for government aid and costly preferences in procurement. Yet it is rarely acknowledged that for the past thirty years, U.S. steel makers have received a steady stream of taxpayer-funds subsidies," Barfield writes.

Subsidies make everything all right. Mismanage? No problem: The government will bail you out. Misprice? No problem: Uncle Sam is here. Fail to invest in new technology that will make your business competitive? How much? We'll write you a check.

Tax breaks, bailouts, and loans, as well as protectionist measures that ban foreign competitors from bidding on lucrative government contracts under "buy American" provisions, are given out because the US steel industry has a very big chit it can cash in: its 1.2-million-member union. Wearing political lenses, that's 1.2 million votes. Remember that number throughout this chapter. It is the sine qua non reason, rationale, and trade-off for all this maneuvering.

It would be far more efficient and far better for the US economy to let the free market take over. Job losses plus steel price increases are what hurt the US economy so much. But there are those 1.2 million votes to consider . . . just ask the United Steelworkers Union.

China's massive steel subsidies allow that country to produce steel at far below the cost of steel from the United States and many other foreign producers. This in turn means that Chinese steel should be had on the cheap and we should be able to enjoy lower prices for goods containing steel.

We don't. Instead we get to support the steel industry with what amount to taxpayer-funded loan guarantees, price guarantees, and job guarantees.

It's much easier to blame China than to blame a big voting bloc of the American public for the steel industry's woes.

What's missing in the dialogue between the steelworkers and the government is the steel consumers: us, and those businesses that rely on less expensive steel to manufacture goods. When steel prices rise, fewer goods can be made and fewer people need to be employed to make those goods. We consumers, in turn, buy less of more expensive things. Hence, the economy takes a hit, fewer people overall are employed, and unemployment rises.

To be sure, foreign producers such as China pervert the market with cheap prices and exacerbate an already troubled industry. Still, China is just the banana peel under the crutch. The steel industry is plagued with the bankruptcies of its largest companies, unemployment in the hundreds of thousands, and idle plants. The US steel industry is utilizing just 60 percent of its production capacity.

The legacy of the steelworkers' union, of an America long past, is what is being subsidized to our detriment.

Huge buildings and thousands of acres of riverfront property sit empty and unused as testament to this. Workers like John, my taxi driver who had for decades enjoyed a career in the steel industry, found themselves out of date, out of a job, and without the proper training for much else.

The Heritage Foundation, among others, points out that some 30 percent of all claims to the Pension Benefit Guaranty Corporation have gone to steelworkers. The PBGC is a government program that pays retirement benefits when companies can no longer afford to. It's supported by US taxpayers. The costs of funding pension and health care benefits for approximately 600,000 retired steelworkers is estimated to run between $10 billion and $13 billion.

The Chinese government uses this type of US funding to make its own case for subsidizing steel. "Chen Haoran, executive director of China's Chamber of Commerce of Metals, Minerals and Chemicals, argued that the United States has also subsidized its industry by, for example, removing the pension burdens of many steel companies when they were in bankruptcy," the *New York Times* reports.

Tit for tat, the trade war over steel continues, and it's all about the issue of subsidies—how much, how little, to whom, and for how long.

The US and China have been battling for years over China's undervalued currency. When a country's currency is cheap, so are its goods, and this creates an unfair advantage in the world marketplace. (You can tell when the US dollar is cheap because Times Square is rotten with foreigners.) The US and other governments have been howling at China to raise the value of its currency to no avail. Surrogate trade battles over everything from steel to chicken to credit cards have taken place, with China so far winning the war.

The World Trade Organization is supposed to step in and mediate these battles, but it's been about as effective as the judge who keeps giving Lindsay Lohan bail.

The WTO has launched "investigations" in China to render some type of remedy and relief, but China keeps manipulating those investigations.

"Look," a WTO representative might say, "you are giving steel companies loans."

"No," a Chinese trade representative might say, "we are giving them money so they can live up to environmental standards."

Environmental issues kick subsidies into another corner of rules and regulations, and on and on it goes. From tires to nylons, automobiles to paper to salt, different products are used as surrogates to do battle over subsidies and tariffs.

Domestically, however, these issues have a real effect on lives—our lives.

In a telling case that goes from little issue to big issue, steelworkers had complained to President Obama that cheap tires from China were costing the United States jobs. The steelworkers' union is the same union that represents tire factory workers (and, as such, part of that sacrosanct bloc of voters). Obama caved and imposed caps on tire imports from China. As the *Washington Post* explains, in China that was "seen as a move pandering to the United Steelworkers who had helped get President Obama elected, and as a violation of the U.S. president's promise to other G-20 leaders that he would avoid protectionist measures. On Internet bulletin boards, public sentiment about the United States turned ugly, and there were widespread nationalist calls for China to start dumping its vast holdings of U.S. Treasury bonds."

Dump our Treasury bonds and interest rates go up—as well as the costs of our goods. That dings our economy a lot and hurts us consumers.

All this chicanery for tires, which amount to a tiny amount of trade between the United States and China, and a political favor.

Steel costs, which account for about 5 percent of the price of the average car, wind their way into our pockets: That Ford

Explorer you are eying is jacked up by nearly a thousand dollars because of the US-China trade dispute and rising steel prices.

We end up paying for and subsidizing perhaps the largest segment of society that is living the lie and entrenched in an America of yesteryear. In fact, it still gets a piece of the action from those days. Until recently, the US steel industry received a piece of the duties collected by the government from foreign producers. "Despite being ruled illegal under the United States Constitution, the NAFTA agreement, and the WTO agreements, the U.S. Government has persisted in making disbursements" until recently, according to a report by the American Institute for International Steel, a group in favor of free trade.

Big Steel doesn't believe it has to live by the rules and still believes that it can operate in an alternative reality of days gone by. Its pensioners from bankrupt companies receive retirement payments, as well as full dental and medical. Corporate owners get tax breaks and kickbacks. And presidents lobby other nations on their behalf to gain political favor. In 2001, for example, President Bush asked world leaders to lower the global output of steel to help US steelworkers. All this for companies that do not believe they must adhere to free-market principles.

As the Corporate Research Project reported, in an article titled "Big Steel on Steroids":

> A country's steel output has traditionally been considered a primary indicator of its level of economic development. In the United States, the rise of the industry proceeded in tandem with the growth of the entire economy. American steel producers dominated the world market from the end of the 19th

century through the 1950s, when European and Japanese producers began to mount an effective challenge. In fact, the expansion of production capacity overseas, especially in developing countries such as Brazil and South Korea, has given rise to the view that the U.S. no longer needs a large domestic production capability.

What remains of Big Steel and the Steelworkers are not about to succumb quietly to the logic of globalization. For the past three decades, the industry has been complaining that foreign producers use subsidies from their governments to dump output on the U.S. market at artificially low prices.

If a country's steel output is indeed a primary indicator of its economic development, how did our system become backward and out of touch with the rest of the world?

There's an iconic black-and-white photograph from the 1930s showing an American steelworker sitting on a girder of the Empire State Building in New York City. His feet are dangling over the edge and he is eating his lunch out of a lunchbox. The picture seems so very America. So very "ideal."

I went to New York and looked up from the sidewalk to where that worker may have hung over Fifth Avenue. The smell of hot dogs and the smoke from roasted chestnut vendors invaded my senses. The street was thick with pedestrians. No way a steelworker would be allowed to dangle over the crowd today. He'd be strapped onto the building with the latest, safest regulator-approved equipment.

Still, the old false imagery is what the steel industry still clings to. Subsidies help to sketch this image. They are part of the grand illusion that the America we live in today is somehow immune from foreign influence, foreign trade, and foreign competition, as well as technological advancements.

But to understand the rise of subsidies and how they grew, much like the Empire State Building itself, when they grew bigger and bigger and taller and taller, we must go back to that time and explore the policies that created today's malfunctioning government spending machine.

CHAPTER FIFTEEN

THE GROWTH OF SUBSIDIES

It was during the depths of the Depression, in 1932, that Franklin Delano Roosevelt took over the US presidency. The Empire State Building, completed less than a year before, had become a symbol of America's commitment to rise again.

With many businesses virtually out of business, the only player to step in and create work was the government. And it did—along with a new deal, namely, FDR's New Deal.

FDR created the largest government spending programs in history. This created Big Government. And one of the first things Big Government did was help Big Business. But not in the usual way. The stock market crash had been a great lesson in cutting off the head of the economic snake. Instead, the government started at the bottom, with the basics, the necessities: food.

The New Deal hastily doled out money to farmers and got right down to creating the subsidy programs we know today.

As I walk around the Empire State Building, through the crowds of tourists milling (I now see why some New Yorkers want a "tourist lane" on the sidewalks; they get clogged with bystanders), red double-decker buses line up at the building's entrance. Leaflets are handed out. It's a cold day, but the sidewalks are jammed. Traffic is constant, taxis form lines, horns blast, and the low roar of New York's unmistakable cacophony continues—on and on.

I lived around the corner from here years ago. The lights from the Empire State Building would shine through my windows and change the hues on my walls to red, white, and blue.

I see those colors now as standing for debt, not democracy.

The Empire State Building, when it was completed in 1931, was the tallest building in the world. As a symbol it remained, even though it was eclipsed by the Twin Towers. The former World Trade Center, of course, is gone. But subsidies and the Empire State Building remain.

Subsidies over the past century have grown in dollar terms from the millions to the billions, and the beneficiaries have changed over the years from a cause to an industry to individuals to major corporations. From the Reclamation Act of 1902, which provided water to western states, to the $300 billion 2008 Farm Bill (oh, did that slip by the public?), which increased the subsidy for the production of ethanol (which we now know was a dumb idea), subsidies have been an endemic part of the economic and political landscape.

Still, the programs put into place by FDR were breathtaking in terms of their sheer lust for and celebration of subsidies.

Here's how it went down: FDR ran on a campaign promise of hope (sound familiar?) and tried to restore the confidence of America. This was the context for the famous words he delivered during his first inaugural address: "The only thing we have to fear is fear itself." Right after this speech, in his first 100 days in office, he enacted 15 major pieces of legislation that established his New Deal policy. Among these, he created the Federal Deposit Insurance Corporation, designed to protect bank deposits, and the Agricultural Adjustment Administration (AAA), to protect farmers.

The FDIC actually does protect bank depositors and has lived up to its name (although arguably it has never really been tested, as there hasn't been a massive run on the banks since the FDIC was formed).

The AAA, however, hasn't lived up to its name and protection guarantees. Far from protecting farmers, it has hindered their progress and pretty much handed their businesses over to big corporations that, in turn, have lapped up all those billions of dollars in government-funded price supports.

The AAA was designed to help farmers by paying them *not* to farm. It imposed a special tax that was paid to farmers so they could rest easy and grow less, which also raised the price of their goods. This had the added benefit of reducing their costs.

It was a sweet deal for farmers. Too sweet, the Supreme Court found, and overturned the law three years later, in 1936.

Refusing to let them go down, FDR, the Rocky Balboa of price supports, pushed for another law—the Agricultural Adjustment Act of 1938. This act, while raising a middle finger to the Supreme Court, made price supports *mandatory* for corn, cotton, and wheat to keep supply in line with market demand. The USDA says the act established government supports for butter, dates, figs, hops, turpentine, rosin, pecans, prunes, raisins, barley, rye, grain sorghum, wool, winter cover-crop seeds, mohair, peanuts, and tobacco.

Seems like a lot of price supports, eh? But that wasn't all. Not by a stretch. FDR also underwrote farm labor, extended farmers' credit, and created an insurance program backed by the federal government in case crops failed. These farm programs all added up to a no-lose situation for the American farmer and are at the root of the problem the United States faces in dealing with the rest of the world under World Trade Organization agreements. The WTO is supposed to create a fair world trade marketplace so that no single nation can dominate or bully others by dumping cheap (and subsidized) products on the world market or raising tariffs so high that it unfairly shuts out foreign goods. Anyone who knows anything about the WTO knows that the organization doesn't work. In fact, whenever there is a WTO meeting anywhere in the world, it is always the subject of protests. Many protestors believe the WTO only has the interests of rich nations and big, multinational corporations in mind when it sets rules.

FDR probably didn't foresee this when he enacted his massive farm aid packages. After all, this was a time when the farming community made up a big chunk of the US population. Farming wasn't associated with corporate interests or anything elite back then.

While FDR was growing up, almost half the US population worked in the agricultural sector. Relying on the land was how people fed themselves and their families. It was how they earned their incomes. Other industries hadn't matured. The Depression had sunk many a hope and dream. People, then, proudly worked the land—until other opportunities came along.

By the time he was president, the agricultural community was still 21.5 percent of the workforce, and agriculture brought in 8 percent of total US gross domestic product. That was still a formidable amount. So it can be said that it was the American people to whom his programs were aimed.

The slide had begun, however. In 1945, 16 percent of the total labor force was employed in agriculture, and its share of total GDP had dipped to 6.8 percent. By 1970, only 4 percent of the employed labor force worked in agriculture, and its share of total GDP was down to 2.3 percent. By the year 2000, less than 2 percent of the employed labor force worked in agriculture, and its share of total GDP was less than 1 percent.

As the population urbanized and farms became businesses, you'd think that subsidies would lessen. Nuh-uh. They grew!

The original half a billion dollars allocated to the farm industry has grown to more than 400 times that amount *per year* when everything is tallied.

The first subsidy recipient was a family farmer who received subsidized water, land, and eventually price supports for his hard work. Today it's likely a multinational corporation that receives all kinds of funding to artificially grow and enhance productivity to determine prices on the world commodities markets. We've gone from agrarian America to corporate America and institutionalized a system of payments along the way that bedevils the world.

I mentioned in chapter 4 how Jesse Jewell was the first true integrator of the agribusiness model. He was a poultry pioneer who combined all the phases of the business, such as raw materials, processing, and distribution, into a single, powerful company. Jewell the chicken rancher eventually grew to become the largest chicken producer in the world, and the business was sold to a group of investors. His story is analogous to the growth of the entire agricultural industry—from farmer to factory.

How the farming industry grew from a bunch of cooperatives to a multinational business armed with corporate lobbyists is an intriguing tale full of characters like Jesse Jewell. But behind them all were subsidies, their essential form of livelihood.

Those who analyze such programs say they wish there were a few periods in time that were turning points and resulted in a shift in the way government involved itself in the business of agriculture.

"It's depressing to me how little things have changed over the years," Dan Griswold, director of the Center for Trade Policy Studies at the Cato Institute, in Washington, DC, laments to me. "I'm not sure that there have been any major turning points in programs that haven't changed in 75 years."

Griswold is correct: Subsidy programs haven't much changed over the years. Still, there are some moments worth mentioning.

The first point was during the 1960s. Until this time, the policies enacted in the 1930s held firm, and farm support was still determined by acreage and by prices only. Farming techniques largely remained the same.

The 1960s were different. According to the USDA, farmers in the 1960s were in the midst of a technological revolution that was decreasing the number of farmers while greatly augmenting the productivity of those remaining on the land. The agency said new forms of fertilizers, pesticides, and machinery, as well as farming methods, enabled farmers to set new production records.

Of course, the surplus affected prices big-time and meant the government had to deal with supply-versus-demand issues.

The Kennedy administration decided to dispose of surpluses through donations of food to the poor. In fact, President Kennedy's first executive order directed the secretary of agriculture to immediately expand the program of food distribution to needy persons. A pilot food stamp plan was also started. In addition, steps were taken to expand the school lunch program and to make better use abroad of American agricultural abundance. These programs eventually morphed into the Food and Agriculture Act of 1965, and the foundations for our school lunch, food stamp, and USAID programs were laid.

Cut to the late 1960s. Expenditures were rampant. The corporate camel's nose was full under the tent. Subsidies reached a new peak of $3.8 billion in 1969. There was also concern about the very large payments that some farmers were receiving. Even back then, people had become wary of just who was receiving these large subsidy payments.

The government then sealed the deal on its preference of working with Big Ag: Grain farmers with fewer than 25 acres were not to receive special treatment by the government, it was announced. That meant only big farms need apply.

In any case, the USDA reports that:

> By 1973, the position of agriculture had changed profoundly from where it had been a decade before. World crop shortages and a falling dollar sharply escalated the trend toward greater export demand for American crops. Following the Soviet grain sale of 1972, grain exports nearly doubled ... and total agricultural exports increased by over 25 percent. Government grain stocks, which had hung so long over the market, were virtually liquidated. Even higher output by grain farmers was quickly absorbed by the market. For example, corn production increased by some 25 percent between the late 1960s and 1973 but Government stocks of corn disappeared completely in

1973. For the first time since the Korean War, it appeared that
demand had fully caught up with supply and that demand would
continue strong for at least several years. Along with strong
demand, however, came higher prices and this, in turn, made it
difficult to justify programs designed to limit production.

Griswold notes that sugar programs were abolished
between 1974 and 1981. The result? Domestic sugar controlled
60 percent of the market rather than the 85 percent it controls
today, after protectionist sugar programs were reinstituted.

In any event, the USDA reports, "price controls on food in
the early 1970s had only limited success in holding down consumer costs. Food price inflation and the growing importance
of agricultural exports to the general economy made agricultural policy of greater interest than it had been for many years."

In 1973, a new concept of target prices was introduced to
replace price support payments. This was historic and important. Indeed, then-Secretary of Agriculture Earl L. Butz pro-
claimed that target prices represented "an historic turning
point in the philosophy of farm programs in the United States."

Enter President Ronald Reagan. Reagan didn't like target
prices one bit. Target prices paid farmers a certain amount even
if market prices went below those amounts. They meant some
fictitious number was driving the farming industry, not actual
market prices.

Butz was correct: This was an historic turning point. It
brought farmers into the world of fiction.

Reagan fought to control the budget and slash costs. He
tried to do away with target prices and devised a plan to cut farm
program allotments. But Big Ag had already dug in its heels.

Eventually a compromise was agreed on that moved away from target prices but included compensation for inflation.

These policies remain despite Farm Aid concerts and farm industry public relations campaigns that would have you believe the farm industry was starving.

The next big point to take notice of was the Farm Security and Rural Investment Act of 2002, also known as the 2002 Farm Bill. This brought the farming community into our diets and linked energy and the environment to agriculture.

Danger, Will Robinson, danger.

The act increased government spending by a smashing $90 billion—and that's above the hyperinflated budgets of previous acts. It included more money for conservation and incentives for producing more ethanol (as opposed to food) from corn and soy.

This was all passed in the wake of September 11, when the nation's attention was, of course, elsewhere. Still, free-trade advocates did sound off—even if few were listening. They said the act pushed through excessive subsidies and measures that violated WTO agreements.

As if that wasn't insulting enough, the Food, Conservation, and Energy Act of 2008 (a.k.a. the 2008 Farm Bill) dolloped another hundred billion dollars on top of that, laying out $288 billion for five years. The act spends money on alternative energy, conservation, nutrition, and rural development. It also includes increased spending for food stamp benefits and increased support for the production of ethanol.

So that's where we are today: paying out tax dollars to loan, credit, cajole, punish, and produce our food. From assisting half the population to a select minority, and from an industry that was made up of family farms to one where the vast majority of subsidies go to major corporations and the average farmer's income is 50 percent more than the average American's. This is a land far, far away from what FDR could have imagined—and one that, in my mind anyway, hasn't done justice to that steelworker who labored so hard on the Empire State Building. What he was building, I imagine, was a symbol of a strong America whose backbone would be people, everyday people, not the elite and corporations who take government handouts.

The farmer of yesteryear is gone, whittled down to a small minority, while the "average farmer" today is a corporate executive.

Interestingly, the current owner of the Empire State Building, Anthony Malkin, can trace his family's real estate business interest to the exact time when the landmark was built. His grandfather, Lawrence Wien, started the family real estate business in 1929 and created the concept of real estate syndication in 1934. Real estate syndication operates like a cooperative, in which shares of ownership are sold to multiple investors. Syndication opens the doors to people and values and prices, whereas handouts—given to the chosen few—keep the doors tightly shut. It's like allowing everyone standing before me out on 34th Street to ride up on the Empire State Building's elevators, or selecting a chosen few for the ride to the top.

In the next chapters we'll see how being shut out of an open market hurts us and how giving handouts to a chosen few does us harm. We'll see how the tax steroids we give to the farming industry affect us as taxpayers and consumers. First and foremost, we'll see how they've come to make us poor.

CHAPTER SIXTEEN

WHY THEY MAKE US POOR

Two hundred eighty-eight billion dollars. Today that's the
number on the table. It's how much we spend to give a boost
to our food supply under the Food, Conservation, and Energy
Act of 2008. To be fair, that amount is spread over five years.
Quick math: 288 divided by five is $57.6 billion per year.

Do some additional math and divide that figure by the
number of households in the United States and you get a flat
$576. On one program, $576 per household per year. That's
more than a month's worth (five weeks) of food costs for the
average person.

Now let's get really fancy. According to many sources, the
maximum savings that can be attributable to current food subsidies is 5 percent of the retail price. Five percent of a year is equivalent to about two and a half weeks' worth of food costs. Above I
showed how the Farm Bill of 2008 costs you five weeks' worth of
food. If we are paying through our taxes, for just one program,
the equivalent of five weeks' worth of food, yet we are getting just
a 5 percent price savings, then it can be said that the very program that purports to help us is ripping us off . . . and that's just
one program! Estimates triple the $57.6 billion being spent by
the Farm Bill, since other indirect subsidy programs are in
place (such as federally underwritten energy, water, and land

grants and insurance programs). So let's say we are being ripped off by seven or eight weeks' worth of food costs by paying more with our taxes than we are receiving through the price cuts they sometimes engender. There is a serious disconnect in this country between what we pay for and what we get.

But let's get away from theories and math and get down to brass tacks (and tax!). The average tax bill in America is $17,000. Know how much the average farmer receives in myriad federal tax subsidy schemes? Seventeen thousand dollars.

That was a startling comparison to me. We each pay almost exactly as much in taxes as a farmer receives in federal subsidies.

We have seen over the course of the past few chapters how the business of subsidies has evolved to where it is today. We have seen how the few are getting rich off the backs of the many. And by reading those chapters, you might believe that the farmers are mere puppets of government policy. They are. It was the government that began this mess and used farmers to exert its influence over the economy and other countries. Still does.

Take a look at where we are today in terms of our agricultural exports and you'll see how we wage influence.

Turn the export screws on Nigeria and make them poorer. Turn the export screws on Mexico and make them poorer, too. Ditto Egypt and the Philippines. I chose just these few countries because not only are they top importers of American agricultural products, but they are also places where food riots broke out as recently as 2008.

Take a look at Ethiopia, Peru, Colombia, Pakistan, and other nations struggling financially. There are, of course, political and hegemonic reasons for many of our heavy-handed

THE TOP U.S. EXPORT MARKETS AS OF 2010:

WHEAT	SOYBEANS
Japan	China
Nigeria	Mexico
Mexico	European Union
Philippines	Japan
South Korea	Taiwan
Taiwan	Indonesia
Venezuela	Turkey
Colombia	South Korea
Ethiopia	Egypt
Indonesia	Thailand

CORN	COTTON
Japan	China
Mexico	Turkey
South Korea	Mexico
Taiwan	Indonesia
Egypt	Thailand
Canada	Vietnam
Venezuela	Taiwan
Dominican Republic	South Korea
Peru	Peru
Colombia	Pakistan

trade relationships. But keeping the world's poor hungry certainly has its commercial advantages if you are a food producer.

The same holds true for the poor here at home.

A detailed study on subsidies by the American Enterprise Institute concludes that subsidies impose "costs on taxpayers far in excess of the benefits they deliver to either rural America or the nation as a whole." Moreover, they vanquish more people into poverty, unemployment, and dire financial straits. If global barriers were to come down, farm exports around the world would be 74 percent higher in 2015, and the US would reap about $60 billion more in farm income. As the Heritage Foundation says, "If farm subsidies were really about alleviating farmer poverty, lawmakers could guarantee every full-time farmer an income of 185 percent of the federal level ($38,203 for a family of four) for less than $5 billion annually—or *one-fifth* the current cost of farm subsidies [italics mine]."

A financially healthier farming industry—for example, one that got a $60 billion surplus and was globally more competitive—would mean more people employed and fewer people forced to sell their family farm or seek income elsewhere. But subsidies work against this credo. According to the USDA, the majority of small family farms in America earn 85 to 95 percent of their income "off-farm." In other words, they cannot afford to live off the monies farming brings in and have to turn to alternative sources of income.

The brainwash of farm subsidies, however, pressures politicians to keep subsidies on the books. Even though less than 2 percent of the employment sector is in the farming industry, we still refer to "nonfarm" payrolls. Listen next time the business news is on or you're reading the *Wall Street Journal:* The term *nonfarm* is everywhere.

But who exactly *is* "on the farm"? Archer Daniels Midland, Boise Cascade Corporation, Caterpillar, Chevron, Deere & Company, DuPont, and dozens more multinational corporations. They receive the biggest benefits from US subsidies. Last year, Archer Daniels's revenue was $61 billion, Boise Cascade's was $3 billion, Caterpillar's was $32 billion, and Chevron's was $171 billion. Not exactly the sort of financial distress we associate with farming. These companies sell the seeds, equipment, fertilizers, and pesticides and have a stake in almost every aspect of farming—without the risk of getting their hands dirty by actually farming.

There are two million farms in the United States, and the majority of them are family-run. They just don't make anywhere near the kind of money non-family farms make. Besides residential and lifestyle farms (small farms whose operators report a major occupation other than farming), which constitute the largest chunk of farmland (and 822,000 actual farms), the next biggest group of farmers is the small family-run farm, with sales of less than $100,000 per year. There's about a half-million of them. Retirement farmers make up the next biggest group of farmers; they number about 300,000. Small farmers that garner sales between $100,000 and $250,000 per year come in next, numbering 170,000. Then it trickles down to the few and, ironically, those that produce the most in sales for America: the corporate-run farms. There are fewer than 50,000 of these in the US.

Corporate-run farms bully the system and step on their smaller brethren. Competition is moot, as these behemoths simply buy up anything that gets in their way. According to the nonprofit group Farm Aid, whose mission is to keep family farmers on their land and who famously stages concerts to raise awareness, between 1974 and 2002, the number of corporate-owned US farms increased by more than 46 percent. It reports that every week 330 small farmers leave their land, and as a result of this trend, there are now nearly five million fewer farms in the US than there were in the 1930s. Of the two million farms that remain, only about a half million of them are family-run farms. Moreover, there isn't a younger generation of farmers that can step in and run the family farm, even if the farm ownership trend were to reverse itself: Half of all US farmers are between the ages of 45 and 65, and only 6 percent of all farmers are under the age of 35.

Still, 71 percent of farm subsidies go to the top 10 percent of the large corporate farms. The bottom 80 percent of recipients average only $846 per year, while those at the top get millions in federal subsidies. For every five cents that the average taxpayer pays to the government, less than half a penny finds its way into cost savings on the shelf.

Yippee!

The federal subsidy system that determines who gets what and how subsidies get paid is anything but straightforward. There is a dizzying amount of money in loans, grants, and payments that winds its way from every taxpaying American's bank account to federal government coffers to committees to agencies to a multitude of third parties before it eventually can do its job of reducing prices. As you can imagine, by that time there isn't a whole lot of money left to make much of an impact at the checkout line. Instead, a huge amount of money is lost in the middle.

So far, we've seen exactly how much we pay in *direct* corporate farm subsidies alone: $12.2 billion. That's a no-brainer. The government even puts out these numbers. But what about other, indirect subsidies? Crop insurance. Food aid programs, domestic and abroad. Land grants. Disaster relief. These and other assistance programs also add to the subsidy tab we pay.

Tally it all up and the federal government spends the $57.6 billion that the most recent farm bill budgets per year *plus* billions more on indirect subsidy programs.

According to the Green Scissors Campaign, a coalition of consumer groups that seeks out wasteful government spending programs, we dish out $200 billion a year on subsidies that are "wasteful to taxpayers, harmful to the environment and bad for consumers."

What are we getting for our hard-earned dollars? Not much, says the American Enterprise Institute.

Take crop insurance. Taxpayers dole out some $7 billion a year for crop insurance and billions more in disaster payments, enabling some farmers to collect more than double—as much as $2.73 for every $1 they paid in crop insurance premiums. And, as the AEI observes, "it's a remarkably inefficient program: the government pays $1 for every 60 cents farmers receive." It notes that "between 35 and 40 percent of every tax dollar spent on crop insurance goes toward program delivery."

"Program delivery" means administrative costs. That means almost half the money spent is wasted on what amounts to administration. You wouldn't (and shouldn't) give money to a charity that only puts half your donation to work. Nor should we pay subsidies that do the same.

Moreover, the costs have crept up, and up, and up. During the 1970s, the annual cost of disaster assistance was less than $500 million. In the 1980s, the annual costs of disaster and crop insurance had climbed to $1.5 billion. And by the 1990s that liability had risen to \$2.5 billion. During this century, the costs have eclipsed \$7 billion annually.

Even more wasteful are US food aid programs (which must come from domestic food producers that are almost always subsidized by the government). According to the AEI, "Logistical costs eat up 60 percent of the US food aid budget; in contrast, Canada spends only 32 percent on logistics. These high costs are a result of requirements that food be purchased and transported from the United States, and shipping, bagging, and processing be undertaken by approved contractors. Such mandates can produce absurd inefficiencies." In some cases, it would be far easier to ship food from, say, one part of a Third World country that's experiencing disaster to another part of the same country—and not import food from a faraway place like the United States. Instead, numerous news accounts detail how food has to make its way from America's shores in expensive and roundabout ways to get to poor countries in need of help and food relief.

For example, law stipulates that Great Lakes ports cannot ship food aid cargo (because of complicated and politically charged maritime laws governing shipping and handling of freight). Food must be moved by truck or rail through the Great Lakes region before it is then transported by land to another US port for overseas shipment.

That's a waste of food, money, and taxes.

The Great Lakes could and should be a more important center of commerce. I traveled to the biggest, Lake Superior, to investigate the closest port of call to farm country, from which a large portion of our commodities (other than food aid) are shipped.

I wended along the shores where the rails meet Lake Superior. The port in Duluth, Minnesota, is a fascinating place that centers on world trade. Here, in the middle of the country, flags on tankers from foreign nations float by. It's a drab place. The port has a few museums showcasing trade and the history of the Great Lakes. There's an aquarium. Nothing fancy. Nothing glamorous. Nothing too "international" in any sophisticated sense of the word. Yet the port manager told me that tankers come from as far away as Japan, and many more from other parts of Asia—increasingly so.

I was taken by this international commerce. Ships came and went routinely. They anchored, unloaded their cargo, and rose taller from the water. Trade—world trade—occurred before my eyes. It would be simple to do the reverse and send food aid overseas from here. It would easily save money—tax dollars. But inertia trumps efficiency when it comes to government subsidies.

Being surrounded by all the freshwater at the Great Lakes got me thinking about water subsidies, too. Total federal outlays on water treatment and waste disposal have averaged some $3 billion per year. "With respect to water treatment investments, it further appears difficult to justify federal involvement," writes research analyst Mitch Renkow. He says the use and the benefits accrue most on the local level. And locals are perfectly willing to pay for improved water quality. So why get the federal government involved and use federal funds? As we should know by now, the answer lies in politics: It's all local.

The money for farmers pours out of the federal spigot in so many ways it is difficult to track. And we are taking our crazy show on the road; we are now subsidizing farmers in foreign countries with US tax dollars. The Environmental Working Group explains: "The improprieties of our farm subsidy system have become such a problem in world trade that the Obama administration has recently inflicted a new subsidy affront on U.S. taxpayers. In order to avoid politically awkward reforms in America's cotton subsidies, which have been found to contravene World Trade Organization rules, our government has 'settled' matters by agreeing to subsidize Brazil's cotton farmers to the tune of a half-billion dollars over the next several years."

That's a good one, ain't it? It isn't enough that we underwrite farmers who really don't need the money, at the expense of those who do here in America. We are building other versions of a rotten America in different countries!

"We lack billions of dollars needed to make school lunches healthier, maintain an adequate food safety net for low income Americans, promote local sustainable and organic food systems or tackle agriculture's truly daunting environmental and conservation problems... policy should make agriculture more sustainable, should be fiscally responsible, and should be fair and equitable for the diverse interests in the U.S. food and fiber system," the EWG notes. We shouldn't be putting money into more farm subsidies. Rather, we should be putting that money into programs that work, or back into taxpayers' pockets.

"There is a role for government support," says Ken Cook, EWG's president. "There is plenty of room for it. But it should be smart." As it stands, Cook says, government subsidies are stupid. "The farm program has gotten completely off track," he says. "It's time for reform."

So does the US farm policy that sets us back billions of dollars really make us poor, as I posit?

One thousand five hundred dollars per household in tax payments to support these programs isn't anything to shrug off. But it likely won't break most people's bank accounts. However, paying for things that do not give utility does, in fact, damage the country. And ultimately that boomerangs back to us individually. The Federal Reserve Bank of St. Louis examined the costs of subsidies to us. Citing data from a 2006 Organization for Economic Cooperation and Development (OECD) report, it found that "US farm subsidies added $12.3 billion in food costs and $91.1 billion in taxes per year from 2003 to 2005, which translates into an annual average of $109 in food costs and $812 in taxes per household." (It's more now.)

The Congressional Budget Office says the 2008 Farm Bill will cost more overall than the previous Farm Bill in 2002. It says that while crop commodity subsidies will cost about $5 billion less per year, food-cost savings will be lost due to higher prices. The next Farm Bill is scheduled for 2012. One can only guess what that will bring.

What, then, do we really get out of our subsidy payments? I know what farmers get: The new bill establishes Average Crop Revenue Election (ACRE), an optional program that might add further protection if farmers lose revenue. We lose; they don't. That's what's what.

But don't take my word for it. Using USDA figures, you can see exactly what you get for what you pay in subsidies: An $8,400 subsidy payment for a grain farmer works out to an eight-cents-per-dollar savings. A $26,500 subsidy payment to a cotton farmer works out to a 10-cents-per-dollar savings. A $3,000 payment to a vegetable farmer is less than a penny-per-dollar savings. Fruit and nut growers that get payments of $721 provide you with a half-penny-per-dollar savings. Greenhouses and nurseries given $157 in subsidy payments produce just one-tenth of one cent in savings. A cattle rancher given $1,100 in payments gives you four cents per dollar in savings. Dairy farmers given $9,700 give you three cents per dollar in savings. Etc.

It's paying a lot to get a little in return.

Overspending and perverting our global trade has managed to make the United States of America, as noted earlier in this book, a 101 percent debtor nation. It means that we US citizens are bankrupt.

Doing away with billions of dollars in subsidy programs could get us back on track to prosperity.

Unfortunately, in this country, we don't get to pick and choose where our tax dollars go. They just go. When it comes to subsidies, you, I—everyone—writes checks for large amounts.

For that, we don't so much get cheap prices as we get cheap food. And the results of that are far more damaging in the long term than debt.

As I watch a lone tanker leave the port of Duluth and head toward the channels and locks that will allow it passage to the ocean and beyond, I realize that it could be carrying oats or flour or apples or any number of food products that we export abroad. All of these commodities are relatively healthy foods and ingredients.

I wonder where all the junk food is, so I go looking.

CHAPTER SEVENTEEN

WHY THEY MAKE US FAT

I'm at McDonald's, the new McDonald's, the one that feels like a health food restaurant, where calorie counts align next to price tags on the menu board, where there's an array of salads from which to choose, where oatmeal is advertised on banners as being good for your morning breakfast, and where smoothies are served up fresh in front of you.

Most of the people who come in and out of this particular McDonald's restaurant in Los Angeles aren't overweight at all. They look . . . healthy. Of course, this is LA, where there's a term for even the skinniest of girls who have body fat—"skinny fat"—so I checked out McDonald's in different parts of the country: East Coast, different parts of the West Coast, down south. All operate the same. All attract the same type of customer: guys with names on their shirts, families with little kids, and, most abundantly, senior citizens.

My experiences, of course, are post–*Super Size Me*—the movie that showcased how the giant-size meals at fast food restaurants like McDonald's were contributing to the obesity problem in America.

Now, McDonald's may have changed its theme to be more health conscious, but you can still become quite the chunky monkey if you load up on the products it serves. Still, you could say that about lots of places in America. And subsidies have a lot to do with the reasons why.

We are being served fake food in America: plumped-up chickens, fattened hogs and cattle, and produce treated with pesticides and fertilizers that aren't products of Mother Nature. Pile that on top of our man-made junk food and soft drinks.

The great majority of food produced in the United States comes from factory farms that artificially enhance agricultural products.

A majority of subsidies goes to factory farms.

More than 60 percent of Americans carry in their bodies seven or more pesticides from the foods they consume, according to Centers for Disease Control monitoring. These, make no mistake, are the traces of fake foods in our diets. Agribusinesses and pesticide companies are not required to test for chemicals that might be found in people, not even for compounds that widely contaminate the food supply.

Fake food, as I call it, isn't only dangerous (pesticides can be toxic); it also makes us fat and unhealthy.

In a cover story examining the benefits of organic food, *Time* magazine reported, "The biggest reason not to ignore the food purists is that in a lot of ways they're right. Our diet is indeed killing us, and it's killing the planet, too. Earlier this month [August 2010], the Centers for Disease Control and Prevention in Atlanta released a study revealing that nearly 27% of Americans are now considered obese (that is, more than 20% above their ideal weight), and in nine states, the obesity rate tops 30%. We eat way too much meat—up to 220 lb. per year for every man, woman and child in the U.S.—and only 14% of us consume our recommended five servings of fruits and vegetables per day. Our processed food is dense with salt and swimming in high-fructose corn syrup, two flavors we can't resist. Currently, enough food is manufactured in the U.S. for every American to consume 3,800 calories per day—we need only 2,350 in a healthy diet—and while some of that gets thrown away, most is gobbled up long before it can go stale on the shelves."

The bottom line is that we eat too much, and we eat too much crap manufactured (a more appropriate word than *grown* or *raised* these days) by factory farms.

When we pay subsidies via our tax dollars to corporations that churn out food as a product, we are giving them incentives to churn out volumes of low-quality food at the lowest prices possible. Corporations are in business to make money, not to make nice, healthy meals. Lower costs and more money. Following that line of thinking, the way to lower food costs is to use cheaper ingredients and utilize cheaper ways to grow or raise or *manufacture* food with fertilizers and growth hormones, and completely man-made "sweeteners" for taste.

The woman in front of me in line at McDonald's, for example, is interested only in the items listed on the dollar menu. And for that, she has many choices: chicken, beef, fries, soft drinks. If she bumped up her budget by a few bucks, she could get even more: A value meal—burgers, fries, and Coke— is just $4.99. The sign says the whole meal contains between 920 and 1,160 calories.

Cheap, in most cases, doesn't mean better. And when it comes to food, it certainly doesn't mean healthier. Cheap, when it comes to food, usually means artificial growth enhancements. When these artificial ingredients start entering the food supply chain, look out: Others will follow. Cheap food, too, infects us, in perhaps the unhealthiest of ways. Case in point: high fructose corn syrup.

You cannot whack into a husk of corn and watch the syrup ooze out, like you can, say, by chopping into a maple tree. High fructose corn syrup is a made-up concoction. Scientists mess with corn enzymes to produce a sweet compound. Because corn has been so heavily subsidized, it makes it cheap to produce this stuff—a lot cheaper than cane sugar or maple syrup itself. (Actually, the supply of US maple syrup is shrinking, and prices are rising as global temperatures increase and Canada takes over the market. Canada subsidizes its maple syrup market. But that is another story.)

High fructose corn syrup (not to be confused with plain old corn syrup, which is a different type of food enhancer) is made by changing one type of sugar (glucose) in cornstarch to another (fructose). HFCS is not only cheaper than cane sugar; it also extends the shelf life of processed foods. Sounds like a win-win from a business perspective. Hence, it's become a popular ingredient in many sodas, fruit-flavored drinks, and other processed foods. In other words, the most popular food items on the shelves.

The acclaimed food writer Michael Pollan wrote about this in 2007 in the *New York Times,* saying that subsidies are to blame for the growth in cheap artificial sweeteners and other processed ingredients:

> The farm bill as currently written offers a lot more support
> to the cake than to the root. Like most processed foods, the
> Twinkie is basically a clever arrangement of carbohydrates and

fats teased out of corn, soybeans and wheat—three of the five
commodity crops that the farm bill supports, to the tune of
some $25 billion a year. (Rice and cotton are the others.) For the
last several decades—indeed, for about as long as the American
waistline has been ballooning—U.S. agricultural policy has
been designed in such a way as to promote the overproduction
of these five commodities, especially corn and soy.

Simply, it's cheaper to manufacture artificial sweeteners
(corn syrup) that contain more calories and produce more food
that isn't good for us, because subsidies coax businesses to do so.

A lot has already been written about corn subsidies and
their responsibility for the advent of corn syrup, which has
come to replace cane sugar, and how that development parallels
obesity rates in America.

Most of this stems from a research study published in the
American Journal of Clinical Nutrition in 2007. The study
tracked federal data on obesity, linking it to the increased usage
of HFCS in our diets.

It found that "fructose serves to reward sweet taste that
provides 'calories,' often without much else in the way of nutrition. Second, the intake of soft drinks containing high-fructose
corn syrup (HFCS) or sucrose has risen in parallel with the epidemic of obesity, which suggests a relation."

The analysis goes on to say, "The intake of dietary fructose
increased significantly from 1970 to 2000. There has been a
25 percent increase in available 'added sugars' during this
period."

To put this into context, before America was even discovered, humans ingested just a few sugary items, reports the

AJCN. "For example, honey, dates, raisins, molasses, and figs have a content of less than 10% of this sugar, whereas a fructose content of 5–10% by weight is found in grapes, raw apples, apple juice, persimmons, and blueberries. Milk, the main nourishment for infants, has essentially no fructose, and neither do most vegetables and meats, which indicates that human beings had little dietary exposure to fructose before the mass production of sugar," it says.

Today, "Most fructose in the American diet comes not from fresh fruit, but from HFCS or sucrose (sugar) that is found in soft drinks and sweets, which typically have few other nutrients," the *AJCN* reports. "Soft drink consumption, which provides most of this fructose, has increased dramatically in the past 6 decades, rising from a per-person consumption of 90 servings per year (approximately 2 servings per week) in 1942 to that of 600 servings per year (approximately 2 servings per day). More than 50% of preschool children consume some calorie-sweetened beverages. Children of this age would not normally be exposed to fructose, let alone in these high amounts. Because both HFCS and sucrose are 'delivery vehicles for fructose,' the load of fructose has increased in parallel with the use of sugar."

Now let's see how fructose turns into fat.

Sugar, as we should know by watching a child go bonkers after eating a candy bar, provides energy. Sometimes too much. The extra amount turns into fat. Medically speaking, sugar provides energy for cell functions. After food is digested, sugar is released into the bloodstream. In response, the pancreas secretes insulin, which directs the muscle and fat cells to take in that sugar. Cells either obtain energy from sugar or convert it to fat for long-term storage.

Too much sugar and not enough energy expended makes Freddy fat.

This connection—from corn to HFCS to Fat Freddy—has been slammed by many researchers because, they say (and rightly), subsidies' effect on retail prices is marginal (as we have seen in this book), and eliminating subsidies wouldn't do much to stem the price and, by extension, the ability of Fat Freddy to gobble down as much unhealthy food as he wishes.

"The magnitude of the effects of U.S. farm commodity subsidy policy on obesity must be very small," researchers at the University of California, Davis say. "Farm subsidies have had small effects (up or down) on most farm commodity prices, much smaller effects on retail prices, and even smaller effects on consumption. Compared with other factors, the policy-induced differences in relative prices among various farm commodities have played only a tiny role in determining excess food consumption and obesity in the United States. U.S. farm subsidies have many critics. A variety of arguments and evidence can be presented to show that the programs are ineffective, wasteful, or unfair. Eliminating farm subsidy programs could solve some of these problems, but would not even make a dent in America's obesity problem."

Even USDA researchers now call into question the relationship between HFCS and obesity.

What I am about to say I mean: For a bunch of smart people, they sure are stupid. It isn't about the *price* of food, you ninnies; it's about the *cost* of making food. And this didn't begin today—it began decades ago, when corn was super cheap. The model well in place, the machine began to turn out fake food by the ton. There is no disputing the amount and the kind of food most Americans eat. The question many are struggling with is whether this matters.

HFCS proponents say sugar is sugar, whether corn or cane, and therefore the caloric count and result (fatness) is the same. That argument actually sounds rather logical. That is, until you back up and remember that HFCS is artificial and cane isn't.

A research study at the University of Southern California's Keck School of Medicine discovered why that matters. The study shows that HFCS "is delivering a megadose of fructose (a sweeter and more harmful form of sugar)—far higher than previously thought. . . .

"Contrary to prevailing assumptions, the findings show that the HFCS (a mixture of glucose and fructose produced from corn) in popular sodas may be as high as 65 percent fructose, nearly 20 percent higher than commonly assumed.

"'The elevated fructose levels in the sodas most Americans drink are of particular concern because of the negative effects fructose has on the body,' explained study author Michael Goran, Ph.D., professor in the departments of preventive medicine, physiology and biophysics, and pediatrics at the Keck School."

HFCS delivers more fructose than cane sugar—lots more—according to the USC study.

The World Health Organization took up the argument of whether increased subsidies equal increased calories. Surprise, surprise: It found that they do matter. "The studies showed that taxes and subsidies on food have the potential to influence consumption considerably and improve health, particularly when they are large," the WHO reports. In no uncertain terms it declares: "The World Health Organization (WHO) has recommended the use of fiscal policy to influence food prices in ways that encourage healthy eating."

So there you have it. There are, of course, many issues that affect obesity. All of them make sense. We are less active than in previous decades, choosing to watch television or play video games or participate in other sedentary activities more than we move about. This means we use less energy and burn off less sugar. We eat more. And here's the real kernel (sorry) of the story: Manufacturers use more cheap (artificial) ingredients.

The WHO explains: "The current obesity epidemic reflects an increasingly 'obesogenic' food environment and long-term changes in activity levels and energy expenditure. Currently, financial incentives favor the consumption of highly processed, energy-dense foods since it is consistently cheaper, in terms of energy content for a given price, than less energy-dense and often more nutrient-rich foods. Taxing less healthy foods could create a financial incentive for consumers to avoid them. Studies on the effect of manipulating food prices show that both individual consumers and population groups do respond as predicted."

I must admit that it was a gallant effort, this fake by corporate America—the corn growers—and Big Government to dissuade public opinion from believing that HFCS (more of it anyway) is in any way tied to obesity. And that—say it isn't so—subsidies of corn that we turn into HFCS are at the bottom of it all. But the fact is, subsidies make you fat.

Now, here's how. Just as a chicken is pumped full of antibiotics that are meant to add body weight, we are also pumped full of artificial ingredients that make us gain weight.

Subsidies encourage the production of massive amounts of food because farmers get more subsidies that way. This manifests as more bad food. The "quota" encouragement that subsidies provide leads food producers to figure out ways to produce more products at cheaper costs. Whatever the price at the checkout counter is, it doesn't matter. The subsidy, by then, is spent.

Wanna risk using more expensive ingredients or feeds or fertilizers? Why? That risk doesn't make good business sense.

Many books have been written about the benefits of "organic" and "natural" eating. Maria Rodale's *Organic Manifesto* is one. In it, she writes, "We are all in the same situation to varying degrees. We are all being poisoned, contaminated, sterilized, and eventually exterminated by the synthetic chemicals we have used for the last 100 years to grow our food and maintain our lawns, to make our lives easier and 'cleaner' and our food 'cheaper.'"

That's alarming prose. Now add obesity into the mix and there is reason to be afraid, very afraid, of subsidized, i.e. fake, food.

After reviewing the major studies and research on the subject, the WHO concluded that "food taxes and subsidies can influence consumption in high-income countries and that imposing substantial taxes on fattening foods may improve health outcomes such as body weight and chronic disease risk. The findings support current recommendations that taxes and subsidies should be included as part of a comprehensive strategy to prevent obesity."

The policy the WHO recommends is almost exactly the opposite of the one we have in America. We subsidize and give tax *breaks* to food producers that manufacture "products" we eat that make us fat. Therefore, call me crazy, we should really be weaning ourselves off fake food and getting back to the real stuff—and taxing the bad stuff if we must.

Weight gain and the associated diseases that come with it aren't the only physically harmful things that go along with subsidies. Subsidies engender violence. Indeed, they connect the fat with the fanatical.

CHAPTER EIGHTEEN

WHY THEY MAKE US HATED

The frustration and despair caused by these [agricultural] policies undermine American security. Many people who depend on agriculture for their survival, both as a source of nourishment and a means of acquiring wealth, perceive U.S. farm policy as part of an anti-American narrative in which Washington wants to keep the rest of the world locked in poverty. Indeed, in a survey of anti-American sentiment around the world, the Pew Research Center found a majority of respondents in more than a dozen countries were convinced that U.S. farm and trade policies increased the "poverty gap" worldwide. These sentiments transcended geographic, ethnic, or religious boundaries. In such an environment, terrorist ringleaders find fertile ground for their message of hate and violence.—*Daniel Griswold, Stephen Slivinski, and Christopher Preble, "Six Reasons to Kill Farm Subsidies and Trade Barriers"*

The above is how the Cato Institute in Washington explains how farm subsidies can be linked to terrorism against America.

The dots are rather simple to connect: We fund certain artificial prices that result in overproduction. Our subsidized export product gets shipped overseas. This corrupts those markets. The local producers there get pissed off at us. They lash out in violent ways.

Eviscerate hope from the shelves and people will latch on to other goods as a means to survival. In inner-city neighborhoods in the United States, drugs and crime collide in a world without hope. In some foreign countries, terrorism becomes the drug *and* the crime.

Our agricultural policies seed this environment. Government policy is what terrorists use to justify and rationalize their sick behavior. Subsidy policies emotionlessly take swipes at entire groups of *people*. Those *people* then swipe back—at us *people*. Often we don't even fully understand our government policies, let alone the anger they ignite. Yet we suffer from them just the same.

As natural resources become ever more scarce and commoditized, American agricultural policy is increasingly important in the global picture. The human factor, or human quotient, becomes, then, more and more important to consider, along with the effect of what we do and what that does to the world. Improvements in technology, innovation, and transportation have given us great benefits as a society. But they also have their pitfalls. And those at the bottom of society's income ladder feel the steps mankind makes the most—because all too often, those steps land on the tops of their heads.

Farming and terrorism may seem like unlikely bedfellows. So too may fishing and piracy. The networks are there, however. And it's time that we tune in to the connection between arms and agriculture.

Let's first take a look at how the largely subsidized commercial fishing industry promulgates piracy: Off the coast of

Somalia, international fishing fleets have set up shop because, well, they can. There isn't a Somali coast guard to prevent overfishing or enforce maritime law. In fact, the United Nations, in a report, says the lax sea policing has caused a fishing "free for all" that illegally plunders Somali stocks and freezes out local fishermen. Ishaan Thardoor, writing in *Time* magazine, cites another UN report that estimates that $300 million worth of seafood is stolen from the Somali coastline each year:

> In the face of this, impoverished Somalis living by the sea have been forced over the years to defend their own fishing expeditions out of ports such as Eyl, Kismayo and Harardhere—all now considered to be pirate dens. Somali fishermen, whose industry was always small-scale, lacked the advanced boats and technologies of their interloping competitors, and also complained of being shot at by foreign fishermen with water cannons and firearms.

"A 2006 study published in the journal *Science* predicted that the current rate of commercial fishing would virtually empty the world's oceanic stocks by 2050," the *Time* story notes. Somalia is part of what is known as the Horn of Africa, comprising that country as well as Ethiopia, Eritrea, and Djibouti. The waters off this coastline boast some of the most fertile fishing grounds in the world. Unlike other parts of the Indian Ocean, where fishermen have to resort to extreme measures such as dynamite fishing to haul in fish aplenty, the Horn offers a variety of fish in abundance—attractive bait for international commercial fishing fleets.

I traveled to the Horn of Africa. Most of the 100 million people who live in the region go without at least one meal per day.

Besides the fish off their coasts, coffee, bananas, and live-stock are the countries' biggest exports, although it's difficult to track these things, because most trade is unofficial and undocu-mented. Facilities are worn, and regulation is sparse. Despera-tion, of course, abounds.

It hits you as soon as you land: From the airport in Ethio-pia to the capital, Addis Ababa, for example, the roads are strewn with people walking. The luxury of transportation—whether private or public—escapes the masses. Dirt roads bounce you through ramshackle neighborhoods and dead fields. The farmland isn't arable. Soil, like the people, finds it hard to get proper nourishment.

Bounce you go, on bald tires unfit for driving and shocks that remind you just how close the roof is to your head. Out on the street, children swarm, though not as in other parts of the world where I've been. They swarm like bees at the hive, pleading for a coin, a pen, a piece of paper—anything that is tangible and that could, come barter time, mean life. One man offers me his child to take with me. "To take care of. For a better life in America."

Off the coast, the tragedy continues: High-seas trawlers from countries as far-flung as South Korea, Japan, and Spain have operated down the Somali coast, often illegally and without licenses, for the better part of two decades, the UN says. Pub-lished reports discuss how these ships often fly flags from nations such as Belize and Bahrain, which further helps them skirt international regulations and evade censure from their home countries. *Time* quotes Tsuma Charo of the Nairobi-based

East African Seafarers Assistance Program as saying flat out that "illegal trawling has fed the piracy problem."

Now think about piracy in the larger context of terrorism. Parallel lines can be drawn between fishing and farming. The difference is that with farming, we don't go to another country, overexploit the land (instead of the sea), and skip off with our bounty. With farming we overexploit our own land and ship off our bounty. Ironically, this has the same result in many of the same places: It destroys markets and jobs and turns people into festering haters.

Broken down to its basic meaning, "hate" is an intense hostility deriving from fear, anger, or sense of injury. When people fear for their lives or livelihoods, hate ensues. When people are angry over US policy, hate ensues. And when people feel that they have been personally injured due to the damage caused by that policy, hate ensues.

In attempting to explain the question of "Why do they hate us?" President George W. Bush said, "They hate our freedoms—our freedom of religion, our freedom of speech, our freedom to vote and assemble and disagree with each other." And in perhaps his most elegant address to the nation, Bush said, "America was targeted for attack because we're the brightest beacon for freedom and opportunity in the world. And no one will keep that light from shining."

In their book *Why Do People Hate America?* authors Ziauddin Sardar and Merryl Wyn Davies provide a foreign (they live in London) perspective on the question.

According to them, "In rhetoric and symbols it is the *idea* of America, America's idea of itself, that has been at the centre

194 THOMAS M. KOSTIGEN

of national consciousness since the events of 11 September. Love of one's homeland is not unique to America, nor is it to be derided. What is at issue is how this sense of identity is employed to limit or act as a substitute for political debate about the policies and actions taken in the name of the nation at home and abroad."

Their point is well taken: Just as we are proud to be American, a Somali is proud to be from Somalia. Insert any countryman and his country here. Therefore it is not the jealousy of our freedoms that creates hate; it is our ignorance of and intrusions upon the freedoms of those abroad.

New York Times columnist Thomas Friedman took up this issue in a column titled "Farm Subsidies Help Feed Terrorism." He wrote that when subsidies banish more people into poverty, terrorism rises. "Sure, poverty doesn't cause terrorism—no one is killing for a raise. But poverty is great for the terrorism business because poverty creates humiliation and stifled aspirations and forces many people to leave their traditional farms to join the alienated urban poor in the cities—all conditions that spawn terrorists." Friedman quoted Robert Wright, author of *Nonzero*, as saying, "If the sons of American janitors can go die in Iraq to keep us safe, then American cotton farmers, whose average net worth is nearly $1 million, can give up their subsidies to keep us safe. Opening our markets to farm products and textiles would be critical to drawing many nations—including Muslim ones—more deeply into the interdependent web of global capitalism and ultimately democracy."

For all of his willingness to create messages of hope and establish dialogues with nations opposed to the American way of life, President Obama is no better at diluting hate from abroad. In fact, when it comes to farm subsidies, the government under his watch is actually less forthcoming than previous ones, which further promulgates the system of mistrust that can turn into hate.

According to the Environmental Working Group, whose data I've leaned on for this book, its 2007 database "used previously unavailable records to uncover nearly 500,000 individuals who had never been identified as farm subsidy recipients. Many had been shielded by their involvement in byzantine mazes of co-ops and corporate entity shell games. . . . Unfortunately for our 2010 update, the data that provided such a revelatory account of just who receives the billions paid out in the maze of federal farm subsidy programs is no longer available to us."

Why? you ask.

EWG quotes Chris Clayton, an editor at the DTN/ Progressive Farmer Ag Policy news service: "That's because Congress changed the wording of the 1614 provision in the 2008 farm bill from USDA 'shall' release such data to USDA 'may' release such data. USDA has since decided not to release the information. According to USDA officials, the database can cost as much as $6.7 million to produce, and Congress did not appropriate money to compile the database."

Amazing, the effects of one word change on EWG's—and our—ability to see why farm subsidies are so corrupt. Moreover, this furthers ignorance. When we don't know the sources of corruption, how can we the people demand change? We can't. We end up looking for other sources and causes of hatred toward America—religious, political, and cultural enmity. Obfuscation shifts the plate away from food and other subsidies.

But let's take a real hard look at a case in point.

It was the following story reported by National Public Radio that actually got me going to find out how subsidies "here" can lead to hate for Americans "over there":

> In northern Mozambique, cotton farmer Americo Candido Asan says US subsidies drive prices ever lower, making it difficult for him to make a profit.
>
> Candido, 35, plants five acres of cotton each year. He does all of the work in his fields by hand. Once a year at harvest time, the local cotton company sends a four-wheel-drive truck to pick up his sacks of cotton.
>
> "Here in Mozambique we don't have any help from the government," Candido says. "So if they have subsidies, it means American farmers have everything prepared for them. But here we are using our own money, our own labor, and the price always becomes lower and lower because of them—the Americans—it's not fair." . . .
>
> Cotton exporters say this part of northern Mozambique should be able to sell cotton at competitive prices. It has plentiful rainfall. Labor, at about $1 a day, is cheap. The main roads have been rebuilt after a lengthy civil war and are in excellent shape, by African standards. There's a functioning railway linking the area with a port on the Indian Ocean.
>
> But growers complain that they're barely making a living from their crops, and in recent years, several large cotton companies have gone out of business.

The bottom line the story points out is that US subsidies hamper African farmers' ability to farm.

An Oxfam report on the hypocrisy of subsidies is also eye-opening: According to a 2003 story in the United Nations' online magazine *Africa Recovery,* "In West Africa, losses in export revenue outstrip the amount of economic assistance provided by Washington. Mali received $37.7 million in US aid in 2001 but incurred losses of $43 million, due in large part to US subsidies, Oxfam reports." Such practices cancel our goodwill around the world—not just in developing countries.

Canada and Mexico are none too pleased with American subsidies, either. Canadian officials are upset—and that in and of itself takes some doing. They say Canada is being forced to respond in kind to the types of subsidies the United States forks over to farmers. According to published reports, officials are also mad about our decision to impose big tariffs and duties on Canadian lumber. A quick look to America's southern border doesn't bring a happy picture, either. Mexico is unhappy with what it feels is an abrogation of the North American Free Trade Agreement for many agricultural products—such as sugar, as discussed in chapter 7.

No matter the place on the planet, ill will can turn to hate or worse. According to an article in *Scientific American* dissecting the psychology of terror, "Most terrorists are not mentally ill; rather they rationally weigh the costs and benefits of their actions and conclude that terrorism is profitable."

Speaking to this point: former Canadian finance minister John Manley observes that the United States would find it hard to persuade Afghan farmers to switch from growing lucrative poppy crops (profits from which help to fund terrorist organizations) to less lucrative food crops when the Americans are busy subsidizing their own farmers by tens of billions of dollars a year. "We want these people not producing opium. We want them producing food and selling it into the world markets, and then maybe we'll find less of a draw on overseas development assistance and charity from countries like Canada and the United States," he said.

Nicholas Stern, chief economist at the World Bank, is blunt about America's leadership role. Quoted in the UN's *Africa Recovery,* he says, "It is hypocritical to preach the advantages of free trade and free markets and then erect obstacles in precisely those markets in which developing countries have a comparative advantage."

"Poor countries don't want our pity; they want our respect," the Cato Institute reasons. "To the extent that American security depends on the expansion of liberal democratic institutions and free market economics, Washington must be particularly sensitive to policies that exacerbate poverty in the developing world. . . . The long-term interests of Americans as consumers, producers, taxpayers, and citizens of the world should not be sacrificed for the short-term interests of a small minority of farmers."

Far out in the hinterlands of Ethiopia, along the border with Somalia, a farmer stands by the bank of a dry riverbed. He tells me that he hopes to grow sorghum. I look around at the little plot of land he's working. It's dry as a bone. Weeds he'll pick, and soil he'll turn. He's hopeful. A large-brimmed sun hat keeps away some of the heat. His pants are rolled up to the knees, and his shirtsleeves are ripped off. He stands, leaning on one hip, and twists a dry piece of weed between his fingers.

The area, he tells me, used to be quite fertile. So much so—he points to a ruined palace on a faraway hill—that the country's rulers would come and watch over the land as it was tilled.

No more.

I think to myself that even if the land somehow magically transformed itself and became arable again, other factors would slap him back down and put him out of business.

Even during times of famine, Ethiopian farmers had warehouses full of surplus grain. "A group of Ethiopian farmers and grain traders sent a petition to the prime minister's office, urging the government to seek money from donor nations to buy local grain for food-aid distribution before bringing in more from outside. The petitioners warned that if warehouses aren't cleared out soon, there won't be money to pay for this year's harvest or space to store it. Domestic prices will collapse. Loans will go unpaid, farmers will plant less next year and the cycle of famine will spin on," the *Wall Street Journal* reported in an article, "As U.S. Food-Aid Policy Enriches Farmers, Poor Nations Cry Foul." It said, "Rival exporting powers such as the European Union and Australia charge that Washington uses food aid to dump surplus commodities, in effect subsidizing U.S. growers."

Indeed, it is not just we citizens of the world who suffer at subsidies' long arm—it is the world itself. The planet is being unduly affected by subsidies.

CHAPTER NINETEEN

WRECKING THE ENVIRONMENT

It's a hard hike. I'm in Southeast Asia, in the jungles of Borneo, skirting along the border between Malaysia and Indonesia. It's the rainy season, and the mud gets like quicksand in places—sticking me hip-high so I can't move.

My translator and native guides and I take turns helping each other out. My trail shoes, despite the tight laces, slip off constantly. We wheeze, sweat, and trek for hours, deeper and deeper into the rain forest. Even with the thick tree cover, the mud is like wet cement. What's happened is deforestation. It has corrupted the soil, making it soft where it should be hard, weak where it should be strong. Deforestation here is the worst in the world. It has not only weakened the planet's ability to make oxygen (as we know, plants help make the air we breathe); it has a much more "touchable" effect: It wrecks the ground we walk on.

I sweat through my clothes, take a seat on a felled piece of timber, and look out at the scorched acres all around me.

Dirt. That's what it comes down to. We're subsidizing the destruction of the ground beneath our feet, the air we breathe, and the water we consume in myriad ways—all because we aren't tending properly to the earth's soil.

Only 8 percent of the earth's land mass is arable. That means the entire world population is directly reliant on a very small sliver of dirt for its food. And we're overworking it, result-ing in massive erosion.

We lose approximately 1 percent of our topsoil every year due to farming. In fact, humans are responsible for around 80 percent of all land degradation, according to various esti-mates. It isn't easily replaced: Soil regeneration takes between 200 years and a million years.

When we create incentives via subsidies for farmers to overproduce on their land, it wreaks havoc on dirt.

E–The Environmental Magazine reports that "one reason why agriculture can be so detrimental to soils is because of the sheer scale of most farming operations today. According to USDA, since 1900 the number of farms has fallen by 63 percent, while the average farm size has risen by 67 percent. In 1900, the average farm size was less than 100 acres; in 2002 it was more than 400 acres. Farm operations have also become increasingly specialized, from an average of about five commodities per farm in 1900 to an average of one per farm in 2000. Most impor-tant, the USDA says that all of this has taken place with no vari-ation in the amount of land being farmed. . . .

"While individual farms have shrunk, yields have increased, thanks to growing reliance on pesticides, herbicides and fertil-izers. But while this practice has allowed farmers to control pests and nutrients in the short term, the net result is artificial enrich-ment of overworked soils that often lose stability."

That means that repeatedly planting the same crops on the same land is bad for soil.

We are, at current regeneration rates, losing 40 times as much soil as is being replaced around the world. In Borneo, as I've described, it's very apparent. But all over, soil degradation negatively affects cropland, slighting productivity by 29 percent and sweeping 39 percent of our rangeland productivity away. In dollar terms, soil erosion costs America alone $37.6 billion. Worldwide, damage from soil erosion is estimated to cost $400 billion per year in losses, researchers at Cornell University calculate.

Yeah, that got my attention, too. How much are we spending on subsidies each year again? And what are we getting in return?

It is thoughtlessness and idiocracy that will cause the earth to become unsustainable for us to live on. We're abusing our rights. It's high time we exercised them to do what is right and good for the planet we live on—our future.

By eliminating most subsidies, we could, with the stroke of a pen, get the environmental movement to shut up. Wouldn't that be nice? I am one of the ones out there in the world yapping about conservation, recycling, and whatnot. I would like nothing better than to be able to zip it.

This is why I can't: Worldwide, we subsidize more and more of our existence without regard to consequence. We haven't thought through the interdependence—the ecology—of all that we consume. We need to, right down to the last bit of dirt that is needed to grow our food—before it's blown away. Just one teaspoon of dirt, to make my point, contains more creatures than there are humans on the planet.

Dirt is linked to our freshwater supply, our clean air, and, of course, our food supply.

When it rains, soil traps and absorbs that water for us, whether in plants or by filling our aquifers, rivers, lakes, and streams. If not for soil, rainwater would run off the land and into the oceans; continents would be barren wastelands.

This is what is happening in Borneo, the most species-rich place on earth. The coastal wetlands are being ruined, animals are being forced from their land. And the mangroves that serve to protect people and communities from storms are being washed away.

When trees are knocked down, the soil beneath them weakens. And don't think for a second that this timber isn't somehow tied into US subsidies. According to the *Christian Science Monitor,* an elaborate scam has been devised to take advantage of American taxpayer dollars while at the same time increasing deforestation around the world, even in a faraway place like Borneo.

It is in fact a scam called "splash and dash," according to the *Monitor,* that takes advantage of the $1-per-gallon biofuel subsidy. Here's how it works: Palm oil grown on Malaysian Borneo is shipped to the US, where it's mixed with petroleum diesel to produce "biofuel." This makes it eligible for the federal subsidy program.

Palm oil comes from palm trees; knocking them down creates deforestation and land degradation. Let's remember, soil serves to produce oxygen—the air we breathe. To grade-school it, plants store carbon that gets converted into organic compounds (with the help of the sun) and produces oxygen. No soil, no land plants. Healthy soils can also act as important carbon sinks themselves, storing carbon that might otherwise enter the atmosphere. More carbon dioxide, more global warming.

The circle goes round and round, and until we put a stop to the earth's biggest interrupters, we are in for a big loss of life.

Cornell University's *Chronicle Online* discussed a study on erosion: " 'Soil erosion is second only to population growth as the biggest environmental problem the world faces,' said David Pimentel, professor of ecology at Cornell. 'Yet the problem, which is growing ever more critical, is being ignored, because who gets excited about dirt?'

"Almost 100 percent—99.7 percent, actually—of human food comes from cropland, which is shrinking by more than 10 million hectares (almost 37,000 square miles) a year due to soil erosion, Pimentel reports, while more people than ever— more than 3.7 billion people—are malnourished. . . .

"The United States is losing soil 10 times faster—and China and India are losing soil 30 to 40 times faster—than the natural replenishment rate."

To be sure, we need agriculture. But farming at the rate we do is plundering. It's also how we farm and what we use to farm that is causing environmental degradation of such magnitude.

"It's all about the soil," Jules Dervaes told me. Dervaes is an "urban homesteader." He turns out factory-farm-like yields from his small patch of land in Pasadena, California. On just one-tenth of an acre, he produces more than 350 vegetables, fruits, and berries, adding up to a 7,000-pound harvest annually!

I visited Jules's little farm, but I had to drive by twice to make sure that I was in the right place: You'd never know it was a commercial farm. The Dervaes "farm" is on a typical suburban street. His neighbors have similar homes to his. But on more careful inspection, you take note of the soil: Every bit of it is taken up by some type of producing species. The front yard is home to flowers, herbs, and spices. The driveway is lined with berry bushes. Even the often-lost space between sidewalk and street grows Swiss chard.

It's all about the soil.

Jules's daughter Anais works the front-porch stand, where Meyer lemons and navel oranges were for sale the day I was there. A family had driven all the way up from San Diego to visit the farm and try its organic produce. Anais, the daughter, was excited to inform me that the farm had surpassed 7,000 pounds of product in 2010. "And that's just produce," she said. "Not eggs."

I reminded her what Jules had told me about the importance of soil. "We were just talking about that last night. It's not just what grows on top, it's also what grows on the bottom and underneath that matters," she said. Indeed, the Dervaes homestead is one and a half feet higher than their neighbors' homes because of all the composting and soil turnover they do.

As most farmers know, growing the same crop in the same place season after season disproportionately depletes the soil of important nutrients for plant growth. Doing what Dervaes does—a practice called polyculture—provides a variety of benefits to the soil. It helps avoid the buildup of pathogens and prevents pests that often attack single-species farms. This kind of rotation also balances out the fertility demands on crops because it avoids the excessive depletion of soil nutrients that a single variety demands. Another benefit to the soil comes by alternating deep-rooted and shallow-rooted plants.

But farmers aren't subsidized the same across crop varieties. Not even close. Not even close to close. Just five crops amount to 90 percent of the total subsidy payments the federal government doles out to farmers each year. Rotating a variety of crops, therefore, isn't in the best financial interests of farmers.

Still, pillaging the land like this over time hurts farmers, too. They can't grow their crops on dead soil. They know that.

Dervaes enlists a number of methods to work the earth and keep the soil alive and strong, including companion planting, saving seeds, and raising certain livestock for manure.

Big agricultural businesses that own factory farms and provide us with most of the food in our diets don't cave easily—even to Mother Nature.

Enter artificial fertilizers and pesticides. Lovely stuff, these toxins. They allow Big Ag to keep planting in places nature would have disallowed decades ago.

Pesticides have been around for thousands of years. Forty-five hundred years ago, sulfur was used to ward off pests. Mercury, lead, and arsenic have also been used. Indeed, arsenic was the pesticide of choice until the "pesticide era" kicked in, in the 1940s. Then artificial pesticides were born and the world became a very different place, a more toxic place. And a place where natural rules no longer apply. But wait, there's more.

In the early part of the 20th century synthetic fertilizers began to be mixed with artificial pesticides such as DDT, and became a toxic cocktail that got farmers drunk on their use: crop production went through the roof.

Emboldened by federal subsidies that paid them to grow, grow, grow, farmers lapped up fertilizers and pesticides, increasing their use twenty-fold and fifty-fold, respectively.

Now, more than 100 million tons of artificial fertilizer gets used annually, and some 2.5 million tons of pesticides.

Similarly, agricultural production rose dramatically, so much so that America had a great deal more to export and began to dominate world markets.

All well and good, you might believe. What is wrong with artificial crop stimulants that increase—relatively inexpensively, by the way—our ability to grow food? We need to feed a growing population, right? We need to increase our trade and exports.

If the ramifications of artificial fertilizers, pesticides, and growth hormones, which also came into fashion in the early to mid-20th century, weren't so bad for us and the environment, it would certainly be right to say, "Have at it." But that isn't the case.

According to the Stockholm Convention on Persistent Organic Pollutants, 10 of the 12 most dangerous and persistent organic chemicals on earth are pesticides.

Gentle reminder: This is the stuff used to grow our food that we're talking about.

As if ingesting indirectly these things wasn't bad enough, most of the sprayed insecticides and herbicides—upwards of 95 percent—end up landing someplace other than where they are supposed to land, including on other crops, air, water, and soil. This is called "pesticide drift." It's a major cause of water and soil pollution.

The truly bizarro thing is that—straight out of a science fiction flick—pests can develop resistances to pesticides, necessitating that new pesticides be created. Otherwise, look out: three-headed monster!

Remember that awful disaster in Bhopal, India? The chemical spill at that plant that ended up killing thousands of people was a pesticide.

Synthetic fertilizers, which rely on petroleum for their composition, also lead to environmental problems, drying up land, increasing the amount of ammonia runoff (a by-product), and increasing the amount of greenhouse gases in the atmosphere.

Climate change and scorched earth may not be the best results one could hope for by farming. But in an economic and political environment that encourages overproduction, those are the results of today's big farms.

Cato's Daniel Griswold qualifies the environmental destruction created by subsidies. In a 2005 article for the Property & Environment Research Center, he wrote,

> A central if unstated purpose of US farm policy is to maintain "the rural way of life," which translates into promoting production of commodities that would not be economical under competitive, free-market conditions. This often means producing selected crops under conditions less favorable than the land and climate in other countries. As a result, trade barriers intensify production in countries that do not have a comparative advantage, necessitating more intense use of fertilizers and other inputs. Similar national priorities explain why farmers in Japan, Korea, and Switzerland on average use far more fertilizer per acre than those in Australia, New Zealand, and less developed countries where the same crops can be grown under more naturally favorable conditions.
>
> According to the World Resources Institute, agriculture is the biggest source of nutrient and pesticide runoff into rivers and lakes in the United States. . . .
>
> "Even where fertilizers and pesticides are not used intensively, the mere act of plowing soil eliminates forest and grass cover, leaving soil exposed for weeks at a time and vulnerable to erosion. Erosion can result in the buildup of silt in nearby rivers and downstream lakes.

Worldwide, agriculture accounts for two-thirds of freshwater use, mostly for irrigation of cropland. In the United States, subsidies for agricultural water use amount to $2 billion or more annually. Those subsidies prop up uneconomical types of farming (such as growing cotton in the Arizona desert), divert water from residential and industrial users who would be willing to pay market rates, and further damage the environment. According to one study, 25 percent of irrigated farmland in the United States suffers from excessive salinity caused by irrigation. Ending farm subsidies and protection, as well as related water subsidies, would reduce environmental damage while freeing water resources for more economically justified uses.

The higher prices for farmland raise the cost of acquiring and maintaining environmental preserves, parkland, forests, or other land-use alternatives that are more likely to preserve habitat and biodiversity.

And subsidies do no better at sea.

Farm subsidies directly lead to ocean pollution, a number of researchers say. Fertilizers and pesticides kill the oxygen in oceans, seas, rivers, and lakes. Especially along shorelines. These smothered-to-death areas are the so-called dead zones. And they are growing at an alarming rate. Dead zones now encompass at least 14,000 square miles of ocean—bigger than the state of Maryland.

They are patchy. The Environmental Working Group, in an analysis, "found that the vast majority of [Gulf] fertilizer pollution comes from a relatively small area of heavily subsidized cropland along the Mississippi and its tributaries where tax-payer funded commodity spending overwhelms water quality related conservation spending by more than 500 to 1. Shifting a modest portion of commodity subsidies, particularly the por-tion that goes to the largest and wealthiest growers, into pro-grams that encourage more careful fertilizer use, wetland restoration and the planting of streamside buffers of grass and trees to absorb runoff, could reduce dead zone pollution signifi-cantly while also boosting the bottom line for family farms."

The EWG analysis showed that farmers flush more than $300 million of nitrogen fertilizer down the Mississippi River each spring.

Nice to know where your tax dollars end up, isn't it?

Gulf residents, already suffering the consequences of our thirst for oil, get to enjoy the literal shit that we underwrite via our taxes and that makes its way downstream. And it doesn't stop there or with them.

Across the ocean, to the shores of lands far away, our sub-sidies go. The people and places there find no better treatment. They end up living with our government-funded death zones offshore and different kinds of death zones onshore.

In short, our subsidies produce very bad things and incite very bad people. They are bad for us, bad for foreign countries, and bad for the planet.

In Borneo, I have to scramble out of the rain forest I am in because the timber operators are due back. These are the gang-sters who chop down the trees and add so much to the earth's troubles. If I'm found investigating them and the land they destroy, they'll kill me, I'm told. They are famously called the "timber mafia" in these parts, and I'm keen not to have to come face to face with any of them, as I know that I'd end up face-down in the dirt somewhere. They benefit enormously from our subsidies that encourage demand for biofuel and the palm oil that is famously shipped from Borneo to America.

I make it out of the jungle safely at sunset.

The locals I am with say they are shut out from the market by the timber mafia. And they are more afraid of storms, because the trees are no longer there to protect their homes. In unimaginable ways, these are our tax dollars at work.

Letting the long light shine down on those who reap the most from America's subsidy programs may further enlighten us about the real America in which we live.

So let's cut to the chase and name names.

CHAPTER TWENTY

WHO BENEFITS

Those who benefit the most from subsidies are powerful interest groups, corporations, and institutions that actually don't need the money at all. Sure, the federal assistance helps make business strong and facilitates growth. But tax breaks, exemptions, quota payments, land deals, and direct payments are boardroom topics—strategies put together by men and women in dark pin-striped suits, not the people whom subsidies were designed to help.

"You probably were sitting next to a farmer at the Metropolitan Club today," says EWG's Ken Cook. I had just regaled Ken with my experience of lunching at the "coat and tie required," "no cell phones allowed" club in downtown Washington, DC. It's a very fancy place where the rich and the political establishment hobnob. "Farmers today are businessmen."

Picture businesspeople gathered around a table in a conference room, making decisions based on the numbers and data put before them in some PowerPoint presentation. These aren't farmers in overalls, workers in blue-collared shirts or hard hats. They aren't the types of people we would ever think of when we hear the words "federal assistance." These people are the polar opposites of those who stand hat-in-hand in a food line. In fact, the biggest recipients of subsidies *profit* from those standing in food lines. (The federal food stamp program is littered with subsidy recipients who use the program as another way to sell their products at artificial prices.)

Big corporations and wealthy individuals. Year after year, they take billions of dollars from the Internal Revenue Service and spend it, or save it, or invest it, as the case may be.

Multinational energy and steel companies, as we've seen, profit immensely from lucrative subsidy programs. Big Ag, too. "From 1995–2009 the largest and wealthiest top 10 percent of farm program recipients received 74 percent of all farm subsidies with an average total payment over 15 years of $445,127 per recipient—hardly a safety net for small struggling farmers," Cook's EWG found in an analysis of farm subsidies. This top 10 percent earns on average $268,227 a year. That's household income. And that's for very large farms. Not bad take-home pay.

Meanwhile, the bottom 80 percent of farmers received an average total payment of just $8,682 per recipient, according to the EWG. These farmers earn on average less than $50,000 in household income, according to the USDA. That sits at about the national average. Still not so bad.

I always get a little lost in the numbers and percentages thrown around by data firms. And the adjectives *large* and *wealthy* don't conjure up much for me, either (except a fat, rich guy), so I went looking for a better image of a federal subsidy recipient.

Well, there's Ted Turner, the largest landowner in the US and the billionaire behind CNN. He gets federal subsidy money. There's a Rockefeller. Sports stars. Even late-night talk show host David Letterman received a federal subsidy. These aren't anomalies.

Residential/lifestyle farms are by far the biggest share of all farms in America, comprising almost half of all farms in the country. Lower-sales operations and farms worked by retired individuals (retirement farms) account for the next big share of farms—more than 30 percent of the total. All in, that's more than 80 percent of all farms.

Yet big farming operations receive the most in government subsidies, with the smallest number by percentage—5 percent—receiving the most.

But let's get real and look beyond the dollar signs. Wealthy individuals own the bulk of farmland, which they then lease to farmers, reaping federal subsidy dollars along the way. This makes for sensational headlines, but it isn't the type of business I'm talking about—which is the *real* business behind subsidies. Wealthy owners are a good fake, but they're small-time.

Multinational corporations such as Monsanto, Cargill, and Archer Daniels Midland are the real players in the subsidy business. Collectively, they and a few others are known as Big Ag. They control as much as 80 percent of certain grain exports from the United States. They sell their seeds, which are then used to plant fields around the world. It's their chemical fertilizers and pesticides that are used to facilitate crop growth, and their artificial hormones that make livestock grow bigger. And, too, they own those animals, which feed off the grains and are then butchered into the meats we eat. It's a business philosophy known as "seed to shelf." And it's these corporations that reap the most benefits from subsidies to grease their wheels and make the food system as we know it go round and round.

From tax exemptions to export subsidies to price supports, these multinational corporations win out—big. And it gives them an edge in the world markets.

Step outside the podunk world of Farm Aid. Get your head out of Kansas. The actual big winners from the billions of dollars in subsidies we hand out could come straight from the pages of a good spy novel.

Look at ConAgra. You might know it better as Hunt's, Chef Boyardee, Hebrew National, Slim Jim, Peter Pan peanut butter, or one of the other dozen brand names it owns. It's run out of Omaha, Nebraska, but has 25,000 employees all over the world. Its revenues exceed $12 billion a year, and it's publicly traded on the New York Stock Exchange. Behind gates, ConAgra's corporate headquarters has 750,000 square feet of office space on 45 acres of land. It's no farm.

They have on staff scientists, lawyers, and lobbyists who hobnob with the super-rich and the political elite—powerful decision makers. Now, here's where it gets interesting in that behind-the-scenes kind of way: "With diversified interests ranging from 'farm gate to dinner plate,' a ConAgra subsidiary can be found along most links of the food chain," Dr. William Heffernan at the Department of Rural Sociology at the University of Missouri wrote in a report to the National Farmers Union. "ConAgra," he said, "is one of the three largest flour millers in North America and ranks fourth in dry corn milling in the U.S. The company produces its own livestock feed and ranks third in cattle feeding and second in cattle slaughtering. It ranks third in pork processing and fifth in broiler production and processing."

And that is just the outright food part. ConAgra, according to its own corporate description, is a leading distributor of crop-protection chemicals, fertilizers, and seeds in the United States, Canada, the European Union, Mexico, and Chile. It has joint ventures in Africa and is a leader in the distribution of new biotechnology products, principally seeds.

Heffernan reported, "In the handling and transportation of grain, ConAgra owns about 100 elevators, 1,000 barges, and 2,000 railroad cars."

Despite ConAgra's long history of being a vertically integrated company that operates from "seed to shelf," it doesn't operate alone. It works with other conglomerates to render control of the food supply. One example of this offered by Heffernan is ConAgra teaming with DuPont in a group of joint ventures. "DuPont has relied heavily on ConAgra for the initial commercialization of its new high-oil corn. Once United Agri Products found farmers to grow the corn under contract, ConAgra's chicken operations bought the grain," he said.

This is the type of big-business wheeling and dealing that benefits most from federal farm programs and subsidies. It's conglomerate control, influential through virtually every aspect of our lives, right down to our cereal in the morning and our gas at the pump.

Farmers buy their seeds from Big Ag, they buy their feed from Big Ag, and they sell their stock to Big Ag. Big Ag trades and deals among its members. We pay the bill.

ConAgra, Cargill, and ADM are some of the biggest beneficiaries of ethanol subsidies in America. Combined, they earn about $8 billion a year. They themselves don't need subsidies. But they work quietly to keep subsidies flowing to producers.

Subsidies feed the little people, the farmers on their supply chain. And Big Ag needs to keep them indentured.

As Tufts University's Tim Wise explained to me, the big agricultural corporations aren't really in the farm business. Sure, they, or one of their subsidiaries, might receive some farm program subsidies here and there. But that isn't where the action is. It's selling the seeds on the front end, the chemicals and equipment in the middle, and then taking a profit on the back end, the retail side, where all the big money is made.

"Big Ag doesn't want farmers to profit too much or lose too much. They want to keep them barely hanging on," Wise said. "That's your best type of customer."

These "customers" are essentially serfs who provide inexpensive raw materials to food processors. They have been conditioned to believe that they aren't growing food any longer. They are growing elements that giant companies turn into food. As such, giant food companies want subsidies to keep flowing to the farming community so their raw materials remain cheap. Then, using this, say, cheap corn, they can—presto, slammo, stir it up in a bottle—make high fructose corn syrup and whatnot, and pop out Snickers bars and gummy bears ad infinitum without having to worry about running out of supply.

Farmers who reap subsidies are still at the mercy of grain elevators, commodities traders, exporters, and service providers. Farmers around the age of 65 who are seeing their businesses abandoned or sold to bigger operations are especially vulnerable. For farmers who aren't making money off their farms and have to take on second jobs to support their families, it's even worse. These farmers suffer at the subsidy trough while others lap up the good stuff and enjoy the good life.

According to the USDA, commercial farms with $250,000 or more in farm income are the big winners when it comes to subsidies; they get the most—the majority of all federal payments.

The USDA admits that this disturbing trend is increasing as small farmers go bust.

"U.S. farm production is shifting to larger operations, while the number of small commercial farms and their share of farm sales continue a slow, long-term decline," the USDA reports. "Larger farms have a competitive advantage over smaller farms in most commodities because the average cost of production per unit declines as the size of the operation grows (referred to as economies of size). In addition, many of the operators of small commercial farms are at least 65 years old and are leaving farming as they grow older."

So if small farms aren't benefiting from subsidies, yet big farms are, then what will it take to turn things around?

Craig Cox, senior vice president of agriculture at the EWG, told me that the recession has forced policymakers to take a hard look at subsidies. He expects change. Both in terms of the amount of subsidies handed out and the types of subsidies given.

"We'll get rid of direct payments," he predicts. Instead, more disaster relief programs will appear to help farmers manage risk.

Even in Iowa, a farm state, the state agricultural committee is talking seriously about nixing direct subsidy payments and creating more effective risk management programs for farmers with taxpayer money, Cox says.

Our giant food conglomerates probably wouldn't much care about this change, as they are much more concerned with getting a steady supply of raw materials for their goods than with the actual price of those goods, Cox notes. Prices, I suppose, can always be passed along to consumers.

As taxpayers, we certainly don't benefit from the subsidy system, nor will we likely benefit from any change. A shift in *how* subsidies are paid doesn't mean that we won't pay.

Our subsidy system is a "safety net for extremely wealthy people" as Cox says. And that net may rise or lower depending on the whims of Congress and the types of subsidy programs that are in place. But the size of the net won't change. It will support big landowners and big commercial farmers, as it always has. It will indirectly support the multinational conglomerates that feed off them, and the energy suppliers that feed *them*— and, coming full circle, the politicians that dole out the funds to begin with. All funded by the US taxpayer under the guise of lowering our food bills, or more altruistically bailing out the poor farmer.

"Calling farm subsidies a bailout is an insult to bailouts," Cook says.

Indeed, we've supported via taxpayer funds far more farmers than autoworkers or even, of late, Wall Street investment bankers. And we continue to support the same farmers over and over.

EWG's data show that six of the top 10 recipients of commodity payments in 2009 were also among the top 20 recipients in both 2007 and 2008. Of the top 20, eight were in the list all three years, and three more were in 2009 and one other year.

These are operations such as California's SJR Farms, which receives more than $2 million in federal funds. Or Louisiana's Balmoral Farming Partnership, which gets $1.9 million. Or Arizona's Gila River Farms, which receives $1.7 million.

Serious dough. Enough, of course, to look a little deeper at the numbers.

Those three farms are all large operations that produce a variety of crops, from cotton to citrus. They are in politically appealing neighborhoods—congressional districts whose representatives sit on powerful agricultural committees—and grow politically appealing crops. Balmoral is probably the most interesting recipient: It's a pass-through vehicle for 17 individuals, 10 of whom received more than half a million dollars each in federal subsidy payments alone.

This type of structure is called a "Missouri Christmas tree" in subsidy-speak. Cook explains that the structure is formed as a pyramid. The most common of these is created when a farm family hangs on to the subsidy it's been granted and doles it out to family members who no longer really work on the farm. "They lease it out," he explains, usually after a parent dies. Maybe one brother visits it now and again, and another writes something once in a while for the farm's Web site, and a sister checks the books. That, apparently, is enough "working the farm," in the government's eyes, to keep the checks coming—even if the kids live far away in a city. "Go to our Web site and enter a Chicago or Manhattan zip code. I bet a whole bunch of 'farmers' live there," Cook says.

Still, these are just the direct beneficiaries on the first floor of the subsidy tower. The owners of the tower itself, the multinational corporations, indirectly receive the most benefits from the subsidy system. And then there are the cronies.

In 2009, a full 60 percent of farm subsidies flowed to states represented by senators serving on the Senate Committee on Agriculture, Nutrition, and Forestry, the EWG found.

Congressional districts represented on the House Committee on Agriculture received 37 percent of all farm subsidies that year. And members representing four out of the top five districts in terms of farm subsidies serve on the House Committee on Agriculture, it said.

Ten states—Texas, Iowa, Illinois, Kansas, Minnesota, North Dakota, Nebraska, California, South Dakota, and Missouri—accounted for the greatest amount of subsidies in 2009.

Most of our agriculture is grown in those ten states, and their representatives would be daft to call for subsidy reform. But is that in the best interests of the rest of the country?

"In a time of growing federal budget deficits and increasing populist anger over government spending, it would seem prudent to trim wasteful agriculture programs. Instead, Congress—at the behest of the biggest agriculture interests representing just five commodity crops—has constructed a system that ensures profits for the largest growers of corn, cotton, rice, soybeans and wheat," Ken Cook wrote in an EWG report.

Big profits, in fact. The Koda family farm I visited in California, for example, enriched its patriarch so much, I discovered, that he opened California's first Bank of Tokyo branch, of which he became a founding director. From farmer to financier, the story of riches isn't an anomaly.

Subsidies enrich many people at taxpayers' expense. Exactly who these people are is what I'll look at next.

CHAPTER TWENTY-ONE

POWER PLAYERS

The mythical K Street, where lobbyists transform moneyed interest into political interest, comes closest to Capitol Hill at North Capitol Street. There, you won't find many lobbyists, or politicians for that matter. K Street, you see, is like Wall Street: The physical location's shadow and reach extend beyond mere geography.

At the intersection of K and Capitol are a Baptist church, a parking lot, and the DC offices of the managed-care consortium Kaiser Permanente. But there, past the US Government Printing Office and the National Postal Museum, stands the Capitol dome.

The list of powerful people linked via subsidies to this virtual intersection is long and vast. Their web circumscribes the finely angled street layout that is DC and envelops it. These power players draw the lines and work their connections to ensure that subsidy policies remain intact. You'll see below why these powerful players have vested interests in keeping the subsidy system alive and, of course, who these people are.

I've broken the power players into three groupings: lobbyist groups, industrial complexes (including executives), and politicians. I'm grouping the USDA chief and US trade rep into the spectrum of politics, even though these are appointed, not

elected, officials. It should also be noted that the biggest beneficiaries of subsidies are those who receive them indirectly. Big
agricultural companies get to purchase subsidized products—
corn, wheat, soy, rice, etc.—from subsidized farmers. This
enables them to buy commodities at artificially low, or "fake,"
prices . . . and inflate their profit margins.

Politicians get the benefit of subsidies indirectly as well
(although in some cases, members of Congress do receive
direct subsidies). They support the programs that benefit their
biggest donors.

To that end, let's begin with arguably the most powerful
person in America when it comes to deciding on subsidies and
doling them out: the chair of the Senate Agriculture, Nutrition
and Forestry Committee.

The current chair of the Agriculture Committee is Senator Debbie Stabenow, a Democrat from Michigan. Stabenow is
forging new ground on the committee: She isn't from what's
thought of as a traditional farming state—as most agricultural
chairs have been—although she is quick to point out that agriculture is Michigan's second-biggest business and responsible
for one out of four jobs in the state.

Stabenow grew up in a small town in central Michigan,
and her folks weren't farmers (her father was a car dealer, her
mother a nurse). Stabenow was elected chair after Senator
Blanche Lincoln, a Democrat from Arkansas, was defeated in
her reelection bid.

Lincoln was a staunch subsidy defender (and recipient).
The jury is still out on Stabenow. But in her very first remarks
as chairwoman, Stabenow hinted that she won't be taking away

subsidies anytime soon: "As we look forward to writing the next farm bill, I am fully committed to a strong safety net," she said.

Her predecessor, it's worth mentioning, was more than fully committed to a strong safety net of subsidies: She wrapped herself in it. Check this out:

> Members of Congress must report sources of income totaling more than $200, but most get payments through partnerships or other entities, so it can be difficult to learn which ones receive the subsidies. Recipients are searchable by name on www.ewg.org, but, for example, payments to Sen. Blanche Lincoln, D-Ark., are listed under her maiden name, Lambert, at a Virginia address near Washington. Records show Lincoln and her family members collected $715,000 from 1995–2005, the most recent year complete data are available. She said she personally received less than $10,000 a year, and the subsidies ended in 2005 when her land was sold.

That was reported in the November 13, 2007, *USA Today*—two years *before* Lincoln was named chair of the committee. Now, that's powerful interests at work.

Stabenow's counterpart in the House of Representatives is Chairman Frank Lucas, a Republican from Oklahoma.

Lucas is an ardent subsidy supporter. He argues and votes against anything that could dent the rural community. He is the first Oklahoman to chair the panel and has stated that "the Obama administration is no friend to agriculture."

Oh, boy.

Lucas was born on a farm and has deep roots in western Oklahoma. He still runs his own farm and ranch and is "proud" to support subsidies.

The US trade representative is Ron Kirk. He represents American interests in the world and at the World Trade Organization. Coming from Texas, where he was mayor of Dallas, Kirk's farm-and-energy interests and support are obvious. He was at one time a highly paid lobbyist for Energy Future Holdings Corp. And he regularly sidesteps the issue of farm subsidies, or I should say he avoids addressing policies that would harm US farm subsidies. Kirk's impression of the world therefore can be construed as pro-farm and pro-energy. Which, at day's end, means pro-subsidy.

Tom Vilsack is the secretary of Agriculture. As former governor of Iowa, he joins the tradition of USDA heads who've been appointed from farm states. Vilsack is pro-ethanol and pro-GMO—and he's met opposition for his pro-corporate farming views. The Organic Consumers Association opposed Vilsack's nomination as secretary. Energy and environmental reforms were key points of the Obama campaign, and Vilsack exhibited no signs of wanting to reform either one. The OCA said he has repeatedly demonstrated a preference for large industrial farms and genetically modified crops. For example, he originated a seed preemption bill as governor, effectively blocking local communities from regulating where genetically engineered crops would be grown. Vilsack was also the founder and former chair of the Governors Biotechnology Partnership. Biotech includes genetic modification.

Now for the real money: Big agricultural conglomerates. For these we have to head outside the Beltway.

Cargill, based in Minneapolis, is by far the biggest benefi-
ciary (even if indirectly) from the federal subsidy system. The
privately held conglomerate employs 131,000 people in 66 countries. It earns some $3 billion a year on revenues of $108 billion.
Cargill spent $1.6 million lobbying Congress and the adminis-
tration in each of the past two years, according to the US Public
Interest Research Group (USPIRG). Its chief executive is
Gregory Page, and because Cargill is private, his compensation
isn't disclosed.

Next up is Archer Daniels Midland, based in Decatur, Illinois. It's a publicly traded company with annual revenue of
$70 billion. It has 28,000 employees around the world, and it pro-
duces foods, seeds, beverages, feed, ethanol, and bioenergy—
that's *ethanol* to you and me. ADM also provides agricultural
storage and transportation services. It spent $1.33 million on
lobbying in 2010, slightly more than it spent in 2009. At least
$400,000 was spent lobbying for ethanol alone in 2010. ADM's
chief executive is Patricia Woertz. She made $15 million in
2009, the last year reported.

Then there is ConAgra, based in Omaha. The food pro-
cessor has 25,000 employees all over the globe, makes revenue
of $12 billion annually, and pretty much owns the food chain,
from pasture to plate. It spent $280,000 lobbying Washing-
ton in 2010 on food issues. Its chief executive is Gary Rodkin.
He earned about $6 million in compensation in the last
reported year.

Last but not least is Monsanto, based in St. Louis. With
$11 billion in revenue and 21,000 employees, it's the Bobby
Brady of the Big Ag bunch, the smallest. Monsanto makes
herbicides, pesticides, and crop seeds. It's the genius behind

much of the genetically modified food on earth and the cre-
ator of the "terminator seeds." These seeds produce plants
that have sterile seeds, so they do not flower or grow fruit
after the initial planting. Why? So farmers have to buy more
seeds. It spent $2.5 million lobbying Washington in the first
quarter of 2010 alone, and more than $6 million more
throughout the rest of the year. Its chief executive is Hugh
Grant (not the actor). He earned about $11 million in the last
reported year.

To be sure, there are other multinational corporations that
operate in the food or seed or chemical businesses. DuPont,
based in Wilmington, Delaware, and others team up with Big
Ag, as well as develop their own agricultural products. General
Mills, in Minneapolis, is a giant in the food business, too. But
the four conglomerates above are the top of the lineup when it
comes to power in the subsidy business. They get their way—
and have the employees and political power to prove it.

The food industry at large spent more than $107 million
lobbying in 2009 and gave more than $36 million to congres-
sional candidates in 2008.

Here is where lobbyists and trade associations come into
play. They are the conduits between power and politicians.
Their currency is money.

The National Cotton Council, in Cordova, Tennessee, is
the power behind the cotton industry. It represents producers,
ginners, warehousers, merchants, cottonseed makers, cooperatives, and manufacturers—essentially anyone and everyone
who has anything to do with cotton. Its 35-member board is
made up of the most powerful cotton industry executives in
the world.

The NCC wears its power on its sleeve—okay, its Web site: "Cotton is grown in 17 states, stretching from Virginia to California, covering more than 12 million acres or about 19,000 square miles. From this combined acreage, the nation's cotton farmers annually harvest about 17 million bales or 7.2 billion pounds of cotton. Business revenue stimulated by the crop in the U.S. economy is estimated at some $120 billion."

Its Web site's wording is as charged as the power it displays: "The cotton industry is an important consumer. At the farm level alone, the production of each year's crop involves the purchase of more than $5.3 billion worth of supplies and services . . . stimulating business activity for factories and enterprises throughout the country. In a typical year, U.S. cotton farmers invest more than $652 million in fertilizers, $762 million in agricultural chemicals and $238 million in planting seed. They also pay out more than $528 million in fuel and equipment and $610 million in farm labor. . . . Overseas sales of U.S. cotton make a significant contribution to the reduction in the U.S. trade deficit."

Its power goes local, too: "In addition to offering a national perspective on the industry, the World of Cotton data provides state, congressional district and county profiles as well. The number of businesses, jobs and the revenue they generate is available for each cotton-producing state."

Politicians, in other words, take note.

The corn industry is represented by the National Corn Growers Association in Chesterfield, Missouri. It represents more than 300,000 growers across the country. Wooba—that's a lot of farmers. On their behalf, it lobbies for more ethanol use under the guise of "protecting national security." It is also the leading voice for corn growers in the promotion of biotech products—genetically modified products—to US and international government leaders. It also promotes better trade policy for the corn industry (as if it isn't in corn's favor already) and, curiously, improved transportation systems. A head-scratcher, until the NCGA explained, "Presently, the U.S. enjoys a comparative advantage in corn production worldwide, and the per-ton cost for transporting corn in the United States is lower than in other countries. But the United States has allowed its transportation infrastructure to deteriorate. At the same time, our competitors are making major investments in their transportation systems. Thus, our international competitiveness is in jeopardy. Unless our nation invests in major improvements to our aging transportation infrastructure, U.S. agriculture will pay the price."

There are just 15 members on the NCGA's board.

Meanwhile, the National Association of Wheat Growers, based in Washington, DC, operates through a series of committees and organizations in 21 wheat-growing states. Its organization is unique in the way it raises issues. I'd say it's even grassroots, but that would be an awfully trite way to describe a farming organization. NAWG's policy comes up from the countryside through county committees, which send ideas and resolutions to state associations, which set their policy and bring priorities to NAWG's board of directors. As such, and as the NAWG itself puts it, "Farmers who step up to represent their state associations on NAWG's Board of Directors serve as the crucial link between individual wheat growers, the state organizations and the national organization in Washington, D.C."

The NAWG is a strong advocate of direct-payment sub-sidies and has long lobbied to preserve them. It also advocates more ethanol (from its wheat) and more protectionist poli-cies. In perhaps the most forthright of ways, it launched a Web site (farmpolicyfacts.org) to push for the issues it believes in. It's designed "to educate Congress and Ameri-cans about agriculture's contribution to a strong and vibrant United States."

The American Soybean Association, based in St. Louis, makes no bones about its mission: lobbying. "A primary focus of the American Soybean Association is policy development and implementation," is how it describes itself. "Policy develop-ment starts with the farmer/members and culminates at an annual meeting of voting delegates. ASA is tasked with accom-plishing the policy goals established by the farmers/members/delegates. ASA does this by testifying before Congress, lobby-ing Congress and the Administration, contacting members, and meeting with the media."

The 90-year-old association represents 22,000 soybean farmers and has nearly 50 directors on its board. (There's even one from Canada.)

According to www.farmfutures.com, the ASA's top pri-orities in 2010 included "the enactment of a retroactive exten-sion of the biodiesel tax incentive, enactment of pending free trade agreements, and ensuring that producers are not adversely impacted by climate change legislation."

The rice industry is represented by several interest groups, but the USA Rice Federation represents all segments of the US rice industry, "with a mission to promote and protect the inter-ests of producers, millers, merchants and allied businesses."

The Rice Federation is based in Hamburg, Germany. (Okay, I'm kidding—sort of. The federation does list Hamburg as one of its four main offices. The ones closer to home are in Arkansas, Washington, DC, and Louisiana.) The group focuses a lot on education and awareness. To be sure, this dovetails into lobbying efforts. But a unique approach is its nonprofit foundation, designed to educate members and consumers. It also came up with a program called R.I.C.E.—Rice Information to Communicate/Educate.

The program is a call to action and gives the rice industry power via its tens of thousands of members. Its mission is twofold, the federation says. First, it's to provide a suggested legislative or regulatory message, and second, it provides the means to deliver the message quickly. How? It blasts the contact info for congressmen.

Imagine thousands of calls going out simultaneously to members of Congress about to vote on an issue. That's power.

The National Dairy Council has a lot of political and business muscle, as we have seen in the pages of this book. It was established in 1915, and through its network of state and regional dairy councils disseminates lots of research and information about the nutritional qualities of milk. Its mission, it says, is to get people to drink at least three servings of milk per day.

The American Sugar Alliance boldly proclaims that it does not take any subsidy "checks." Careful language. It also cherry-picks dates to show when sugar policy didn't cost American taxpayers "a dime."

"The world sugar market is a thinly traded, heavily subsidized dump market and is the world's most volatile commodity market," the ASA says. It also takes swipes at food manufacturers, saying they don't pass along sugar savings to consumers. The ASA is the most vocal and aggressive group I came across in writing about subsidies. I suppose it has to be, in order to keep sugar prices artificially high.

On pretty much the opposite side of the spectrum is the National Fisheries Institute. On its Web site, it features recipes. Still, the group represents the entire seafood supply chain, from vessels at sea to local seafood restaurants. The recipe for blackened salmon is a nice, soft cover for a hard-core industry interest group.

But on to the real hard-hats: The United Steelworkers Union, based in Pittsburgh (where else?), is the largest industrial labor union in North America, with more than 1.2 million members (read: lots of votes).

Begun in 1942, it has a storied past and has held numerous strikes pitting it against corporate America's most powerful business interests. Where they conjoin, however, is on the issues of subsidies. The union believes that subsidies equal jobs (even though this book and others have shown this isn't the case), and therefore it muscles Washington for higher import tariffs and more protectionist policies.

The head of the USW is a Canadian, Leo Gerard. He was elected in 2001, and has pushed the union to expand to other countries, giving it even more power in world trade. In 2008 the USW merged with the United Kingdom/Ireland–based union Unite to form a new global labor entity.

Like the steel industry, the energy industry has its sway, too—both in the form of its trade association and directly.

The American Petroleum Institute is the "thank you for polluting" energy lobby. It represents all aspects of the oil-and-gas industry and produces the greatest amount of media of any lobby group I encountered, including its own radio program. From advertising to social media to its own videos and software applications, the propaganda casts a wide net.

However, the Big Three energy companies don't leave anything to chance and are power players in their own right. Royal Dutch Shell, ExxonMobil, and BP are the most profitable companies in the world. Repeat: Royal Dutch Shell, ExxonMobil, and BP are the most profitable companies in the world. They are headquartered in the Netherlands, Texas, and London, respectively.

The power of the Big Three is evident in their bank accounts. The oil-and-gas industry donated nearly $19 million in 2010 to politicians. In terms of lobbying efforts, the industry spent $75 million.

I saved the best part for last. The politician who received the most money from the oil-and-gas industry in recent years? Senator Blanche Lincoln. Not the head of the energy committees, not politicians from big energy states such as Texas and Louisiana (although they did get money, too); but the former head of the Senate Committee on Agriculture received the most money.

It's worth repeating how much money the big energy companies make.

Royal Dutch Shell has revenue of nearly $300 billion a year and earns more than $12 billion a year; ExxonMobil has revenue of $310 billion a year and earns almost $20 billion a year; and BP has revenue of $246 billion per year and earns more than $16 billion annually.

The interests that align between power and money are strong. And it's difficult to see where our taxpayer interests get served. Certainly it's not through the tax system itself—we pay dearly. And certainly it's not through more jobs, better national security, or cheaper consumer prices.

Notice that not one consumer group is mentioned above. While we might not be able to lobby or donate millions of dollars to politicians to support our interest, there are ways to better use our means to create a more fair America.

At the corner of K Street and Capitol, eager students from the nearby community college hustle into cafés and open their books. They count their change and buy their coffee. They are price sensitive. Yet they are left out of the matrix that confines prices. Consumer groups aren't represented on K Street. Consumers are too fragmented. Concentrated interest groups count on this. They fight to win subsidies without contenders.

What we can do to change that and the power structure is what we discuss next.

CHAPTER TWENTY-TWO

WHAT CAN WE DO TO CHANGE?

Going up against Big Government and corporate America to effect changes to the federal subsidy system isn't easy. In fact, it's downright daunting.

Rick Swartz thought he was up to the task, however. He'd enlisted big funders, nonprofits, and groups with large constituencies—all with an eye toward subsidy reform. The journey he went on and the lessons he learned jell into an interesting case study for anyone looking to try to get changes made in Washington, DC, or even at home.

When I was in DC, I looked Swartz up. He's an affable guy, generous with his time. We agreed to meet for breakfast at Twigs, in the Capital Hilton, one of those power breakfast spots where deals and coffee brew at equal speed.

Swartz is an interesting character; he's an outsider inside political circles. A self-described part-time, left-leaning issue advocate and full-time activist and lobbyist, he's worked on numerous political issues in the district for decades as a Lone Ranger of sorts, through his solo practice, along the way forming alliances and contacts at the highest levels of government.

"I'm a bridge," he tells me. "And someone just told me that because I am a bridge I get run over and walked on a lot." He has the salt-and-pepper hair to prove it. His stories explain why.

"I used to speak with [Speaker of the House] Nancy Pelosi all the time," Swartz says. "We'd speak at 11 o'clock at night, meet all the time." This was when Swartz was looking to reform the 2007 Farm Bill (which eventually was delayed so much, it turned into the 2008 Farm Bill). This was in the months leading up to it, when Pelosi was also anti-subsidy and pro-reform. This was before "Nancy Pelosi cut our legs off," as Swartz says.

Let's back the story up a tad. Swartz had been working on immigration reform issues on behalf of Dick Gilder, a well-known Wall Street investor and philanthropist with an activist bent. "We had met some success," Swartz says of his relationship with Gilder. That was about the time that Gilder was approached by the CEO of the Environmental Defense Fund, Fred Krupp. Krupp wanted to get Gilder involved with climate change legislation. Gilder wasn't much interested. "They couldn't agree on anything except that crop subsidies suck," Swartz says. Which got them both thinking.

Gilder hooked Swartz up with the EDF to create a game plan as to how to tackle subsidy reform and to create an ad hoc alliance.

The Cato Institute, the Heritage Foundation, EDF, church groups, Oxfam, and others all came together under one umbrella: the Alliance for Sensible Agricultural Policies.

"We didn't have a Web site or anything," Swartz says. The groups were nervous about coming together in a public way. Imagine left-wing groups such as Oxfam aligning with right-wing groups such as the Cato Institute, and right-wing groups like the Heritage Foundation aligning with organizations like Bread for the World. Crazy. What would people say? These Romeos and Juliets from different sides of the tracks didn't want to get caught out in public together. But behind the scenes, behind closed doors, they had the same mission in mind: to reform government spending.

The alliance raised $15 million and was hell-bent on changing the nexus between Big Government and Big Ag.

"There was common ground in fiscal sanity," Swartz says. He lined up support from senators and congressmen. He got some businesses behind the alliance. Editorial boards even took up the cause. The *Wall Street Journal* wrote at the time, "With grain prices soaring, farm income at record highs and the federal budget deficit widening, the subsidies and handouts given to American farmers would seem vulnerable to a serious pruning."

The *Journal* cited Swartz and the formation of his nascent alliance:

"'We decided to put on a game,' says Washington lobbyist Rick Swartz, who organized the alliance.

"Some groups argued that farm subsidies hurt poor, unsubsidized farmers in the developing world. Others argued the programs can't be justified with the federal budget deficit as large as it is. Still others blamed the commodities subsidized in the farm bill for contributing to obesity, diabetes and heart disease.

"Antipoverty group Oxfam America tapped into a grassroots network around the country to raise awareness of the issue. It paid for television ads that ran in the nation's capital and in targeted states, including Minnesota, home to Democratic Rep. Collin Peterson, chairman of the House Agriculture Committee."

The vote for the Farm Bill was getting close. Things looked promising for Swartz and his group. There was a new administration, new energy coming into Washington that on the face of it—that big smiling face of hope—was for reform. And that's when Nancy Pelosi cut the proverbial legs off the movement, as Swartz put it.

I take another sip of coffee, enthralled with all this behind-the-scenes, backdoor maneuvering.

He goes on to say that Pelosi and Rahm Emanuel, the White House chief of staff, didn't want to alienate the rural-community voters and thereby potentially lose seats in Congress. So Pelosi did an about-face. She squared off against subsidy reformers like Representative Paul Ryan, a Wisconsin Republican. "We got rolled," Ryan told the *Wall Street Journal.* "The agriculture community circled the wagons."

Pelosi, Swartz claims, told other House members that the reform issue "was a personal one" with her. Personal, one can imagine, if one's job as House speaker is at stake.

Indeed, corporate America and Big Ag bucked subsidy reforms and spent $80 million fighting changes. That was just on lobbying alone. Swartz reckons that the total tab spent by the food-and-agricultural industry was many times the $15 million he had raised. "They hit back hard," he says.

The $288 billion 2008 Farm Bill was $14 billion higher than the 2002 Farm Bill and included $16 billion in new spending provisions. It included a new revenue-based subsidy program instead of subsidy payments based on politically set target prices. President George W. Bush vetoed the bill in 2007 because he didn't like the high cap on payments to people earning more than $750,000 annually; he thought that amount of earnings was still too high.

Swartz and the various groups that composed the Alliance for Sensible Agriculture wanted to roll back spending and payment caps and reform the bill dramatically to include more funding for the food stamp program and foreign assistance. It wasn't going to happen. Not because it wasn't right or just. Because of politics.

Congressmen agreed, and many were upset at the thought of the subsidy bandwagon continuing. "At some point, you have to step back and ask, 'Does this make sense for the American taxpayer?'" Representative Ron Kind told the *Journal*. He had sponsored a measure that would have slashed about $10 billion in subsidies over five years. It, along with other reform suggestions, namely by Swartz and his group, got crushed on the House floor.

Lesson learned. But also lessons to be learned.

Swartz lays out a six-point plan for members of the educated public who get angry about an issue such as subsidy reform and want to do something.

1. Google which organizations are working on reform issues and find the ones that you can plug into. "Even by joining a letter-writing campaign, you'll find like-minded people," Swartz says.

2. Meet with staff or your elected official in their home district. "You don't have to travel to Washington to be a citizen," Swartz says. Bringing other voters or groups—such as church groups—will get attention. "Work through local networks," he suggests. Lobbying at home is more effective than lobbying in DC. "The echo back home is much more important than the day in and day out of what's going on in Washington," Swartz says.

3. Go public. Anybody can write a letter to the editor or an op-ed for their local newspaper—and Swartz suggests people do. "You don't have to be a professional publicist to speak out," he says.

4. If you have the means, contribute to politicians who think like you do. Political action committees and big money are welcomed by politicians, but so is money from voters, especially when it comes from their home district and is attached to a person, not just an institution.

5. Advertise. "Name names," Swartz suggests. It's an edgier tactic, but "the last thing a subsidy recipient getting $150,000 a year wants is publicity." But do it locally. Washington is where this type of hardball game is played. Rarely is it played out on the local level. Billboards are good for this, too.

6. Boycott. It's the most difficult tactic, but if big enough, they hit corporations where they hurt most—in their bank accounts. Swartz warns, though, that "they're really hard to organize, and unless there is a major institution behind it, you can't pull it off. There is also the danger that the boycott becomes an idle threat—if not enough people participate, your cause looks weaker."

Going up against powerful interests can be futile. Speaking up and out might make you feel good, or get things off your chest, but the message more often than not falls on deaf ears. Especially when it comes to subsidy programs that have been around for decades. The entrenched interest groups involved have experience and know how to play the power game based on years of practice. Take the National Corn Growers Association. "You want my vote, senator?" a member might ask. "Well, how would you like to meet 300,000 of my little friends ..."

The food writer Michael Pollan and the "slow food" chef Alice Waters are creating a type of food revolution that could be a powerful voice in how food is grown—sans subsidies that go to corporate farmers. But until that revolution takes hold, powerful people with a lot of followers have to be fought by other powerful people with a lot of followers.

"The silver bullet to all this is really Rush Limbaugh," Swartz says. "We need him or someone like him to call out conservatives for their financial hypocrisy. The angle then becomes just pure shameless hypocrisy."

That would get attention and spawn a form of activism the likes of which Washington hasn't seen.

Indeed, on January 24, 2011, David Rogers wrote on *Politico*: "As eager as they are for a fight with the White House, Republican budget cutters have a problem in their own back pasture: what to do about a system of farm subsidies that's still pumping billions into GOP districts at a time of record income for producers." Tea Party activists and members even more so.

Monica Mills, director of government relations for the DC-based Bread for the World, a powerful nonprofit group comprising a collective of Christian organizations, agrees with Swartz in that local voices matter and politicians are being held accountable. "People often pooh-pooh that, but it's a huge deal," she says. And while, as Swartz says, a person doesn't need to travel to DC to be a citizen, traveling to Washington to meet with members of Congress gets attention.

"Every year, we have a lobbying day in June, and it's fantastic," Mills says. She says people come from all over to meet with members of Congress, and usually it's with the members themselves. "It's tremendously powerful," she says. "The members literally hear the voices of the people."

Bread for the World also deals with foreign assistance. And I asked Mills how she deals with getting those voices heard—people from foreign countries with no dog in the race, no voting influence or consuming power to sway things on their own behalf.

"You cannot just talk about policy, you have to talk about how policy affects a person," she says.

Mills cites examples of poor farmers in places like Haiti falling victim to US trade policy (the United States sells rice for about half the price that local Haitian farmers can, because of the benefits of subsidy assistance, as noted earlier in this book).

She says letter-writing campaigns can be effective if they hit two areas: first, morality ("Say it's the right thing to do") and, second, national security. Farmers put out of work can result in a backlash against America (as we saw in chapter 19).

No matter what, Mills says, the key to change is connecting, letting the powers that be know that policy affects people, real people with names, faces, and voices.

"The best way to attack subsidies is to shine a spotlight on them," says Dan Griswold. But, he says, "they are hard to dislodge." In the end, "it's up to people engaged in the messy world of politics to change things." And that likely isn't going to happen anytime soon.

Revolt may be necessary to change the subsidy system as we know it. I'm not talking about a violent or bloody revolution, as it were. I am merely speaking of a revolution in the way we think about food, farming, and different kinds of subsidies. Perhaps "evolution" is a better way to put it—evolving toward a more transparent, fair, and just economy accomplished by a chorus of people calling for change. Otherwise we may encounter a revolution of the bloodier sort.

I've encountered several of these. Outside Puebla, Mexico, was the first time and place I encountered such a revolt. People marched, waved flags and banners, and stood in protest of their country's food policy. They were Zapatistas.

The Zapatista movement in Mexico has been around in various forms for 100 years. The name comes from Emiliano Zapata Salazar, a leading figure in the Mexican Revolution of 1910. Zapata was an agrarian reformer who revolted against land progressively going to fewer and wealthier landowners because of government policies. His trademark saying was "It's better to die on your feet than to live on your knees."

I kept a low profile during the protests, because some of the revolt had to do with US trade policies, especially those that affect the rural Mexican farmer. If you'll recall, there have been "tortilla riots" in Mexico due to US corn policy. (At the riot I saw, the American flag was being stomped on.)

I see traces of that type of activist revolutionary tendency in America, even with the Tea Party. No matter what you think of the Tea Party's policies, speaking up and out should be saluted. Sure, many Tea Party activists are dimwits, crackpots, and radicals. But the general thesis of what they stand for—if you could get one of them to articulate it properly, which is a challenge—holds true.

When I asked Griswold about change in the subsidy system, he brought up the Tea Party movement (without any leading or prodding from me). "The Tea Party movement, whether or not you agree with them, may have an effect on subsidies," he said. "Reform may be a welcome casualty."

Shining the spotlight on government spending may well put subsidies in the spotlight and circle them for reform—especially with the 2012 Farm Bill looming.

Government accountability is something that we should all agree on. Change will come only when people rise up and speak out. Change will come only when those voices are heard and joined by others and the power of the people is wielded through their representatives in government.

"No taxation without representation" was one of the tenets of the American Revolution. It stemmed from the lack of direct representation in the British Parliament, in which people were denied their rights, yet—and this is a big *yet*—were being taxed all the same. In short, it was about having no say in what was being paid for with people's taxes.

This is exactly what is going on today with most subsidies. As Griswold said, "People pay for subsidies and are not even aware of what they are paying for. And those who are aware don't care enough to do anything about it."

We shouldn't let subsidies continue out of apathy. With any luck, as corporate spending becomes more of an issue in future elections on the back of massive budget deficits, a light will be shone on subsidies; our taxes will be represented and the real results of what we pay for will be shown for what they are.

With such light, a new and more real America may begin to dawn.

It's up to us, though, to first turn on that light.

Back at the Capital Hilton in Washington, I wrap up my breakfast with Rick Swartz. I look around at the other tables, and the powerful deals may have gotten done. It would be nice if deals actually got done about the true cost of the breakfast itself, however—without subsidies. For a gander at that, we have to conjure up a new type of existence. Next, let's see what that would look like.

CHAPTER TWENTY-THREE

WHAT WOULD THE WORLD LOOK LIKE WITHOUT SUBSIDIES?

Take a look around at all the things in your life. The average American home, which is 2,400 square feet, has approximately 11,000 items in it. Each month, the typical American household spends $40 on water, $104 on electricity, and $84 on heating and cooling. Outside, we step into our cars, which we average Americans typically spend $28,400 on. We drive on average 13,476 miles per year at an average cost of $1,986.

At our work, we earn $52,000, the average American annual gross salary, and we pay about $17,000 in federal taxes. We work eight hours per day, and we have one child to attend to.

Now let's break down the average American food bill and find out what we spend.

We spend $3,753 on food that we eat at home, and $2,619 on food outside our homes—either for takeout or fine dining sit-down meals. Total hit to the bank account: $6,372 per year.

For meats, poultry, fish, and eggs, the annual total amounts to $777 per household. For dairy, it's $387 a year that we spend. For fruits and vegetables we spend $600 a year. And for other food at home, we spend $1,241 a year. I'll take this "other food at home," specified by the Census Department's Consumer Expenditure Survey, to mean soda, cookies, and other junk food.

All of the things I have just described, all of the money we spend and the items we spend our money on, are part of a grand illusion—a fake America that is designed to cater to our whims, concerns, vulnerabilities, and ignorance. The America described above in hard statistical data is not how America could or should look. It's an artificial landscape of figures calculated by a government that spends in order to get votes and by corporations that manufacture or grow goods based on cost rather than benefit—in any rational sense of the word.

Completely left out of the picture of our lives today is a very simple question that we often ask in this country: "Do we get what we pay for?" It means, or should mean, "Do we get the best product at the best price?" In the context of subsidies, "What are we getting exactly for our tax payments?"

We worry most about jobs, taxes, and national security, as well as education for our kids and health care. Still, sitting way high at the top of all of our concerns is money: first, how we get it (via jobs), and then how it's being taken away (via taxes and government spending). Yet the ability for us to climb to the top of the pyramid and reach our goals as well as have our concerns addressed is taken away ever more by Big Government and corporate America. The ladder always seems to be missing a few rungs just below the window into how government money gets funneled to corporations and the wealthy.

At the end of the day, this book is meant to be that window.

But let's take a look at how a typical day in America might play out without subsidies.

You wake up in the morning on a fine pair of cotton sheets and a pillow—a 400-count, made-in-the-USA name brand. It's warm, cuddly, safe-feeling. You yawn. Your day is about to begin. Everything around you looks pretty much the same, but it isn't real. You might as well still be dreaming. This is the start to our false existence.

You probably paid $120 for those sheets you were sleeping on, for instance. The same cotton set without subsidies would cost 10 percent more. That means, in a world without subsidies you'd be short-sheeted by more than 600 square inches of cotton. Put another way, the king-size bed you were sleeping on would be a queen size in a *real* America.

In the bathroom, the water you use costs $375 per year. Not really. The $4 billion the Environmental Protection Agency spends to keep water supplies clean and safe as well as to support infrastructure, plus local and city funding, mean that water costs in America are artificially low. Water costs are patchy across the country. In Chicago, water costs are the lowest of the major cities in the nation, running at about $25 per month for the average American household. In Dallas, water costs are twice as much as in Chicago, and in Atlanta six times that of Chicago—$150 per month. It makes sense, I suppose. Chicago has the largest surface source of freshwater at its front door: the Great Lakes. And Atlanta almost ran out of freshwater a couple of years ago. Still, the amount of subsidy support we can find in our water bills amounts to, as a rough estimate, a few gallons of water per day. That's one flush of a modern-day toilet, a few minutes' worth of a shower, the amount of water for a shave or to brush your teeth three times per day. To pay the same bill without subsidies, you'd have to nix one of those things from your daily activity. (This may provide some insight as to why people from other countries don't wash as much as we Americans do; we use twice as much water per person as the rest of the world.)

Time to get dressed? Okay, how about those socks you are about to put on—get rid of them. Just as with your sheets, your clothing, too, will suffer from the subsidized hand of the US government when it comes to cotton and other textiles. Socks, especially, get a helping hand. President George W. Bush, one might even say, had a sock obsession: He wanted them made in the USA with the full support of the federal government. The Bush administration claimed that socks imported from Honduras were hurting sock manufacturers in North Carolina and Alabama, and imposed a tariff on socks shipped to America. Result? The price of socks remains artificially low. In a world without subsidies, you'd have to forgo them anyway to account for the added cost of your wardrobe (10 percent more). I mean, you'd have to lose something. It's the socks or . . . go commando. Your choice.

Breakfast time. Is that bacon I see in the frying pan? An egg on the skillet? Some toast? Coffee? Sugar? OJ?

In a world without subsidies, for the price you'd typically pay for the most important meal of the day, you could be served an extra portion. Sure, the bacon itself ostensibly would cost more in this world—13 percent more. Eggs would likely go for 25 percent more, too. And your toast, an extra quarter. But you'd save at least 50 percent on the price of sugar—netting you a tidy 12 percent gain on your meal.

By the way, you'd have to cook a few seconds faster if you used natural gas to cook your meal, a few minutes faster for electricity. Otherwise, for the same amount you pay, cooking for the same amount of time, your eggs would be wet and your bacon a bit raw. In the world of subsidies, natural gas is supported a little and electricity is supported a lot.

If you happened to turn on the A/C or heat while you were cooking, then you'd have to turn the temperature up or down a degree. That energy also used to be subsidized. Not anymore.

Okay, now that you're fat, cold, and barefoot, it's time to go to work.

Your car is no longer a minivan from Kia—it's a fancier Mazda. Your Chevy Malibu is now a souped-up Camaro. If you had the standard model of your car, look out, neighbors—the sport package and a high-end stereo system now sit in your driveway. Get ready to go cruisin'. Steel prices affect the price of your car by 5 percent. Since the United States is in a steel dispute with China, we consumers are hit with an extra $1,420 tab on the price of the average car sold in America. Not in the real world we are conjecturing now. Good-bye, yellow brick road that leads to fat pensions and benefits for bankrupt steel companies, and hello, fair trading with China in the world without subsidies. Hell, spring for the sunroof or the convertible model and let the wind blow through your hair.

Okay, now stop, get out, and walk. You are just over a mile short of your regular commute to work. You can't get there spending the amount you normally would on gasoline: We subsidize 7 percent of the price per gallon at the pump with tax dollars. In a world without subsidies, your gas money won't get you as far.

As you begin to sweat, look up: That's the oil company's private jet flying overhead. Even without subsidies, oil executives can afford to live large. The billions of dollars they used to get in the world with subsidies is a drop in the bucket compared with the tens of billions of dollars they earn no matter which world we live in.

And now you've arrived at your workplace. See, there is actually more work to be had in the world without subsidies— more people have jobs. Because subsidies aren't around to weigh on tax bills, inflate land values, and force small family farmers to go seek "off-farm" jobs for income, there are more jobs to go around. In fact, there is $10 billion more to go around, due to consumer price savings on goods. This puts more money to work in the economy and creates more opportunities. Also, the $30 billion or so in taxes related to subsidies are free to go to work in the economy. A surge of spending of this sort also bolsters the prospects for new and more jobs. The more people spend, the greater the need for goods and services, and the more jobs are required; employment rises. Layoffs would be scant as previously subsidized businesses get more efficient and produce better products for a more competitive economy.

You mean not only will there be more jobs and more money to spend, but better-quality products on which to spend that extra cash? Yes siree, Bob, that's what I'm sayin'. Hap, happy you are, then, during your productive morning at work.

Time for lunch. Let's pretend you eat lunch the Warren Buffett way: hamburger, fries, and a Coke. Warren (and you) would be far happier in a world without subsidies. First, your burger would likely taste better, because the corporate cattle farm doesn't have quite the same incentive to turn out meat en masse. Rather, there is a new emphasis on quality. As such, the subsidized feed it gives its cattle is replaced with grass—a far healthier alternative and not genetically altered.

Warren and you might complain about the price of your burger at first—it's twice as much as what you paid in a world with subsidies—but world market prices are said to be taking hold, and the price is estimated to be coming down. In any case, your doctor is thankful. He says your cholesterol level is lower because you aren't eating as much red meat. Your health care costs are less. And so, in turn, is your insurance bill. Given that Warren owns an insurance company and is a long-term investor, he wears a smile on his face. You mimic him, and are happier and healthier also.

The French fries you're eating taste crispier. The giant corporate farm that grows the potatoes and is one of the largest landowners in the United States has gone back to its roots as a family business and doesn't overproduce and keep as much stock in storage. It's more mindful of transportation costs and manages its operations better. Moreover, it doesn't sell as many potatoes through the food stamp program and is shuffling to get more out the door to the private sector to compensate. The prices of those "chips" didn't change from one world to the other, either. Even though the federal government subsidized potatoes in the fake world, growers never really incorporated that price discount into the retail price of the spud, which was, of course, another waste of your money.

The real lunch treat you get in a world without subsidies, however, is your Coke. It's the good kind, made with cane sugar. Without price supports, there's no incentive for makers to use high fructose corn syrup as a replacement additive. The sugar price that went into the can in your hand got sliced by more than 50 percent when subsidies were eliminated. Now there is no such thing as a "Mexican Coke" anymore in America—it's *all* good.

That little bump of sugar actually gets you through the end of the day. And today is payday, so your mood improves even more. Why? Your paycheck is bigger, because you don't have as high a tax bill going to pay for subsidies. The elimination of $50 billion or so in direct farm and energy subsidies, plus the cutting of indirect subsidies and federal program costs, puts hundreds of dollars back into your bank account. Savings on direct energy and farm subsidies alone put more than $500 back into your pocket. "Tax Freedom Day" comes earlier in the world without subsidies.

With some of your burden lifted, you can enjoy some more time off. The good news is that you aren't as fat, because you aren't plumping up on the excess junk food manufacturers are making, because it's not so cheap anymore, and therefore you don't have to head straight to the gym after work. You can head home early and treat your spouse to a nice bottle of wine you paid for with the extra tax savings you received.

Sticking with your new healthier diet, you might have chosen a bottle of white wine rather than red to go with the fish, rice, and vegetables you are having for dinner. You'll be drinking about a half a glass less than you normally would, because the wine costs that much more—subsidies discount full bottles by more than 10 percent of their price. You want to make sure that the wine is good, because overall the meal is more expensive. The fish is 20 percent more expensive, and the rice costs 12 percent more. You can heap on a healthy amount of vegetables, though, to make up for the protein and starch you're sacrificing, because you paid roughly the same amount for the vegetables on your plate: carrots and string beans.

You wonder why you never ate or drank this healthily before. You don't feel drunk or bloated. You remember the diet your doctor recommended, and it's curiously more in line with the way you eat now. A little sugar, oil, and salt for the next smallest food group in your new diet: meats, dairy, nuts, and legumes. Then a bigger portion of fruits and vegetables. And then slightly more grains in your diet than those fruits and veggies.

The healthy diet consideration makes you want to skip dessert. Besides, you want to get in front of the television quicker: Your budget allows for 15 minutes less tube time. You turn it off earlier than you used to and read—your bedside lamp uses ten times less energy than your TV, so you can stretch your energy costs longer.

Eventually those lights have to go out too, however, and you snuggle a little closer in your smaller bed with your spouse. You sleep better now. Fear doesn't invade your sleep patterns, and you rest easier now, knowing that there is less chance of a terrorist attack.

Third World farmers who suffered at the hands of US subsidies in their home countries and were put out of jobs are working again and compete in the world market rather than view it as a form of American oppression. Because they are not unemployed, angry, and idle, they are less susceptible to recruitment by terrorist organizations.

Without those nightmares and fears to think of, you dream of what you'll do over the weekend with the extra spending money you have thanks to your tax savings. Maybe you'll take in a movie or rent one. You hear that *Food, Inc.* is pretty good.

CONCLUSION

A conclusion to a book this broad in scope is impossible to write; the story goes on and on and on. So this book really doesn't conclude—it hopefully will trail into more work: other books, articles, data, information, and activism.

The web of attachment that subsidies create for our lives is vast. Take the Food Safety Modernization Act signed into law January 4, 2011, by President Obama. It, by most accounts, is a much-needed piece of legislation that mandates better oversight and inspection of our food supply. Its requirements will go a long way toward stemming food-borne illnesses, which affect about 50 million Americans each year. But guess what? These new, stringent requirements are costly to adhere to, so much so that smaller farmers may not be able to afford to abide by them.

Food contamination, of course, can come from any size farm. But large-scale operations that push out millions of products—and any contamination within them—can affect a bigger portion of the population. Bigger farms also receive the bulk of US subsidies. So what now, brown cow? How do we discriminate effectively? If we support through subsidies big farms and not small ones, should we be asking the same requirements of both? The subsidy web extends, and often brings up many more questions than solutions.

This morning I listened to a report on National Public Radio about a \$2 million federal subsidy for a fish factory. It's being used so Asian carp can be cleaned and shipped . . . back to China for sale. Wrap your brain around that one. Asian carp are invading the United States like never before, threatening the way of life for American indigenous aquatic species as well as the ecosystems in which they live. Perhaps that is an apt metaphor for what is occurring in this country with all of our goods: Foreign goods are abundant and invading our shores, and we are spending taxpayers' money to (futilely) ward them off and send them back home, with no seeming benefit to us American consumers.

The disconnect is that we are spending good money for bad business practices and our own bad habits. It's our habits that must change. They connote mindless rituals that we partake in to get through life. We need, instead, conscious decision-making and less habitual recklessness.

Transparency is the key to ending the subsidy system as we know it. We ought to know line by line and item by item exactly where our tax dollars go. In fact, we should get a statement in the mail from the government after we pay our taxes to that effect. When I pay for any other type of good or service I am handed a receipt stating exactly what I paid and what I received in return. Why not for taxes?

This proposition should not be perceived as persnickety. The idea is to create a basis for education and activism. Clearly we are a more activist citizenry since the recession crimped our lifestyles; we were forced to reconcile our individual economic states and (often) statuses. Our eyes went toward government spending, and what we discovered was and is appalling. We are now a debtor nation. We need to know what's what in order to know what to really spend on. We have for too long been writing checks in the dark.

Government subsidies can be and should be the first stop on the train of government accountability.

In chapter 22, where I discussed what we can do to change the subsidy system, I laid out some examples of what we can do as Americans to have our voices heard. To be sure, individuals acting alone and partaking in any of the suggested activities likely won't affect the system in any meaningful way. But together there is some power to be yielded. Still, this means knowing what to speak up and out about. That is where transparency—the full disclosure by the government of what we pay for and what we get in return—comes in. Having a statement in hand of who received how much and why from the government coffers is the first big step in reform.

While I see the benefit of eliminating subsidies altogether, it isn't going to happen. Not in my lifetime, anyway. Maybe never. My hope, however, is that this book will begin to chip away at the needless subsidies spent on corporations and wealthy people who don't need the money to operate better. The benefits of these "do-aways" will be felt not only in our pocketbooks but in our doctors' offices and at our security checkpoints.

"Without your health, life isn't worth living," my mother would often tell me.

We as a nation might be able to survive a recession or a depression, but without our health, none of that matters. It's time we connected the dots—and this is happening to an extent with the work of Michael Pollan, Jamie Oliver, and Alice Waters, among others—between what we pay for and what we eat. The ingredients of our lives are important. Yet education is lacking.

We spend federal dollars on sex education. We teach kids how to add and subtract, as well as communicate. But when it comes to the most basic aspects of life—what we eat and drink to survive; what is good for us!—education is nil. Why?

Way back in time, when hunters taught their young to hunt and gatherers their children to gather, the knowledge of the most efficient ways to obtain food were handed down as first rites of passage. This was primary education. Today, many children do not even know where their food comes from or how things are made.

A recent study on the matter shows that more than 10 percent of all eight-year-olds who were surveyed couldn't say where pork chops came from. Nearly 20 percent didn't know how yogurt or cheese was made. City children, it was found, were twice as unable to identify that beef comes from cows.

Chuckle all you want, but let me ask you: Where do your tax dollars go, and what does the money support?

We need to put the emphasis back on being healthy and wise and not worry so much about the "wealthy" part of that old catchphrase.

I was just as enlightened as the next person by the findings in this book: how we are paying to harm ourselves, mostly by the food programs that we support. Don't even get me going on the harmful effects of our subsidy dollars on poor people abroad, the terrorism and piracy we promulgate, or the environmental degradation attributable to the subsidy system. But will ending subsidies altogether really do the trick of making the world a better place?

No.

Here's why: They are too entrenched in our lives. We cannot lop 25 percent off the market value of land in rural America and expect life for the people who live there to be hunky-dory. We cannot chop the legs off the programs that help people through disasters or fend off anticompetitive dumping of cheap products by foreign producers. To end subsidies, there has to be a global effort. And we need to keep some subsidies alive to keep our seat at the world trade table.

Craig Cox at the Environmental Working Group told me that the complete elimination of subsidies isn't the answer to the problem before us. "I do think that there needs to be some sort of well-managed program that does deal with floods or when storms wipe out farmers. It's tough to withstand that type of thing," he said. "But there need to be well-managed programs for what we have today and for what is glibly referred to as a safety net. [That type of] farm policy is more like guaranteed income."

Beyond the guaranteed-income part of farm policy, which instills gluttony and sloppiness among producers, "distribution issues loom large," Cox says. "What's misunderstood are not only the subsidies but the income distribution of them. A farm household earning $30,000 or one earning $250,000—at some point you have to ask what the need is. And that question is being ignored. At this point—the $250,000 income mark— the subsidy is not a safety net; it's a safety net for extremely wealthy people."

His boss, Ken Cook, suggests a system of carrots and sticks, with some requirements for the preservation of soil and water. Bottom line: "We need better enforcement."

But all is not lost. Tim Wise at Tufts University sees a future in which fiscal pressure is going to force change. He agrees that complete subsidy elimination is not the answer. Wise says sensible policy with better enforcement really is the way to go. "Otherwise land values will plummet and loans will default, and the rural economy goes into a tailspin."

Wise referred me to the National Family Farm Coalition, which has, he says, a sane take on the subsidy issue. What they stand for certainly sounds good: "U.S. farm and food policy must change in order to reverse the economic devastation currently faced by our nation's family farmers and rural communities. In addition, our international trade policy must recognize each nation's right and responsibility to make their own decisions about how to develop and protect the capacity to grow food, sustain the livelihood of food producers, and feed the people in its own borders."

The NFFC seeks to achieve this with policies that restore competition to the farm and food sector; negotiate Fair Trade agreements; promote food security and food safety; hold US government agencies accountable; and minimize the risks of genetic engineering. It's drafted its own version of a farm bill, dubbed the Family Farms Act, to ensure fair prices for family farmers, safe and healthy food, and vibrant, environmentally sound rural communities here and around the world.

That isn't a bad place to start on land. By sea, I asked Dr. Marah Hardt, who researched the chapter on fish subsidies for this book, whether it would be a good idea to end all fish subsidies.

She takes a similar approach to those of Cox and Wise with farm subsidies—removing all subsidies won't work, but there are plenty that can be set adrift. "There are many clearly harmful subsidies that exist simply to boost fishing capacity and make profitable inherently unprofitable fisheries. Things like the Capital Construction Fund and especially fuel subsidies would be the place to start. Consumers might balk at the higher prices, but as fish stocks plummet, prices need to reflect the rarity that is out there. Some species really are a luxury to eat, and we should be paying premium prices for them."

Besides, she says, the money saved could go toward promoting more sustainable fishing practices or greater enforcement, which over the long run would help restore fisheries to more profitable and sustainable levels—something current subsidy programs clearly are not accomplishing. With all the other threats marine life faces, from mercury poisoning to climate change, it behooves us to build up the stocks of fish in the sea to help weather whatever storm is coming. We know marine life rebounds relatively quickly when given half a chance. Slashing half of fisheries subsidies (the $400 million in harmful programs) might just be the chance those fish need.

So how do we decide how much is enough? How big, in other words, to make the subsidy carrot, and when do we enforce by stick?

In 2012, we'll get a chance to voice our opinions when the next farm bill moves through Congress.

We have a unique opportunity at this moment, a time to vote for change. Using the tactics in chapter 22, we can demand accountability—not the least of which is by calling and lobbying our representatives in Washington personally and in groups.

It needn't end there, though. Wall Street and Big Business can field our calls for change as well. Shareholder groups have found success using the power of their stock ownership to exert their power on corporate America. Considering that about half of all American households own stock, shares are in effect voting power to the corporate world. This can make us individuals known in the boardrooms of Big Ag, Big Energy, and Big Steel, too.

Take the nuns. A group of New Jersey nuns, the Sisters of Charity of St. Elizabeth, has lobbied Citibank to better disclose itself. Another group of nuns, the Sisters of Mercy, asked Lockheed Martin to detail how much money it spends developing space weapons. And the environmental group As You Sow lobbied Coca-Cola at a shareholder meeting to stop using potentially cancer-causing BPA plastics in its cans. The same can be done to create a healthier food supply, safer energy policies, and fairer trade agreements.

If a small nonprofit group and some nuns can badger corporate America to change policies, imagine what a force it would be if all of us joined in.

It doesn't take that much to demand better disclosure. Change is a different matter. But let's begin by taking a long, hard look at things out in the open.

In *The Wizard of Oz,* its author L. Frank Baum reveals Oz to be just a man. At the end of the story, Oz floats away in a balloon—the last anyone ever sees of him.

Now that we've lifted the veil off subsidies and exposed the worst of them for what they are, we can similarly make them go away—never to be seen again.

Wendell Berry, the eminent poet and farmer, is suggesting a 50-year farm bill that will take into account health, social welfare, and the environment. In a 2009 *New York Times* op-ed essay, Berry and plant geneticist Wes Jackson wrote, "Thoughtful farmers and consumers everywhere are already making many necessary changes in the production and marketing of food. But we also need a national agricultural policy that is based upon ecological principles. We need a 50-year farm bill that addresses forthrightly the problems of soil loss and degradation, toxic pollution, fossil-fuel dependency and the destruction of rural communities.

"This is a political issue, certainly, but it far transcends the farm politics we are used to. It is an issue as close to every one of us as our own stomachs."

Such a long-term point of view and policy change would be a fitting end to "offenses against the land and the labor by which we are fed." And a new beginning.

SOURCE NOTES

Go online and look it up. That's what I did. And I could simply leave this section on source notes at that.

There are approximately 800 research note references, plus primary research notes, plus general and quoted attributions that we have on file for this book. There are also virtually endless threads of government reports, testimony, and secondary sources on everything I wrote.

I didn't drum all this stuff up in my head. I aggregated and synthesized the data, analysis, commentaries, articles, and information for my thesis. And let me be clear about this: My own ideological bias and views are intentionally woven throughout this book. In some cases, I hitched my wagon to other observers' points of view. In other instances, I diverged from conventional wisdom.

Though I consider myself a raging liberal, much of my source data and opinions comes from conservative organizations and individuals. The point of this book is for it to appeal to both liberals and conservatives. I'm sure I'll piss people off on both sides, but so be it. Big handouts to big corporate interests shouldn't serve any political philosophy. That's why the system is so *fakakta*.

No one has connected the dots in any meaningful way to produce a common perspective on which we all can or should agree. That's what I have attempted to do by weaving the facts together in a way that the average person might: I showed up at a supermarket, took a look around, and began taking notes. I then went home and began to troll the Internet for specific data and information on what I had seen and heard—and about how subsidies might have played into things. That's how I fell down the rabbit hole.

In the process of my online research, of course, I stumbled across great stories, news items, research reports, and opinion pieces that others had written and which jibed with my narrative. Besides the news chronicles, I leaned on a select number of sources for context, data, and points of view. And I will mention these now with great thanks and a recommendation to readers that they, too, turn to them for deeper understanding as well as backup for the myriad positions I've taken in this book:

The Environmental Working Group (ewg.org) was invaluable in its data, reports, and statistics. I have quoted liberally from the executives who work there.

I also leaned on the Cato Institute (cato.org) for perspective, history, and analysis, especially Dan Griswold's.

I have to give it up to *Reason* magazine (reason.com) as well for publishing so many pieces on subsidies. I learned a great deal from it.

The Heritage Foundation (heritage.org) is a conservative organization that I looked to for guidance and framework on various subsidy issues. Senior analyst Brian Riedl has compiled a raft of statistics and research reports on federal spending on subsidies that anyone interested in this subject should read.

James Bovard (www.jimbovard.com) is another to whom I owe credit and voluminous citation for his work in this area.

Much of the background and stories regarding sugar tariffs, along with other wonderful historical insights, can be attributed to him.

Tim Wise and the researchers at the Global Development and Environment Institute at Tufts University (www.ase.tufts .edu/gdae/) were a godsend. They figured out how much of an animal's feed is subsidized, and similar arcane data. Tim's thoughts and guidance also pushed me to seek out new directions and fair farm policies.

Oxfam (oxfam.org) has, arguably, one of the best campaigns to influence sustainable agriculture, making sense while others mince words.

On the government front, I found a great deal of information about subsidies at the Economic Research Service of the USDA (www.ers.usda.gov/), as well as statistics on food expenditures and the like. For additional government info, see the Bureau of Labor Statistics (bls.gov), the Energy Information Administration (eia.gov), the Environmental Protection Agency (epa.gov), and the Centers for Disease Control and Prevention (cdc.gov).

Internationally, the Food and Agriculture Organization of the United Nations (fao.org) houses all sorts of reports and data that I used abundantly; the World Trade Organization (wto .org) has tariff, dispute settlement, and, obviously, trade analysis; the World Health Organization (who.int) is where I learned about everything from obesity to mad cow disease; and the Organization for Economic Cooperation and Development (oecd.org) breaks out country by country data on subsidies and sustainable agriculture and addresses topics that range from the economy to social and welfare issues.

Some of the more issue-specific destinations I used online include steel.org, freetrade.org, organicconsumers.org, open secrets.org, whorunsgov.com, feedingamerica.org, downsizing government.org, and foodandwaterwatch.org. I think their names are self-explanatory.

Speaking of names, I have to mention Michael Pollan, whom I quote on subsidies leading to obesity; Dr. Ussif Rashid Sumaila, whose research on fisheries I fed from; and Brian Trumbore, whose historical context of the Great Depression and tariffs fit exactly with what I wanted to say. John Robbins Food Revolution is revelatory, and I keep going back to food revolution.org for sober analysis of our food culture. On the diet note, I also quote generously from the *American Journal of Clinical Nutrition* (ajcn.org).

Every lobby group has a Web site, from corn to rice to cattle to petroleum. I took them at their word about what they do and how they do it. As well, I trusted the publicly available congressional bios found on official government sites for those officials mentioned, just as I trusted the financial information from publicly traded companies.

I cited many news and opinion pieces throughout the book from respected news organizations. I think this is fair game. For example, Tom Friedman of the *New York Times* wrote a commentary about trade and terrorism abroad. Given that I wrote a chapter on that subject, his comments play into that discussion and are worth pointing out. The *Washington Post,* the *Wall Street Journal,* the *Christian Science Monitor,* National Public Radio, *Time* magazine, and Reuters cover subsidies seemingly more than other news outlets, so I ended up using news stories from them more than others.

Three universities—the University of California, Davis; UCLA; and USC—have done a notable amount of heavy lifting and primary research on food issues, including the effects of subsidies on our food system. UC Davis, in particular, is superb when it comes to agricultural studies.

So rather than frustrate you and list a ridiculous number of URLs that may change or redirect you to a dead link before this book appears on shelves, or which—as I pointed out in the introduction—may produce different numbers because of changing market prices, policy, or any number of other issues, I encourage you to do what I did: Go online and search.

Of course, begin with the sources I mentioned. But you will find other sources, too, out there on the World Wide Web. Use 'em. The Internet makes the availability of information more democratic. And I hope that the aggregated content of this book will add to that notion.

ACKNOWLEDGMENTS

Colin Dickerman and Gena Smith have what few have these days: faith and understanding. I truly appreciate that. Their talent and commitment goes beyond . . .

Also at Rodale I'd like to thank in a huge way Greg Ville-pique, who meticulously went through the manuscript, challenged me, and put in the hours helping me check and recheck sources. Can't thank him enough for that. In addition, James Tyler, Kate Bellody, and Karen Rinaldi are a great group of publishing people.

Susan Raihofer is tenacity defined. I couldn't ask for more in an agent. She rocks.

Margaret Riley is always there for me. Period.

Charles Sharp and Marah Hardt did a bang-up job researching and referencing the text. Many thanks for that and more.

Rick Swartz, Tim Wise, and the gents at the Environmental Working Group helped me navigate through the subsidy maze. I couldn't have done this book without their help, as well as all the help from the resources mentioned throughout *The Big Handout*. I wasn't alone in this.

My wife Jeannie is my sounding board and my safety net. My life would truly suck without her in it.

Last but not least is my enormous family, and I include friends in that definition these days. You all mean so much to me. I am a very, very fortunate man because of each and every one of you.

INDEX

Boldface page references indicate illustrations.

A

AAA, 157
Accountability, government, 246, 259
ACRE (Average Crop Revenue Election), 79–80, 175
Action plan for subsidy reform, 241–42
ADM, 87, 215, 227
AEI research, 167–68, 171–72
Afghan farmers, 197–98
AFL-CIO, 136
Africa, 125–26, 196–97. *See also specific country*
African farmers, 196–97
Agribusiness model, 32–33, 159
Agricultural Adjustment Act (1938), 157
Agricultural Adjustment Administration (AAA), 157
Agricultural experiment stations, 18
Agricultural exports, 166–67
Agricultural industry
  agribusiness model and, 32–33, 159
  agricultural experiment stations and, 18
  artificial farming and, xii-xiii
  artificial injections and, 18
  Big Ag and, ix, 114, 161–63, 207, 214–19, 226–28
  as business, 18–19
  changes in, 158–59, 160, 164, 219–20

competition in, restoring, 262
corporate-run farms, 168–70
crop rotation and, 206
distribution issues and, 261
factory farms, xii, 178–79
family versus non-family farms, 169
fertilizers and, xii, 207–10
growth of, 159–60
job changes and, 158–59
"off-farm" income and, 168
parasites and, 18
pesticides and, xii, 108–9, 207–10
public relations campaigns of, 163
retirement farmers and, 169
"seed to shelf" business philosophy and, 215, 217
soil erosion and, 202–6, 209
supermarket and, 19
water usage and, 210
Agricultural policy, 174, 265
Agricultural products. *See specific type*
Agricultural subsidies. *See also specific type*
  Afghan farmers and, 197–98
  African farmers and, 196–97
  Agricultural Adjustment Act and, 157
  Agricultural Adjustment Administration and, 157
  beneficiaries of, 168–70, 213–19
  carrot-and-stick system for, 261
  cost of, 8–9, 98, 175

Agricultural subsidies *(cont.)*
　creation of, 11–12, 157–59
　crop insurance and, 171–72
　dead zones in ocean and, 210–11
　direct, 170
　eliminating, 9–10, 183, 203
　Ethiopian farmers and, 198–99
　Farm Bill 1996 and, 31–32
　Farm Bill 2002 and, 163, 175
　Farm Bill 2008 and, 156, 163, 165,
　　175, 195, 239–40
　Farm Security and Rural
　　Investment Act and, 163
　financial issues of, 165–76, 220
　first, 159
　foreign, 173–74
　indirect, 170–71
　Kennedy (John F.) and, 160–61
　"Missouri Christmas Tree" and,
　　221
　in 1960s, 160–61
　Obama and, 194–95
　obesity and, 183
　post-World War I acts and, 14–15
　program delivery costs and, 171
　Reagan and, 162
　reforming, 240–42, 261–63
　Roosevelt and, 157–58
　small farmers and, 218–19
　target prices and, 162
　tax breaks, 166
　tax dollars and, 9, 86, 163–64
　terrorism and, 189–90, 194–95
　urbanization and, 159
　USDA and, 14, 16–17, 161–62
Alfalfa, 113
Alliance for Sensible Agriculture,
　240–41
American Bakers Association,
　84–85
American Enterprise Institute (AEI)
　research, 167–68, 171–72
American Petroleum Institute, 134,
　136, 233–34
American Soybean Association
　(ASA), 231
American Sugar Alliance, 68, 72, 232

Antibiotics, 56
Apples, 112
Arable land, declining, 201–2
Archer Daniels Midland (ADM), 87,
　215, 227
Artificial farming, xii-xiii
Artificial sweeteners, 180–81
ASA, 231
Assistance. *See* Subsidies
As You Sow, 264
Australian Broadcasting
　Corporation report, 48
Average Crop Revenue Election
　(ACRE), 79–80, 175
Ayers, Mark H., 135

B

Bacillus thuringiensis (Bt), 108–9
Balmoral Farming Partnership
　(Louisiana), 220–21
Bangladesh, 102
Barfield, Claude, 146
Barnett, Mike, 106
Baughman, Laura M., 145
Baum, L. Frank, 264
Beef
　cattle raising and, 17, 22–24, 26–28
　consumption of, 28–29
　fast-food restaurants and, 26, 29
　hamburger, cost of, 21–22, 25–27,
　　25
　industry, 23
　prices, 21–22, 24–25, 27–28
　retail value of, annual, 23
　subsidies, 22, 24–25, 29
　tariffs, 25
　water needed to produce, 114
Beneficiaries
　of agricultural subsidies, 168–70,
　　213–19
　Big Ag, ix, 214–19
　corporations, multinational,
　　213–17, 221
　of ethanol subsidies, 217
　individuals, wealthy, ix, 214–15,
　　220, 222
　institutions, 213

interest groups, 213
politicians, 221–22
states, top ten, 222
Wall Street, 220–21
Berry, Wendell, 264–65
Beverages, sugar in, 66, 73–74, 184
BGH, 53–54
Bhopal (India) disaster, 207
Big Ag, ix, 114, 161–63, 207, 214–19, 226–28
Big Business, 72, 86, 155, 263–64
Big Chicken, 31, 33–34, 38
Big Government, 72, 86, 114, 155, 185, 248
Big Steel, 151
"Big Steel on Steroids," 151–52
Big Sugar, 68
Black, L.D., 46–47
Bloomer, Phil, 95
Body mass index (BMI), 66
Borneo, 202–4, 212
Bovard, James, 16–17, 69, 268–69
Bovine growth hormone (BGH), 53–54
Bovine somatotropin (BST), 53–54
BP, ix, 131–32, 210, 234
BPA plastics, 264
Brazil, 103–4
Brazilian Cotton Farmers Fund, 104
Bread, 78–79. See also Wheat
Bread for the World, 244
Broiler chickens, weight of, 33
BST, 53–54
Bt, 108–9
Budget deficit, federal, 8
Bureau of Labor Statistics, 28, 269
Bush, George H.W., 62–63
Bush, George W., 140, 151, 193, 250
Butz, Earl L., 162

C

CAFOs, 43, 46, 48–49
California, 90–95, 100
California Environmental Protection Agency, 109
Canada, 172, 197
Cancer research expenditures, 101

Candido Asan, Americo, 196
Cane sugar, 66, 74
Capital Construction Fund, 127
Carbohydrates, refined, 112
Cargill, 87, 215, 227
Cato Institute research, 58, 102, 198, 268
Cattle raising, 17, 22–24, 26–28
Center for Food Safety (CFS), 55–56
Centers for Disease Control and Prevention, 27, 178, 269
Cereal. See Wheat
CFS, 55–56
Cheap food, 5, 26–27, 47, 114–15, 179–80
Chevron, 131
Chicken
    Big Chicken and, 31, 33–34, 38
    China and, 35
    consumption of, 34
    corn for feeding, 33
    corn subsidies and, 35
    free-range versus caged, 37
    industry, 31–35, 37–39
    integrators and, 32
    population, 35
    prices, 36
    Russia and, 39
    subsidies, 32, 34, 37, 39–40
    in supermarket, 36
    tariffs, 35
    waste of, 36
    weight of broiler, 33
China
    chicken and, 35
    fisheries in, 123
    steel and, 144–51
    trade with United States and, 149
Clayton, Chris, 195
Clinton, Hillary, 6
Coca-Cola, 66, 73–75, 264
Cod, 124
Commodities Futures Trading Commission, 84
Commodity markets, 81–86
Commodity traders, 81–83
ConAgra, ix, 216–17, 227

Concentrated animal feeding
    operations (CAFOs), 43, 46,
    48–49
Congressional Budget Office, 29,
    135, 175
Connally, John, 63–64
Continuous casting, 146
Cook, Ken, 174, 213, 220–22, 261
Corn
    for cattle feed, 22–24
    for chicken feeds, 33
    exports, 167
    industry, 70–72, 75, 229–30
    lobbyists, 229–30
    prices, 31
    production, 230
    subsidies, 8, 23–24, 26, 35, 65–66,
        68, 111
Cornell University, 140, 204–5
Corn Refiners Association, 65
Corporate-run farms, 168–70. *See
    also* Big Ag
Corporate Research Project article,
    151–522
Corporate welfare. *See* Subsidies
Corporations, multinational, 213–17,
    221, 228. *See also specific
    name*
Cotton
    Bangladesh and, 102
    Brazil and, 103–4
    consumption of, 104–6
    cottonseed and, 108
    exports, 167
    genetically modified, 108–9
    industry, 101, 103, 105–9, 228–29
    Macy's clothing selections and,
        105
    prices, 101–3
    production, 104, 107
    shirt prices and, 105–6
    subsidies, 10, 101–4, 107
    trade issues, 101–3, 229
    unsubsidized, life with, 249
Cottonseed, 108
Council on Foreign Relations
    report, 98

Countervailing duties, 97
Cox, Craig, 219–20, 261
Crop insurance, 171–72
Crop rotation, 206
Cummins, Wayne, 46

D
Dairy Export Incentive Program, 59
Dairy farming, 54–55, 57
Dairy industry, 51, 53–60, 232. *See
    also* Milk, industry
Davies, Merryl Wyn, 193
Dead zones in ocean, 210–11
Deferrals, income tax, 127–28
Deforestation, 201–4, 212
Dervaes, Anais, 206
Dervaes, Jules, 205–7
Diet, American, 112, 178–79
Dietary fats, 26–27, 112
Direct subsidies, 126, 170, 219. *See
    also specific program*
Disclosure and subsidies, 264
Drewnowski, Adam, 115
Dumping goods, 97, 146, 199
Dupont, 217

E
Economic Research Service of
    USDA, 269
Emanuel, Rahm, 240
Emergency Tariff Act (1921), 14
Empire State Building, 155–56, 164
Energy. *See* Oil and gas
Energy Information Administration,
    133, 269
Environmental issues
    arable land, declining, 201–2
    Borneo and, 202–4, 212
    dead zones in ocean, 210–11
    deforestation, 201–4, 212
    fertilizers, xii, 207–10
    interdependence and, 203
    pesticides, xii, 108–9, 207–10
    pollution, 143–44, 210–11
    soil erosion, 202–6, 209
    "splash and dash," 204
    subsidies and, xii-xiii, 199, 209–12

Environmental Working Group
(EWG) research, 95, 102, 112,
174, 195, 211, 214, 220–21, 268
EPA, 43, 46, 109, 249, 269
Epstein, Leonard, 116
Ethanol subsidies
beneficiaries of, 217
Farm Security and Rural
Investment Act and, 163
oil and gas and, 139–40
sugar and, 70–72
wheat and, 80–81
Ethiopian farmers, 198–99
EWG research, 95, 102, 112, 174, 195,
211, 214, 220–21, 268
Exports
corn, 167
cotton, 167
markets, top US, 166–67
milk, 59
rice, 94, 99
soybean, 167
ExxonMobil, ix, 131, 134, 137–38, 234
Exxon Valdez oil spill, 132

F

Factory farms, xii, 178–79
Fair trade, 100
Fake food, 177–87
Family Farms Act, 262
FAO, 99, 123, 125, 269
Farm Bill (1996), 31–32
Farm Bill (2002), 163, 175
Farm Bill (2008), 156, 163, 165, 175,
195, 239–40
Farm bill (2012), 175, 245, 263
Farm Board, 11–14, 17
farmfutures.com, 231
Farming industry. *See* Agricultural
industry
farmpolicyfacts.org, 231
Farm Security and Rural Investment
Act (2002), 163
Farm subsidies. *See* Agricultural
subsidies
Fast-food restaurants, 26, 29, 69, 177,
179

FDA, 8, 55, 65
Federal Deposit Insurance Company
(FDIC), 156–57
Federal Farm Board, 11–14, 17
Federal Milk Marketing Order
system, 58
Federal Reserve Bank of St. Louis, 175
Feeding America (charitable
organization), 6
Feeding the Factory Farm, 31
Feketekuty, Geza, 17
Fertilizers, xii, 207–10
FFTF, 124
Financial issues
of agricultural subsidies, 165–76,
220
commodity markets, 81–86
commodity traders, 81–83
food, 81–87
forward contracts and, 83–84
speculators, 81–83
subsidies and, 17
Wall Street, 81–87, 220–21,
263–64
Fish
Africa and, 125–26
Chinese fisheries and, 123
cod, 124
consumption of, 121–22
depletion of, 122–23, 191
fertilizers and, 210
fishing fleets and, 125–26
fishing quotas and, 123
health risks of, 122
Horn of Africa and, 191–92
industry, 120, 125–26, 192–93, 233
marketing, 121
orange roughy, 121
overcapacity and, 123–24
overfishing and, 125, 129, 191
pesticides and, 210
research on fisheries and, 126–27
salmon, 128–29
selections, varied, 122
shrimp, 121
subsidies, 119–21, 124–29, 191–93,
258

Fish *(cont.)*
  sustainability of wild, 128–29
  tuna, 121, 128–29
Fisheries Finance Program, 128
Fishermen's Contingency Fund, 128
Fishing fleets, 125–26
Fishing quotas, 123
Food. *See also specific type*
  in American diet, 112, 178–79
  banks, 5
  calorie reduction and, 116
  chain, 114
  cheap, 5, 26–27, 47, 114–15, 179–80
  contamination, 257
  cost of manufacturing, 183–84
  crisis (2008), 3, 81–82, 86–87, 166
  deserts, 117–18
  distribution, 118, 176, 261
  expenditures, 3, 6, 247–48
  fake, 177–87
  financial issues, 81–87
  genetically modified, 109
  healthy, 113, 116–17, 185–87
  hunger and, 4–6
  industry, 7–8, 228
  knowledge about, 260
  logistics, 172–73
  manufacturing, 72, 183–84
  policies, 7
  price controls on, 162
  prices, 3–6, 9, 81–82, 99, 115, 185
  riots (2008), 3, 81–82, 86–87, 166
  scientific aspect of, 18–19
  shopping habits and, 116
  source of, 205
  starvation and, 4–6
  subsidies, 4–5, 113, 165–66, 185–86
  subsidized versus unsubsidized,
    115
  supply, 4, 165
  unhealthy, 25, **25**, 113
  unsubsidized, life with, 250–55
  as weapon, 98
Food and Agricultural Act (1965),
  161
Food and Agricultural Organization
  (FAO), 99, 123, 125, 269

Food, Conservation, and Energy Act
  (2008), 156, 163, 165, 175,
  195, 239–40
Food and Drug Administration
  (FDA), 8, 55, 65
Food, Inc. (2008 documentary), 37–38
Food migration diseases, 18
Food Revolution, The (Robbins), 26
Food Safety Modernization Act
  (2011), 257
Food stamp program, 214
Fordney-McCumber Tariff Act
  (1922), 14
Forward contracts, 83–84
Fossil fuels. *See* Oil and gas
France, 79
Francois, Joseph, 145
Free trade, 100
Friedman, Thomas, 194, 270
Fructose. *See* Sugar
Fruits. *See* Produce

G

Gas. *See* Oil and gas
Genetically modified (GM) cotton
  and food, 108–9
Gerard, Jack, 135–36
Gerard, Leo, 233
Gila River Farms (Arizona), 220–21
Gilder, Dick, 238
Giuliani, Rudy, 62
Global Development and
    Environment, 269
Globalization, x
GM cotton and food, 108–9
Gold Kist Corporation, 45–46
Goran, Michael, 184
Government accountability, 246, 259
Government spending, xi
Grain elevators, 83–84, 87
Grains, 4, 23–24, 33, 57. *See also*
    specific type
Grant, Hugh, 228
Great Depression (1930s), 15, 17, 154,
  158
Great Lakes ports, 172–73
Green Scissors Campaign, 171

Griswold, Dan, 96–97, 160, 162, 189, 209–10, 244–46
Grocery store. *See* Supermarket
Gulf of Mexico oil spill, 128, 132, 210–11

H

H1N1 virus, 42, 48–49
Haiti, 96, 99–100
Hamburger, cost of, 21–22, 25–27, **25**
Haoran, Chen, 149
Hardin, Clifford, 63
Harding, Warren, 14–15
Hardt, Marah, 119–24, 130, 262–63
Hatch Act (1887), 17–18
HealthFocus Trend Report (2009), 70
Health issues. *See also* Obesity
    antibiotics, 56
    dietary fats, 26–27, 112
    fake food, 177–87
    medical costs tied to saturated fat, 27
    pollution, 143–44
    pork subsidies and, 48–49
    recombinant bovine growth hormone and, 54–56
    recombinant bovine somatotropin and, 54–56
    subsidies and, xi–xii, 17
    sugar consumption, 68, 75, 112, 181–83
    supermarket and, 7–8
    swine flu, 42, 48–49
Hedge funds, 84–85
Heffernan, William, 216–17
Heritage Foundation, 148, 168, 268
Hettinga, Hein, 59–60
High fructose corn syrup (HFCS)
    advantages of, 180
    in beverages, 74, 184
    corn subsidies and, 8, 65–66, 68, 111
    development of, 8
    fast-food restaurants and, 69
    fructose and, elevated levels of, 184
    Hunt's ketchup and, 70
    making, 180
    name-change request and, 65
    obesity and, 65–66, 181, 183
    ubiquity of, 7–8
High-Tech Protectionism (Barfield), 146
Hofstadter, Richard, 15
Hog industry, 43–45, **44**, 48–50
Hoover, Herbert, 11, 13, 15–16
Hormel, 51
Horn of Africa, 191–92
House Committee on Agriculture, 8, 222
Household expenditures, average, 247–48
Hunger, 4–6
Hunt's ketchup, 70

I

IGF-1, 56
IMF, 95
Imports
    milk, 59
    rice, 97, 99
    steel, 144–45, 150
Income, average, 247
Income, real, 10
Income tax deferrals, 127–28
Indirect subsidies, 114, 170–71. *See also specific type*
Individuals, wealthy, ix, 214–15, 220, 222
Ingot casting, 146
Insulin-like growth factor 1 (IGF-1), 56
Integrators, 32, 44
Interdependence, 203
Interest groups, 213. *See also* Lobbyists
International Monetary Fund (IMF), 95

J

Jackson, Wes, 265
Jewell, Jesse, 32, 159
Jobs, 71, 144–45, 158–59, 252, 255–56

K

Keck School of Medicine research, 184
Kellner, Irwin, 134

Kennedy, David M., 15
Kennedy, John F., 160–61
Khosla, Vinod, 139
Kind, Ron, 241
Kirk, Ron, 226
Koch, Robert, 18
Koda Farms (California), 92–95,
        100, 222
Krupp, Fred, 238
K Street, 223, 235

L

Lawrence, Robert Z., 98
Letterman, David, 214–15
Life without subsidies, 247–55
    cotton, 249
    food, 250–55
    job creation and, 252, 255–56
    oil and gas, 251–52
    steel, 251
    water, 249–50
Limbaugh, Rush, 243
Lincoln, Blanche (born Lambert),
        224–25, 234
Lippmann, Walter, 16
Lobb, Dick, 34
Lobbyists. *See also specific group
        name*
    commodity markets and, 85–86
    corn, 229–30
    fish subsidies and, 119
    pork subsidies and, 46
    power players, 223, 226, 228–34
    sugar subsidies and, 73
    Web site information, 270
Lockheed Martin, 264
Lucas, Frank, 8, 47, 225–26

M

Macy's clothing selections, 105
Mali, 197
Malkin, Anthony, 164
Manley, John, 197–98
Masters, Michael W., 81
McDonald's, 69, 177, 179
Meat, 23–24. *See also specific type*
Medical costs tied to saturated fat, 27

Menendez, Robert, 135
Merchants of Grain (Morgan), 77
Mercury in fish, 122
Mexico, 73–74, 197, 245
"Miami rice," 99
Milk
    antibiotics and, 56
    bovine growth hormone and,
        53–54
    competition of, 60
    consumption of, 60–62
    dairy farming and, 54–55, 57
    dairy industry and, 51, 53–60
    exports, 59
    government's influence on, 58–59
    Hettinga and, 59–60
    imports, 59
    income loss of producers and, 59
    industry, 61–64
    marketing, 56–58
    Monsanto and, 56
    prices, 58–61
    recombinant bovine growth
        hormone and, 54–56, 62
    recombinant bovine
        somatotropin and, 54–56
    subsidies, 55–59
Milk Income Loss Contract
        program, 59
Milk Price Support Program, 58–59
Mills, Monica, 96, 243–44
Mississippi River Basin, 211
"Missouri Christmas Tree," 221
Monsanto, ix, 54, 56, 109, 215,
        227–28
Morgan, Dan, 77
Morocco, 79
Mozambique, 196

N

NAFTA, 73, 197
National Association of Wheat
        Growers (NAWG), 80,
        230–31
National Chicken Council (NCC), 34
National Corn Growers Association
        (NCGA), 229–30, 242

National Cotton Council, 228–29
National Dairy Council, 60, 232
National Family Farm Coalition
        (NFFC), 267
National Fisheries Institute, 119, 233
National Institute of Food and
        Agriculture, 19
National Marine Fisheries Service
        (NMFS), 121
National Pork Producers Council
        (NPPC), 48–50
National Public Radio reports, 196,
        258
National Research Council report,
        140
Natural resource depletion, 190
NAWG, 80, 230–31
NCC, 34
NCGA, 229–30, 242
New Deal, 53, 155–57
NFFC, 267
Nixon, Richard, 63–64
NMFS, 121
North American Free Trade
        Agreement (NAFTA), 73,
        197
NPPC, 48–50
Nutrition, 116–17, 185, 185–87

O

Obama, Barack, 128, 140, 150,
        194–95, 257
Obesity
    agricultural subsidies and, 183
    body mass index and, 66
    defining, 66
    education and, 115
    epidemic, 26, 185
    factors affecting, 185
    high fructose corn syrup and,
        65–66, 181, 183
    incidence of, 178
    minorities and, 26
    poverty and, 26, 115
    subsidies and, 8
Ocean pollution, 210–11
OECD, 175, 269

Oil and gas
    ethanol subsidies and, 139–40
    industry, 134–37, 233–34
    prices, 4, 131–32, 134–35, 141
    subsidies, ix, 132–37, 140–41
    tax breaks and, 132, 135–37
    unsubsidized, life with, 251–52
Oil spills, 128, 132, 210–11
Omnivore's Dilemma, The (Pollan), 37
Orange roughy, 121
Organic Consumers Association,
        107–9, 226
Organic Manifesto (Rodale), 186
Organization for Economic
        Cooperation and
        Development (OECD), 175,
        269
Overcapacity, 123–24
Overfishing, 125, 129, 191
Oxfam, 94–96, 197, 239, 269

P

Pakistan, 86
Palm oil, 204
Parasites, 18, 108
Pasteur, Louis, 18
Pauly, Daniel, 122
PBCG, 148–49
Peanuts, 112
Pelosi, Nancy, 238, 240
Pension Benefit Guaranty
        Corporation (PBGC),
        148–49
Pepsi, 66, 73
Perkins, John, 95
Peru, 86
Pesticide drift, 208
Pesticides, xii, 108–9, 207–10
Peterson, Collin, 239
Pew Research Center, 189
Physicians Committee for
        Responsible Medicine, 25
Pig farming, 41–43, 45–46, 48–50
Pig industry, 43–45, **44**, 48–50
Pimentel, David, 140
Piracy, xii, 190–93
Pittsburgh, 143–44

Politicians, 221–26. *See also specific name*
Pollan, Michael, 37–38, 180–81, 242–43, 270
Pollution, 143–44, 210–11
Pork
    concentrated animal feeding operations and, 43, 46, 48–49
    consumption of, 41–42
    industry, 43–45, **44**, 48–50
    integrators and, 44
    market share, 44, **44**
    pig farming and, 41–43, 45–46, 48–50
    prices, 47
    subsidies, 42–45, 47–49
    in supermarket, 50–51
    swine flu and, 42, 48–49
Poultry. *See* Chicken
Poverty, 4–6, 26, 115, 194, 198
Poverty gap, 189
Power players
    Big Ag, 226–28
    corporations, multinational, 223, 228
    K Street and, 223, 235
    lobbyists, 223, 226, 228–34
    politicians, 223–26
    power and money interests alignment and, 235
    trade associations, 228–34
Preble, Christopher, 189
Prices
    for agricultural products, 15
    beef, 21–22, 24–25, 27–28
    chicken, 36
    controlled, 34, 162
    corn, 31
    cotton, 101–3
    distortions, 6–7
    food, 3–6, 9, 81–82, 99, 115, 185
    milk, 58–61
    oil and gas, 4, 131–32, 134–35, 141
    pork, 47
    rice, 100
    shirt, 105–6

soybean, 31
subsidies and, xi, 4, 101
sugar, 9, 68–69, 72
target, 162
wheat, 77–79, 81
Produce
    consumption of, 113
    subsidies, 111–13, 115–16
    in supermarket, 117
    water needed to grow, 114
Program delivery costs, 171
ProMar International, 71
Property & Environment Research Center, 209
Protectionism, 6, 9, 14–15, 72–73

R
Rapier, Robert, 138
Rashid, Ussif, 270
rBGH, 54–56, 62
rBST, 54–56
Reagan, Ronald, 162
Real estate syndication, 164
Reclamation Act (1902), 156
Recombinant bovine growth hormone (rBGH), 54–56, 62
Recombinant bovine somatotropin (rBST), 54–56
Reform of subsidies, xiii, 237–46
Rense.com, 86
Retirement farmers, 169
Rice
    in California, 90–95, 100
    exports, 94, 99
    growing, 90–93
    in Haiti, 96, 99
    historical perspective of, 89–90
    importance of, 89
    imports, 97, 99
    industry, 231–32
    "Miami," 99
    prices, 100
    subsidies, 90, 94–95
    in Thailand, 86
    Third World and, 95–96
    trade issues and, 97, 99–100
    water needed for growing, 90–92

R.I.C.E. (Rice Information to
    Communicate/Educate), 232
Rice Federation, 232
Riceland Foods, 94
Riots, food (2008), 3, 81–82, 86–87,
    166
Robbins, John, 26, 270
Rockefeller, John, 214
Rodale, Maria, 186
Rodkin, Gary, 227
Rogers, David, 243
Roosevelt, Franklin Delano, 155–58
Royal Dutch Shell, ix, 234
Russia, 39
Ryan, Paul, 240

S

Salad, cost of, 25, **25**
Salazar, Emiliano Zapata, 245
Salmon, 128–29
Sardar, Ziauddin, 193
Saturated fat, 26–27
Seafood. *See* Fish
"Seed to shelf" business philosophy,
    215, 217
Senate Committee on Agriculture,
    Nutrition, and Forestry, 8,
    221, 224
September 11 terrorist attacks, 163,
    194
Shareholders, 263–64
Sharp, Reneé, 123
Shellfish poisoning, 122
Shirt prices, 105–6
Shopping habits, food, 116
Shrimp, 121
Sisters of Charity of St. Elizabeth,
    264
Sisters of Mercy, 264
"Six Reasons to Kill Farm
    Subsidies," 9–10, 189
SJR Farms (California), 220–21
Slimehead, 121
Slivinski, Stephen, 189
Smoot-Hawley Tariff Act (1930),
    15–17
Soda, 66, 73–75, 184, 264

Soil erosion, 202–6, 209
Somalia, xii, 190–91
Southeast Asia, 201. *See also specific*
    country
Soybean
    exports, 167
    industry, 231
    prices, 31
    subsidies, 31, 33, 35, 111
Speculators, financial, 81–83
"Splash and dash," 204
Stabenow, Debbie, 8, 224–25
Starvation, 4–6
Steel
    abundance of, in everyday life, 144
    in cars, cost of, 150–51
    China and, 144–51
    continuous casting of, 146
    historic perspective of, 143
    imports, 144–45, 150
    industry, 145–53
    ingot casting of, 146
    job losses and, 144–45
    manufacturing, 146, 152
    Pittsburgh and, 143–44
    pollution from, 143–44
    subsidies, 147–53
    tariffs, 144–45
    tax breaks, 147
    union and, 148, 233
    unsubsidized, life with, 251
    uses of, varied, 144
Steelworkers' union, 148, 233
Stern, Nicholas, 198
Stockholm Convention on Persistent
    Organic Pollutants, 208
Stock market crash (1929), 13, 15, 155
Stopgamblingonhunger.com, 85
Subsidies. *See also* Agricultural
    subsidies; Beneficiaries;
    Ethanol subsidies; Power
    players; *specific issues*
    active citizenry and, 258–59
    adjectives describing, 16
    attachment to, 257
    beef, 22, 24–25, 29
    calorie reduction and, 116

Subsidies *(cont.)*
  cattle raising, 27–28
  chicken, 32, 34, 37, 39–40
  connecting dots and, 259–60
  continuing saga of, 257
  controlled prices and, 34
  corn, 8, 23–24, 26, 35, 65–66, 68,
    111
  cost-benefit analysis of, ix, 167–68
  cotton, 10, 101–4, 107
  creation of, 11–12, 155–58
  debt and, 8
  defining, x
  direct, 126, 170, 219
  disclosure and, 264
  eliminating, xiii, 9–10, 40, 116,
    203, 260–61
  environmental issues and, xii-xiii,
    199, 209–12
  expenditures, 8
  farm, 8–10
  farm bills and, xiii
  federal, 127, 170
  financial cycle of, x
  financial issues and, 17
  fish, 119–21, 124–29, 191–93, 258
  food, 4–5, 113, 165–66, 185–86
  food chain and, 114
  food prices and, 4, 9
  food supply and, 165
  globalization and, x
  government accountability and,
    259
  growth of, 156, 159
  Hatch Act and, 17–18
  health issues and, xi-xii, 17
  indirect, 114, 170–71
  life without, 247–55
  long-term view of, 265
  milk, 55–59
  New Deal and, 155–57
  obesity and, 8
  oil and gas, ix, 132–37, 140–41
  pork, 42–45, 47–49
  prices and, xi, 4, 101
  produce, 111–13, 115–16
  quasi, 128

  reform, xiii, 237–46
  revolt and, 244
  rice, 90, 94–95
  sham of, x-xi
  source notes, 267–71
  soybean, 31, 33, 35, 111
  state, 128
  steel, 147–53
  sugar, 65–69, 73–75, 162
  supermarket and, 10
  system of growing food and, 7
  tariffs and, 17
  terrorism and, 189–90
  trade issues and, 6
  transparency and, 258
  truth about, 129
  unhealthy food and, 25, **25**, 111
  violence issues and, xii, 187
  water, 93, 113–14
  wheat, 77, 79–80, 86–87
Sucrose. *See* Sugar
Sugar. *See also* High fructose corn
    syrup (HFCS)
  artificial sweeteners and, 180–81
  in beverages, 66, 73–74, 184
  cane, 66, 74
  consumption of, 68, 75, 112, 181–83
  ethanol subsidies and, 70–72
  fast-food restaurants and, 69
  in food manufacturing, 72
  foreign, 73–74
  fructose, 182, 184
  industry, 66, 68–75, 232
  markets, global, 232–33
  Mexico and, 73–74
  prices, 9, 68–69, 72
  subsidies, 65–69, 73–75, 162
  sucrose, 182
  tariffs, 9, 67, 72, 74–75
  trade issues, 72–73
  in Wal-Mart, 67–69, 74
Supermarket
  agricultural industry and, 19
  in Chicago, 118
  chicken in, 36
  first, 7
  in Harlem (New York), 117

health issues and, 7–8
pork in, 50–51
price distortions and, 6–7
produce in, 117
sales at, 2–3
sham of, 1–3
size of average, 1
subsidies and, 10
as symbol of America, 19
near USDA, 19
world problems and, 6–7
Swartz, Rick, 237–43, 246
Swine flu, 42, 48–49

T

Target prices, 162
Tariff Commission, 16
Tariffs
beef, 25
chicken, 35
post-World War I, 14
Smoot-Hawley Act and, 17
steel, 144–45
subsidies and, 17
sugar, 9, 67, 72, 74–75
Tax breaks, 132, 135–37, 147, 166
Tax dollars
agricultural subsidies and, 9, 86,
163–64
average tax bill, 166
cotton subsidies and, 103
fish subsidies and, 120
foreign agricultural subsidies and,
173–74
people's say in, 246
Taxes and nutrition/health, 116–17,
185
Tea Party movement, 245
Terrorism, xii, 189–90, 194–95, 197
Thailand, 86
Third World, 94–96
"Timber mafia," 212
Trade associations, 228–34. See also
specific name
Trade issues. See also Tariffs
Canada-United States, 197
China-United States, 149

cotton and, 101–3, 229
countervailing duties, 97
fair trade, 100
free trade, 100
Mexico-United States, 197
protectionism, 6, 9, 14–15, 72–73
rice, 97, 99–100
subsidies and, 6
sugar, 72–73
Transparency and subsidies, 258
Transportation infrastructure, 230
Trumbore, Brian, 15–16, 270
Tuna, 121, 128–29
Turner, Ted, 214

U

UCLA, 271
"Unintended Consequences of U.S.
Steel Import Tariffs, The,"
145
United Steelworkers Union (USW),
233
University of Buffalo study, 116
University of California, Berkeley, 140
University of California, Davis, 271
University of Nebraska research
study, 28
Urbanization, 159
USAID programs, 161
USA Rice Federation, 231–32
USC, 271
US Commerce Department
research, 69
USDA
Agricultural Adjustment Act and,
157
agricultural industry changes
and, 160
agricultural subsidies and, 14,
16–17, 161–62
beef subsidies and, 22
Big Ag and, 218–19
Economic Research Service of, 269
Farm Bill 2008 and, 195
household income of farmers and,
214

USDA (cont.)
  "off-farm" income and, 168
  pork subsidies and, 48
  power of, 12
  price controls on food and, 162
  public relations agency of, 109
  supermarket near, 19
  Wall Street's involvement in food
    prices and, 82
  wheat and, 82
US Department of Agriculture. See
    USDA
US Department of Health and
    Human Services, 26
US Environmental Protection
    Agency (EPA), 43, 46, 109,
    249, 269
US Federal Fisheries Investment
    Task Force (FFTF), 124
US food aid programs, 172
US Geological Survey research, 211
US Public Interest Research Group
    (USPIRG), 227
US Supreme Court, 157
USW, 233

V

Vegetables. See Produce
Vessel buyback programs, 128
Vietnam, 42
Vilsack, Tom, 6, 226
Violence issues
  hatred toward United States and,
    193–94
  piracy, xii, 190–93
  subsidies and, xii, 187
  terrorism, xii, 189–90, 194–95, 197
Volumetric Ethanol Excise Tax
    Credits, 138

W

Wal-Mart, 67–69, 74
Walgreens chain, 118
Wall Street, 81–87, 220–21, 263–64

Water
  subsidies, 93, 113–14
  unsubsidized, life with, 249–50
  usage, 90–92, 114, 210
West Africa, 197
Wheat
  ACRE and, 79–80
  commodity traders and, 81–83
  ethanol subsidies and, 80–81
  exports, 167
  food crisis and (2008), 86–87
  forward contracts and, 83–84
  grain elevators and, 83–84, 87
  importance of, 77–78
  industry, 79, 230–31
  prices, 77–79, 81
  shortages, 86–87
  subsidies, 77, 79–80, 86–87
  USDA and, 82
  Wall Street and, 81–86
WHO, 184–87, 269
Why Do People Hate America?
    (Sardar and Davies), 193
Wien, Lawrence, 164
Willmann, Rolf, 126
Wilson, Woodrow, 14
Wise, Tim, 39–40, 218, 262, 269
Woertz, Patricia, 227
World Bank, 125, 145
World of Cotton data, 229
World Health Organization (WHO),
    184–87, 269
World Resources Institute, 209
World Trade Organization (WTO),
    35, 97–98, 103–4, 126, 149,
    158, 174, 269
World Wildlife Fund, 124
Wright, Robert, 194
WTO, 35, 97–98, 103–4, 126, 149,
    158, 174, 269

Z

Zapatista movement, 245